*A Materialist Critique
of English Romantic Drama*

A Materialist Critique
of English Romantic Drama

DANIEL P. WATKINS

University Press of Florida

Gainesville
Tallahassee
Tampa
Boca Raton
Pensacola
Orlando
Miami
Jacksonville

Library of Congress Cataloging-in-Publication Data
Watkins, Daniel P., 1952–
A materialist critique of English romantic drama /
Daniel P. Watkins.
p.   cm.
Includes bibliographical references (p.) and index.
ISBN 0-8130-1240-6. — ISBN 0-8130-1241-4 (pbk.)
1. English drama—19th century—History and criticism.
2. Verse drama, English—History and criticism.
3. Romanticism—Great Britain.   4. Historical materialism.
I. Title.
PR716.W37   1993
822'.709145—dc20   93-13776

The University Press of Florida is the scholarly publishing
agency for the State University System of Florida, comprised
of Florida A & M University, Florida Atlantic University,
Florida International University, Florida State University,
University of Central Florida, University of Florida,
University of North Florida, University of South Florida,
University of West Florida.

University Press of Florida
15 Northwest 15th Street
Gainesville, Florida 32611

For Floyd, Dean, Bonnie, Myra, and Allen
with love, gratitude, and admiration

[T]he whole secret of the modern Jacobinical drama . . . and of all its popularity, consists in the confusion and subversion of the natural order of things in their causes and effects: namely, in the excitement of surprise by representing the qualities of liberality, refined feeling, and a nice sense of honour . . . in persons and in classes where experience teaches us least to expect them; and by rewarding with all the sympathies which are the due of virtue, those criminals whom law, reason, and religion have excommunicated from our esteem.

Samuel Taylor Coleridge, *Biographia Literaria*

[T]he connexion of poetry and social good is more observable in the drama than in whatever other form: and it is indisputable that the highest perfection of human society has ever corresponded with the highest dramatic excellence; and that the corruption or the extinction of the drama in a nation where it has once flourished, is a mark of a corruption of manners, and an extinction of the energies which sustain the soul of social life.

Percy Bysshe Shelley, *A Defence of Poetry*

CONTENTS

PREFACE

This book uses a materialist methodology to investigate and explain some of the historical dimensions of English Romantic drama. It is particularly concerned with the operations of ideology in Romantic dramatic texts, and with the textual formulation and articulation of such matters as gender, class, economics, family, law, property, and so on. I stress this critical orientation because I want to be clear that my interest in historical explanation in this study is not grounded in the particular events and episodes at the conjunctural level of history—I do not seek to recount the details of British society between 1780 and 1832 and then argue for their relevance to the interpretation of Romantic drama. Rather, I am concerned primarily with the way meanings are put forward in dramatic texts produced under the pressures of the structural transformation of British society that culminated in the late eighteenth and early nineteenth centuries. Put slightly differently, I am not concerned here with Romantic drama as a reflection of, or commentary on, preexistent and autonomous historical data; rather, I approach drama as a part of the social history of the period, as a record, that is, of the sorts of social relations, anxieties, struggles, and so on that are constituent features of Romantic culture.

The materialist orientation of this study, moreover, takes for granted that the historical past cannot be brought forward and studied in purely descriptive terms, because the conditions under which criticism operates today are different from the conditions under which Romantic drama was produced. Therefore, one feature and measure of the historicity of Romantic drama is the distance between the past and present. To recognize that distance is to accept that the explanation of Romantic drama is also necessarily an appropriation and use of its meanings. The explanation of Romantic drama, in other words, is political.

I want to mention as well a slightly different matter, namely that in some respects I have written two books: one is a study of isolated plays by a variety of individual Romantic writers, a study that concentrates largely, though not entirely, on issues of gender; the other is a study of Byron, saying little about gender but concentrating instead on such issues as religion, class, and revolution. While the turn to Byron in the latter pages of the study may at first appear to constitute a grating shift away from the preoccupations of earlier chapters, in my view it represents a critical adjustment required by the great power of Byron's accomplishment in drama, and an expansion of the major concerns of the book. Byron's dramas simply cannot be studied in the same way one studies Baillie's *DeMonfort*, Lamb's *John Woodvil*, Maturin's *Bertram*, or Scott's *Halidon Hill*; the scope and vision of Byron's work force a slightly different set of critical interests and emphases. And yet his dramas, as I believe I show, remain distinctly Romantic and, in fact, stand as the greatest and most articulate voice of Romantic drama.

While in this study I examine only a few of the hundreds of dramas written during the period, I believe nonetheless that I am able to demonstrate the historical richness of Romantic drama and illustrate the need for further, more comprehensive, materialist study of the genre. Whatever its aesthetic merits or shortcomings, and however traditional scholars may situate it within the frames of literary history, Romantic drama occupies a critically important position in the social history of Romanticism.

Acknowledgments

This project has benefited considerably from the helpful advice that many friends and colleagues have offered over the past ten years or so. I owe a special debt of gratitude to Terry Hoagwood, who for many years now has shared with me his immense knowledge of Romantic history and literature, and whose encouragement and confidence in my work have sustained me through more than a few moments

of intellectual doubt; to Marilyn Gaull and Michael Scrivener, both
of whom read the manuscript in its entirety and provided excellent,
specific suggestions for revision; to Jerome McGann, whose work on
Romanticism continues to open up new areas of critical investigation
and inspire others to strive for scholarly and critical excellence; to Greg
Kucich, whose friendship, challenging conversation, and outstanding
scholarship have taught me to think in new ways about Romanticism;
to various members of my department, especially Jay Keenan, Sam
Tindall, and Linda Taylor, who kindly listened as I talked through the
ideas of this book and who always talked back in intelligent and in-
structive ways; and to the students in my graduate seminar on Romantic drama during the spring 1991 term, especially Brad Hollingshead
and Andrea Beranek. These students, among other things, taught me
critical and scholarly patience and demonstrated on a weekly basis the
powers of intellectual imagination. I also want to express my gratitude to Tony Rosso, whose knowledge of the politics of Romanticism
and whose respect for the utopian dimensions of Romantic thought
have shaped my ideas about Romantic drama in significant ways; and
to an anonymous friend, who long ago introduced me to historical
materialist methodology and whose example continues to shape my
thinking about literature, history, and politics. Finally, my greatest
debt, still, is to my best friend, Joanna Foster.

Portions of this book appeared previously, in slightly different form,
in various scholarly journals; I am grateful to the editors of these journals for allowing me to reprint those portions here: " 'In That New
World': The Deep Historical Structure of Coleridge's *Osorio*," *Philo-
logical Quarterly* 69 (1990): 495–515; "Class, Gender, and Social Motion
in Joanna Baillie's *DeMonfort*," *The Wordsworth Circle* 23 (1992): 109–
17; " 'Tenants of a Blasted World': Historical Imagination in Charles
Maturin's *Bertram*," *The Keats-Shelley Review* 4 (1989): 61–80; "Thomas
Lovell Beddoes's *The Brides' Tragedy* and the Situation of Romantic
Drama," *SEL* 29, 4 (1989): 699–712; "Violence, Class Consciousness,
and Ideology in Byron's History Plays," *ELH* 48 (1981): 799–816;
"Politics and Religion in Byron's *Heaven and Earth*," *The Byron Journal*
11 (1983): 30–39; "The Ideological Dimensions of Byron's *The De-
formed Transformed*," *Criticism* 25, 1 (1983): 27–39; and "Byron and the
Poetics of Revolution," *Keats-Shelley Journal* 34 (1985): 95–130.

"These Disputed Tracts"

Toward a Theory of Romantic Drama

The recent resurgence of historical scholarship and criticism has, among other things, exposed and created the desire to explore the ideological biases that have shaped studies in Romanticism over the past fifty years or so. In doing so, it has politicized a form of intellectual labor once considered to be culturally innocent. The great and important work of an older generation of scholars—including, for instance, the work of M. H. Abrams, Earl Wasserman, Walter Jackson Bate, and Douglas Bush—has been shown to depend not only upon the excavation of archival materials, the construction of literary traditions, the explanation of the forms of literary production, and the development of critical methods, but also upon exclusions of one sort or another—literary, critical, and political.[1] For instance, the commonplace assumption in traditional Romantic scholarship that lyric poetry is the premier Romantic literary form and thus most worthy of critical and scholarly investigation—along with the massive body of scholarship and criticism that has been produced under that assumption—has entailed the marginalization (and virtual loss for literary history) of other important forms of the period, most particularly narrative and drama, thus effectively narrowing the definition and explanation of Romanticism.

These exclusions, of course, proceed in some measure from the material and ideological conditions under which much Romantic literature itself was produced. Scholars have rightly attempted to reconstruct the actual circumstances and value system of their object of inquiry, and that attempt has helped to determine the ways in which Romantic texts are selected for critical study as well as the meanings that criticism attaches to these texts. But the particular kinds of literature omitted from serious investigation also disclose the extent to which scholarship and criticism since the Romantic period have contributed to and helped to extend certain ideological notions of art, identity, subjectivity, and politics, notions which came to maturation in the eighteenth and nineteenth centuries.[2] In other words, the magisterial work of many of the giants of Romantic scholarship, for all its importance and integrity, is implicated significantly in the structures of value associated with the historical and literary subject matter that it has recovered, reconstructed, and presented to posterity.[3]

Thus, while even the most careful historicist scholars and critics today owe a great debt to the labors of those who have gone before—indeed, serious historical scholarship cannot well proceed without drawing upon the knowledge and methods of an earlier generation—the values, methods, and conclusions that have been handed down can no longer be accepted wholesale. Nor can the current claim that Romantic scholarship and criticism have always been politically charged be made from a politically neutral position. If the intellectual labors of the past are politically significant, then so are the intellectual labors of the present, and criticism must acknowledge and be guided by this fact. Rather than more or less recording, endorsing, and extending without question prevailing Romantic structures of authority and belief—as was often the case in an earlier generation—historical criticism must interrogate the assumptions behind and the relations within those structures. Such a strategy necessarily entails recovering and reassessing what has been marginalized by, or omitted from, literary history (genres, works, writers, ideas); challenging (when necessary) earlier critical notions of literary and aesthetic value; and (if political criticism and scholarship are to avoid dogmatic and dangerous reductions) attempting to construct intellectual principles that are self-conscious, self-critical, flexible, and committed to investigating that terrain where criticism, literature, and politics intersect. To urge Romantic studies to move in this direction is no small effort and is certainly not without risk, but in an academic environment of renewed political and historical interest and in an age of growing historical anxiety and intellectual marginalization it is, arguably, the most worthwhile direction that those studies can take.[4]

One casualty of past scholarly efforts to establish the lyric as the premier Romantic literary form—one small area that might be used as a test site for reevaluating and reshaping our historical understanding of Romanticism and our awareness of the politics of Romantic studies—is Romantic drama, until recently almost universally dismissed as a failure. The study of Romantic drama from a historical and political perspective would not seek to extend existing critical principles to a body of work heretofore placed on the margins of the Romantic canon, but rather to use the drama as a means of demonstrating certain features or dimensions of Romanticism (in its largest, historical definition) that are not so readily seen in the conventional interpretive strategies brought to bear on the high profile Romantic literary forms: namely lyrical forms of one sort or another. In other words, study of the strong features of Romantic drama, rather than simply of those features which traditional criticism has presented as definitive of great Romantic literature, might be one way of challenging conventional interpretive and literary historical approaches to Romantic work, decentering and contextualizing those approaches so that their ideological investments—and their durable political significance—become apparent.

Three recent books suggest that the reassessment and recovery of Romantic drama have already begun. Alan Richardson's *A Mental Theater*, Jeffrey Cox's *In the Shadows of Romance*, and Frederick Burwick's *Illusion and the Drama*, published within three years of one another, offer detailed, systematic, and often exciting interpretive commentaries that place English Romantic dramas in relation to one another or in relation to European Romanticism, as well as providing helpful discussions of individual works. Thus they build admirably upon the earlier work of Joseph Donohue, Terry Otten, and Erika Gottlieb.[5]

While these studies assert the integrity of Romantic drama, put forward new information on the literary history of drama during the Romantic age, and ask historically informed questions that earlier studies had not, they remain committed to conventional interpretive strategies and categories, and therefore do not attempt to explain certain political and ideological issues that a historical materialist methodology would emphasize. (For instance, they tend to accept the Romantic preoccupation with the mind and imagination as the pri-

mary explanatory feature of the drama, rather than focusing on underlying material conditions that might determine the particular shape of
the Romantic mind and imagination.)[6] By proceeding along a traditional path of interpretation and literary historical inquiry, Richardson, Cox, and Burwick eke out the remaining critical, intellectual,
and ideological capital of a perspective that has begun to run dry in the
study of those Romantic texts most frequently seen as possessing literary greatness, seeking to find in hitherto neglected or marginalized
works fresh ground for cultivating old presuppositions—presuppositions that for some time now have been under fire from both textualists
and historicists.

Rather than follow in a critical direction that would shore up traditional values and beliefs by reclaiming a neglected body of literature,
the study of Romantic drama may benefit more, both critically and
politically, from a consideration of two related literary historical problems: first, why did drama, in its *literary* expression, collapse at this
particular historical moment, that is, during the Romantic period (even
while theater was wildly popular); and second, what does this collapse
allow us to discover about literary and social history? Consideration
of these questions not only will very likely disclose the particular historical importance (not to be confused with the purely aesthetic or
literary merit) of Romantic drama, but also might open up an intellectual space for a broader historicist and politically charged critical
practice.

Part of the difficulty in trying to discuss Romantic drama critically
lies in the drama-theater distinction, which became pronounced during the period. Do we mean by Romantic drama those works that were
written for (or were actually performed on) the stage? Or do we mean
poems that were written in dramatic form but never found a hearing
at Covent Garden or Drury Lane? Do we begin from Charles Lamb's
assumption that truly great drama cannot be performed without destroying literary greatness?[7] Or do we begin from the assumption
that a necessary and constituent feature of drama is its suitability for
the stage?[8]

For the most part, the present study is based on an examination of
poetic dramas that did not make it to the stage during the Romantic
period or that had but limited success there (*The Borderers, DeMonfort,
John Woodvil, The Brides' Tragedy, Halidon Hill*, Byron's dramas, and so
on), but I do not wish to make an absolute drama-theater distinction.

Indeed, at least a few of the works included in this study—*Bertram* and *Fazio*, for instance—enjoyed much success onstage. The drama-theater distinction itself is a problem for literary and social historical investigation and should not be accepted on its own terms as a given distinction between types of dramatic expression. My aim, therefore, as this remark might suggest, is not to catalog the differences between drama and theater, or to begin from the assumption that these differences are in some way determining, but rather to investigate in Romantic drama certain historical dynamics that may have *produced* the distinction in the first place and that relegated drama to a position of lower literary value within literary history.[9]

Because what I have written thus far has been largely at the expense of traditional, or liberal humanist, scholarship and criticism, I want to pause here for a moment to add a few words about Marxism and Romanticism, both because I want to argue against some parts of traditional Marxist accounts of Romanticism and because I view my own position finally as falling within the Marxist tradition. A description of my particular differences with the Marxists mentioned here is intended to clarify and provide a sense of direction for the argument about Romantic drama that I am proposing.

Simply put, old-fashioned, economistic Marxism (as well as some recent, noneconomistic Marxist work) views Romanticism as a form of bourgeois individualism and escape from the sordid realities of social life. As Christopher Caudwell writes of Keats: "Keats is the bannerbearer of the Romantic Revival. The poet now escapes upon the 'rapid wings of poesy' to a world of romance, beauty and sensuous life separate from the poor, harsh, real world of everyday life, which it sweetens and by its own loveliness silently condemns."[10] G. V. Plekhanov says much the same thing about Romanticism in general: "The romanticists really were at odds with their bourgeois social environment. True, there was nothing dangerous in this to the bourgeois social relationships. The romanticist circles consisted of young bourgeois[ie] who had no objection to these relationships, but were revolted by the sordidness, the tedium and the vulgarity of bourgeois existence. The new art with which they were so strongly infatuated was for them a refuge from this sordidness, tedium and vulgarity."[11] More recently, John Fekete, in his brilliant history of modern criticism, remarks (again of Keats): "The abandonment of the effort to change the structure of reality appears clearly in Keats. Nature, which in Wordsworth had stood as an alternative to the ugliness of urbanization and as a response to the town-country division and the alienation of fragmentation, expresses a new disaffection from society in Keats."[12]

The difficulty here is not that these remarks are wrong; in many respects they are entirely accurate. Rather, the difficulty is that the assessments are too negative, tending to persuade one that there is little of a critical-political nature to say about Romanticism, except that Romanticism and criticism of Romanticism are hopelessly entrapped in the bourgeois ideological web spun by the subjectivism of liberal humanism.

Marxism, however, has—or should have—much more than this to say about the historical dimensions of Romanticism and its literary forms, and much indeed to say about Romantic drama. What is needed if Marxist explanation is to move beyond tired reductions such as these is a more positive critical perspective than Caudwell and others allow, one that is capable of exploring and articulating the ways in which Romantic drama is a measure or register of the full range of its social and historical formation. The elaboration of such a position must not look first at the question of literary merit (though it is tempting to begin here), but rather at the question of *why* Romantic drama is perceived as inferior to, say, Romantic lyric poetry. This question necessarily directs critical attention to the problems and determining force of history, society, and politics, refusing narrowly textual explanations—which become valid and credible only after the dust of historical controversy has settled.

The best starting point for a materialist consideration of the historical situation of Romantic drama is Raymond Williams's excellent discussion in *The Long Revolution*, a somewhat sketchy but indispensable account of the history of Romantic dramatic form. According to Williams, the changes in the nature of drama, and particularly the historical decline of drama as a literary form, in the eighteenth and early nineteenth centuries correspond directly to the crisis of social class, which involved the transition—in England—from an aristocratic to a middle-class social order. This large sociocultural transformation, Williams argues, "broke up the old forms, which rested on meanings and interests that had decayed,"[13] weakening or exhausting the powerfully expressive voice that once had characterized drama in England. Since the Renaissance, drama had been one means of articulating the consciousness of an aristocratic worldview, but it could not be reformulated by Romantic artists to describe fully and effectively the new class consciousness coming to maturation in the eighteenth and nineteenth centuries.

One consequence of the contradiction between the earlier sensibility of English drama and the developing historical situation was that, as Williams puts it, "the connection between the theatre and literature was virtually lost" during the Romantic period.[14] While drama continued to be produced in great quantity for the stage, and while a few writers attempted to preserve the tradition of English drama by imitating styles and themes from the past (Thomas Lovell Beddoes, for instance, has been placed among these writers), most dramatists were unable to escape the ideological and economic pressures of their own age, surrendering their talents to the extreme popular demand for melodramas and spectacles, or, like Coleridge, turning from dramatic writing altogether.[15] By the first decade of the nineteenth century the spirit of great drama was dead and, as Kenneth Neill Cameron remarks, "the little legitimate drama being acted, whether comedy or tragedy, consisted almost wholly of revivals, especially Shakespeare and Sheridan."[16]

The isolated literary successes in drama—*Manfred, Cain, Prometheus Unbound*—were usually, though not always, confined to the closet (much as the successes or partial successes in epic—another genre caught in a disabling historical bind—were confined to highly satirical or highly subjective forms and expression, as *Don Juan* and *The Fall of Hyperion* attest), where the pressures of public taste and demand were less intense, and where the genre thus seemed more manageable. But even those writers who retreated into the closet did not insulate the drama from the social energies of the age; their works reveal the same anxiety and sense of crisis pervading the period that are found in the melodramas and spectacles favored by the theatergoing public. In fact, as I hope to show in subsequent chapters, Romantic closet drama in some respects represents little more than a "literary" internalization of the interests, tastes, and dynamics that are constituent features of social life during the Romantic period.

For this reason, while division and isolation certainly devastated the dramatic form, as Williams argues, they do not render Romantic drama insignificant, and in fact they direct many works of drama toward a cultural space where certain important dimensions of society at this historical moment become visible. Burdened by the crisis of social class, Romantic drama is inextricably and peculiarly entangled in the radical, disruptive changes of the period, displaying at various levels extreme anxiety that is most fully explained in historical terms. This anxiety is evidenced not only in the omnipresent references to class and social status but also in the fact that, at the level of plot, many Romantic dramas portray (as dramas had done since the Renaissance) the actions of an aristocratic class, while, at another, deeper level, they betray (to a much greater extent than Renaissance drama) an antagonistic consciousness that is necessarily and powerfully bourgeois.

The conflict between the content of the surface structure and a deeper political unconscious [17] registers one of the key features of the Romantic historical moment: namely the difficult struggle that marked the transition from an aristocratic to bourgeois worldview. As Williams writes of the many references to class in the drama of this period: "This exceptional class consciousness, though leading in the short run to little significant drama . . . is a clear sign of a new social order." [18] Even if drama could not be made literarily suitable for articulating the triumph of this new social order, it nonetheless reveals the tensions, anxieties, and ideological struggles surrounding that triumph. Thus, while the conflict between a diminishing aristocracy and an emergent bourgeoisie perhaps took its toll on drama—undoing its status as a premier literary form in British literary history—at the same time it made drama critical to our understanding of both social and literary history, because in this form the class struggle and many of the personal and public conflicts corresponding to this struggle played themselves out.

The literary and class dimensions of Romantic drama become clearer by reference to Lucien Goldmann's comments on the novel, which came to replace drama in the nineteenth century as the dominant form of literary expression. Drawing heavily on Georg Lukács and René Girard, Goldmann argues that the novel emerged alongside a market economy, and that it is characterized by a contradiction between the hero and his world—the same contradiction that exists, Goldmann argues, between the individual and the world under capitalism. While the novel is a product of bourgeois reality, it is unable to express a vision of that reality as full, coherent, and meaningful. "The novel with a problematic hero thus proves . . . to be a literary form bound up certainly with history and the development of the bourgeoisie, but not the expression of the real or possible consciousness of that class." [19] This failure of the novel, however, is not a failure of form, for it corresponds directly to the nature of bourgeois ideology itself, which is "the first ideology in history that is both radically profane and ahistorical."[20] Thus both the experiences and literary products of bourgeois society are *necessarily* characterized by alienation, division, and fragmentation.

One main difference between Romantic drama and the novel (as Goldmann describes it), then, is that, while both forms are characterized by social rupture or division, in Romantic drama these result from a clash *between* ideologies—that is, aristocratic and bourgeois—while in the novel they result from a clash *within* ideology, that is, bourgeois. The rupture that characterizes the novel also characterizes bourgeois reality, while the rupture that characterizes Romantic drama does not. This distinction helps to illuminate Williams's explanation of why literary drama had become a marginal form by the early nineteenth century: it carried within it too much ideological baggage from the past that denied the new content and consciousness of social life, and was thus formally unable to envision that past—or the present—in terms of the bourgeois ideology that had become dominant. The novel was much better situated formally because it was born with, shaped, and enabled by a bourgeois worldview. While this distinction assumes the literary inferiority of Romantic drama, it also helps to focus its precise importance in social and literary history: its articulation of conflict lays bare the dominant forces of social life at a moment of severe historical crisis and exposes what bourgeois consciousness discards, what it redefines, and what it creates anew.

A complex array of issues, themes, categories, and relations unfold alongside this class consciousness in Romantic drama, disclosing the intensity of historic social transformation as well as the various levels of social life at which that transformation takes place. The articulation of the clash between aristocratic and middle-class social networks, for instance, focuses the extent of individual dependence on society for purpose, direction, and even identity, showing that the crises of personal and individual lives are often at once crises of the social forms of human experience. Moreover, in projecting the emergent consciousness of the bourgeoisie amid the desperate and deteriorating structures of an older world, Romantic drama captures the process by which social relations, in the passage from one world order to another, were redefined and reconstituted in bourgeois terms. This process was both irrevocable, despite the nostalgia for older definitions and forms of order, and, when necessary, extremely violent. Indeed, violence and dread of violence are seen in both the aristocratic resistance to change and the bourgeois absolute insistence on change. Even when Romantic drama presents this violence in extremely private or psychological terms (as in *The Cenci* or *Cain*), it usually is traceable to class conflict and social relations of one sort or another.[21]

While not all of these matters appear at the level of plot in every drama of the period, while other Romantic forms contain some or all of them, and while they cannot be said to constitute in a definitive way an aesthetic consciousness of dramatic form, in Romantic drama they nonetheless appear in ways that provide critical and at times unique insight into the many dimensions and governing energy of class struggle in the late eighteenth and early nineteenth centuries, suggesting the determining power of that struggle in both history and literature. Other literary forms of the period—verse narrative, the novel, the lyric—manage more effectively to present a reasonably pure bourgeois consciousness and the turbulent conflicts that exist largely within bourgeois ideology; but the drama—perhaps because during the Romantic period it was a declining rather than an emergent form—captures most painfully the context within which that ideology emerged and the shaping conditions against which it struggled. For this reason it must be investigated not only in terms of public theater and literary history, and not only in terms of literary merit—the traditional ways of studying it—but also in the terms of its class consciousness and social history.

Some of the specific historical anxieties and formal difficulties that both burden and energize Romantic drama can be sketched in a brief examination of Wordsworth's *The Borderers*, an early Romantic drama that exemplifies in many ways the wide range of difficult challenges facing later dramas of the period. While issues of class conflict are not explicitly presented in the drama—as they are, for example, in Joanna Baillie's *DeMonfort* or Henry Hart Milman's *Fazio*—they are present by implication in such plot-level matters as the controversy surrounding Herbert's barony, in the Enlightenment notion of reason (as represented in the character of Rivers), and in the special status accorded to personal affection; and through these matters issues of class touch various relations of social life, ranging from the family and love to law and money.

But the most striking feature of the drama associated with social class, and especially with the emergence of a new bourgeois reality, is the near obsession with language, particularly the relations between language and power. This interest helps to focus an important dimension of bourgeois thought coming to maturation in the late eighteenth century, one that figures prominently in many Romantic dramas: namely the effort to contain the dangers associated with public exchange and to locate the permanent and most valuable structures of human experience at the level of affection and personal life. In the following pages I will consider briefly the connections between language, politics, and ideology that *The Borderers* attempts to negotiate, in an effort to elucidate some of the material conditions within which that attempt was made. My aim is not to offer an exhaustive analysis of language and class but rather to touch glancingly upon certain general features of the historical bind that pressure the drama, thereby showing how the drama's decided resistance to bourgeois intellectualism— its condemnation of the villain, Rivers—leads it ideologically and inevitably into the trap of bourgeois subjectivity and sentimentality.

The Borderers is commonly viewed as a work in which Wordsworth casts off Godwin and the philosophy of "independent intellect,"[22] which had occupied him to the point of emotional collapse in the early 1790s. It is also a work in which he rejects some of his earlier political commitments, particularly his once strong commitment to the principles of the French Revolution and to the use of physical violence to accomplish the ends of the revolution. (His letter to the bishop of Llandaff, 1793, is a vivid and chilling example of his early views on political violence.)[23] The rejection of pure reason and of revolutionary politics lays the groundwork for Wordsworth's nonpolitical poetic vision of the common man and deep human feeling, which characterizes his work of the "great decade." The *Lyrical Ballads*, for instance, steers clear of direct statements and themes that would situate the poems within a framework of political activism, emphasizing instead the integrity of a simple rural life, the generative and compensatory powers of nature, and the threat to both by various kinds of modern intellectual, social, and moral structures of authority. While *The Borderers* is, arguably, not an accomplished piece of poetry (or drama), it is critically important to an understanding of the kinds of political and intellectual issues with which Wordsworth was struggling during the mid-1790s, and to an understanding of the determining power of these issues on his later thought and poetry.

As Reeve Parker and Theresa Kelley have shown, one of the most striking features of *The Borderers* is its studied and systematic handling of language, especially its remarkable assumptions about the determining power of language.[24] During the course of the drama, stories or tales provide the ground and motivation for every significant thought and action. For example, the plan of deception that Rivers (Wordsworth's Godwinian villain) devises for Mortimer depends entirely on a series of stories, which constitute a self-created context exempt from accountability in the world of human exchange and which are subject only to the internal coherence and rhetorical power of the stories themselves. Through such portrayals as this, the drama suggests that language carries within it an authority that is potentially destructive of human compassion and integrity.

But the critique of language implicit in the association of Rivers's villainy with tale-telling does not reject the special status of language, while offering a counterargument for the special status of social life, for example, or even of personal life. Even while Rivers's malicious reduction of human experience and intellect to their linguistic representation is condemned, the drama holds language sacred, as is seen, for example, in the moving stories told by Herbert, or in Matilda's childhood stories that are recalled by Mortimer. Rather, the portrayal of the various plot-level conflicts in terms of the problematic character of language reveals another assumption altogether, namely that—as John Fekete puts it, writing in a different context—language is "the source of intelligibility and of social life, and the locus of the solution to all problems."[25] In other words, the problem of the independent intellect and the nature and role of personal affection that constitute the center of the plot are real issues; but their solution, the drama suggests, is to be found at the level of language rather than social life. Thus the critique that the play offers of one kind of language is at the same time a retreat into another.

The ideological entanglements evident in these competing views of language can be glimpsed by sketching several isolated episodes in the drama. Near the beginning, after Mortimer announces that his character is molded by feeling ("Never may I own / The heart which cannot feel for one so helpless" [I.i.39–40]), Rivers begins to set his trap by relating to Mortimer a tale of the villainy of Herbert (father of Matilda, the woman with whom Mortimer is in love), which includes the accusation that Herbert is not actually Matilda's father. Later, Rivers and Mortimer overhear Herbert telling Matilda of his military exploits, of the way he saved his infant daughter's life, and of his love for his daughter. Thus the story that Rivers tells of Herbert's villainy is set against the story that Herbert tells of his love for his daughter, and the confused Mortimer stands between these stories, looking for the proofs that will show one true and the other false. And Rivers, for reasons that will become apparent momentarily, does not deny what Herbert tells Matilda, but rather fuels Mortimer's confusion by remarking to him that "the blind man's tale / . . . [might] yet be true" (I.i.44–45), and that "in despite of my conviction, / [Herbert] tempted me to think the story true" (I.i.199–200). Further, even if it is not true, Rivers continues,

> The tale of [Herbert's] quondam Barony
> Is cunningly devised, and on the back
> Of his forlorn appearance could not fail
> To make the proud and vain his tributaries
> And stir the pulse of lazy charity. (I.i.52–56)

One aim of Rivers here is to shift Mortimer's attention from the human affection that he actually witnesses between Herbert and Matilda to the stories used to express that affection. That is, he dislodges language from the situation within which it appears, so that the central concern comes to be with the abstract matter of proofs: how does one determine the truth or falsity of the story? To reformulate human issues abstractly, Rivers knows, makes it possible to devalue people, to manipulate them as reified elements or ingredients within linguistic structures that have their own independent logic. That Mortimer allows himself to fall into this intellectual trap is evident; after Rivers prompts him with "There must be truth in this" (I.i.209)—referring to Herbert's tale—Mortimer comments:

> Truth in the story! Had the thing been true
> He must have felt it then, known what it was,
> And thus to prey upon her heart had been
> A tenfold cruelty. (I.i.210–13)

Human need, desire, affection, and experience become subordinate in Mortimer's mind to the problem of "unworthy tales" (I.i.227); and, as Rivers vividly illustrates through the course of the drama, any tale, considered in the abstract, can be shown to be unworthy—or worthy. The material consequences of this intellectualization of language reveal themselves in Mortimer's actions against Herbert.

Rivers's ability to turn Mortimer's interest away from human situations as the starting point for human action to stories and their problematic truth content is the central ingredient in his power, enabling him to weave stories as needed to shape Mortimer's view of specific situations. This is seen, for instance, in the exchange between Rivers, Mortimer, and the garrulous beggar woman, whom Rivers pays to tell tales against Herbert. As she begins, and then strays from, her tale, Mortimer calls her back to her subject with the comment "But to your story" (I.iii.95); and as she moves farther into the false tale about selling her infant daughter to Herbert, she is encouraged by both Rivers and Mortimer with such comments as "You are as safe as in a sanctuary: / Speak" (I.iii.129–30); and again "Speak" (I.iii.130); "Speak out!" (I.iii.133); and "Nay, speak out, speak out" (I.iii.135). As these comments suggest, Mortimer has become entirely enthralled by the tales being spun by the people he encounters. Rather than experience providing the basis for his assessments of linguistic expression, stories come to provide the basis for his assessments of experience. Mortimer's chilling comment reveals the human implications of this perverse hierarchy of values: "I do not think the tale will be believed / Till I have shed his [Herbert's] blood" (II.i.50–51).

One further example will suffice to illustrate the shaping power of stories on the thought of Mortimer. In convincing Mortimer that Herbert has arranged for Matilda to marry the villainous Lord Clifford, Rivers invents a tale about a proposed kidnapping of Matilda to bring her to Clifford. He relates the story to Mortimer once they have arrived on the barren heath, saying that

> I knew it would disturb you,
> And therefore chose this solitary heath
> Here to impart the tale, of which, last night,
> I strove to ease my heart. (III.ii.67–70)

This story is presented by Rivers and accepted by Mortimer as "the proofs" (III.ii.34) of Herbert's villainy. One story proves the other, and all that is left, from Mortimer's perspective, is to bring life into line with the authority implicit in them. As Mortimer says after this newest story has been completed:

> To let a creed built in the heart of things
> Dissolve before a twinkling atom.
> Philosophy! I will go forth a teacher,
> And you shall see how deeply I will reason
> Of laws, of qualities and substances,
> Of actions, and their ends and differences. (III.ii.77–82)

Just as stories are the means by which Mortimer is trapped into villainy, so they are the means by which Rivers finally exposes his own deceit and malice, effectively illustrating the extent to which language has absorbed and controlled Mortimer's thoughts and actions, and, moreover, the ease with which new stories can be spun to redirect those thoughts and actions. After Herbert has been left for dead on the barren heath, Rivers states directly to Mortimer what has been implicit throughout, that "There is a power in sounds" (IV.ii.49). This power is illustrated by Rivers's story of how, in his youth, he was duped by shipmates to leave an innocent ship captain on a desolate island to die, after which "The tale was spread abroad" (IV.ii.75) of Rivers's actions, thus destroying his integrity, his hope, and the possibility of meaningful social exchange. Like Mortimer, he had been convinced by a story which seemed to provide its own self-evident truth about human experience, while in fact it provided no referential proof whatsoever of that truth. Rivers's tale, in short, illustrates the destructive capacity of the power of sound when it is removed from its human context. As Rivers coldly tells Mortimer when his tale is complete: "Think of my story—/ Herbert is innocent" (IV.iii.211–12).

Such tales are set against other, more noble, tales which, the drama implies, exemplify the proper function of language motivated by the affections rather than by the intellect. Such language, apparently, is innocent, and it articulates the common bond of humanity rather than the isolated, manipulative power of the individual. For instance, in recounting to Rivers his love for Matilda, Mortimer notes that when he was a child

> It was my joy to sit and hear Matilda
> Repeat her father's terrible adventures

> Till all the band of play-mates wept together,
> And that was the beginning of my love. (I.i.65–68)

In the exchanges between Matilda and her father too, tales are situated in a context of mutual regard, where the only (and sufficient) proof of the tale is the affection which underlies it. When Herbert describes his past, the loss of his lands, and his efforts to aid his young daughter, he reminds her that

> . . . Thou has been told
> That when, on our return from Palestine,
> I found that my domains had been usurped,
> I took thee in my arms, and we began
> Our wanderings together. Providence
> At length conducted us to Rossland. There
> Our melancholy story moved a stranger
> To take thee to her home. (I.i.159–66)

And finally Wordsworth presents the drama itself as a tale meant to show the dangers of language when it is spun entirely out of pure intellect. After Mortimer discovers that he has been manipulated into killing an innocent man he states: "Raise on this lonely Heath a monument / That may record my story for warning" (V.iii.262–63). The drama implies that such tales as Mortimer's are meant to be seen as uplifting because they do not require reasoned response and are not geared to engage the intellect alone; they are motivated and checked by feeling.

As the foregoing sketch suggests, for Wordsworth in 1795 the problem of the independent intellect was also a problem of language, and thus it had direct implications for his theory and writing of poetry. In *The Borderers* he addresses the relations of language and intellect head on, displaying his willingness, and even eagerness, to abandon certain activist and intellectual principles around which he had once organized his life, as well as the assumptions about language that had informed those principles. At the same time, however, he refuses to condemn the power of language, which is exemplified so disturbingly in the character of Rivers. As a poet, he wished to defend and preserve that power. He sought to do this by dislodging it from the principles of cold reason that had once underwritten his political thought and activity, and situating it instead in the proper sphere of a depoliticized human affection, which, he believed, was permanent and moral.

The implicit assumptions that energize this portrayal of language in *The Borderers* are set out more or less explicitly a few years later in the "Preface" to the second edition of the *Lyrical Ballads* (1800), which provides an important gloss on the earlier work. In the "Preface" Wordsworth attempts to set down in systematic form his ideas about what poetic language—and, more generally, noble or virtuous language—should be. His aim in the *Lyrical Ballads*, he says, was to fit "to metrical arrangement a selection of the real language of men in a state of vivid sensation" (118); to determine "in what manner language and the human mind act and react on each other" (120); and to capture "the best objects from which the best part of language is originally derived" (124).[26] His hope in pursuing this goal was to discover and present "a more permanent and far more philosophical language than that which is frequently substituted for it by Poets" (124).

This position, and the poetic elaboration of it in the poems of the *Lyrical Ballads*, sets the tone for much of the poetry of the Romantic period, and certainly it has, almost single-handedly, shaped critical thinking about Romanticism for much of this century. Its distinguishing characteristic is its assumption that "the best part of language," poetic and otherwise, is located in a prepolitical environment of agrarian or pastoral integrity, virtue, and sincerity, where personal regard is possible. In addition, it assumes (and even fears) that not to work self-consciously to advance the permanent and universal dimension of language—where human feeling can flourish—is to run the risk of having language taken over by "the great national events which are daily taking place, and the increasing accumulation of men in cities, where the uniformity of their occupations produces a craving for extraordinary incident which the rapid communications of intelligence hourly gratifies" (128). Explicitly rejecting the political turmoil and social upheaval in England and Europe, the Wordsworth of the "Preface" defends the possibility of a transhistorical and redemptive sphere of unmediated language.

At the same time, however, in breaking with the decorum and formal restraints of the poetic language of a previous historical period, Wordsworth advances a seemingly progressive and even democratic stance in his defense of "the real language of men," a strategy that seems calculated to allow Wordsworth to have his politics and reject them too. In fact, the gesture of democratic sympathy is one that rejects the hard politics of "the great national events" and "the increasing accumulation of men in cities," and would find the highest human value in a language expressive only of personal life without regard to social exchange, social class, and social struggle. This is exactly the ideological perspective informing *The Borderers*, which not only rejects the language games indulged in by Rivers but also embraces—in the portrayals of Herbert and Matilda, and of Mortimer's tragic lesson— a pure language of the heart, untouched by political reality. The implicit assumption of this view, presented tentatively in *The Borderers* and more confidently in the "Preface," is that all political attempts to disrupt established structures of social authority should be resisted in favor of higher, natural, universalistic forms of commitment.

That this position, which would cleanse language and life of all ideology, is itself ideologically burdened becomes clear when we consider that it presumes an ahistorical and apolitical human nature—which the best language can describe and celebrate—even as Rivers (in *The Borderers*) and the "great national events" of the 1790s (described in the "Preface") emphatically illustrate the politically charged nature of human existence. That is, in giving over the self-interested mind and language of Rivers for the other-interested affections and language of, for example, the narrator in "Simon Lee," Wordsworth escapes into a subjectivist theory of language and life. In denying the virtue of the self-interested intellect, he accepts the virtue of private feelings; in denying the domain of social and political exchange, he asserts a domain of personal exchange; in condemning the misuse of intellectualized language, he celebrates only a language that refuses to intervene in public struggle.

In short, then, Wordsworth's concern with the possibility of a pure, unmediated language in the mid-1790s must be regarded, at least on one important level, as a sign of alienation and anxiety amid the tumultuous changes reshaping the age. While the motivating impulse behind *The Borderers* is a noble attempt to construct a basis for meaningful human relationships, that attempt—as in much drama of the period— took the form, as Fekete puts it, "of a value alternative or surrogate experience outside the dominant social practices rather than the critical edge of transformations within the frame of progress; [thus it became] more a means of evaluation than a means of orientation for social leverage."[27] Once the move in this direction was begun in *The Borderers*, Wordsworth developed its principles fully in the "Preface" and poems of the *Lyrical Ballads*, which are moralistic and value-laden but which find their energy in a precapitalist and preindustrial agrarian world—in a social world whose authority, by Wordsworth's day, had irrevocably passed. To hold up this dead world as an alternative to the admittedly dirty and corrupting world of industrial growth and land enclosures is to minimize the political efficacy of poetry and to maximize its ideological function of diverting historical attention from the prevailing structures of social authority and from the mechanisms of political control.

I am not suggesting that Wordsworth simply selected the wrong topics to write about, but rather suggesting that what he did write about is historically, politically, and socially implicated, and that often it reflects an ideology of the isolated individual within an isolating and alienating world. While the *Lyrical Ballads* may be regarded as Wordsworth's first mature expression of this ideology, *The Borderers* provides an excellent example of the social context within which it arises—of the contradictions, desires, and political struggles (in the form of the Barons' Wars) that might contribute to the privatization of human experience. This social context is the defining mark not only of *The Borderers* but of Romantic drama generally.

The foregoing analysis of *The Borderers* focuses on what is probably the single major difficulty that Romantic drama faced: the issues, and the values underlying those issues, that the drama wishes to explore concern the corruption and loss of social life, and its replacement with personal or subjective life; this shift of imaginative emphasis from public to personal life paralyzes dramatic representation, which depends upon dynamic social exchange for its content. *The Borderers*, in other words, faces the impossible task of dramatizing a negative (or declining) social energy, and an emerging, mainly subjective set of values. The drama attempts to negotiate this overwhelming challenge by displacing social exchange into tales of social exchange, thereby preserving the core subjectivity that is the drama's real concern, while at the same time providing the necessary mechanisms for creating dramatic movement.

The dramatic inadequacy of this maneuver is not without its rewards. The attempt to depoliticize the social nexus, while at the same time drawing upon it for dramatic motive and context, involves the play directly in numerous interesting ideological and political issues that Wordsworth's later lyric poetry conceals more successfully. First among these is the pervasive anxiety emerging from a fear of social life, and the attempt to alleviate that anxiety by retreating into the safer regions of personal life. The valorization of personal life vis-à-vis social entrapment entails a rejection of Enlightenment reason and its language of the head, and their replacement with Romantic subjectivity and its language of the heart. This Romanticization of language, moreover, is necessarily and obviously accompanied by a conservative political gesture, one grounded in the assumption that human fulfillment is entirely a private affair.[28]

While few dramas of the period are as self-consciously intellectual as *The Borderers*, many contain similar sets of issues. They are marked by their sensitivity to questions of individual autonomy, social responsibility, social stability, social transformation, the possibility of human value and fulfillment in a rapidly changing—apparently deteriorating—world. Surrounding these kinds of concern are questions regarding the nature, place, and fate of the family, religion, the state, law, and so on, and the proper relation of the individual to these straitened institutions. In assuming, at the level of the political unconscious, the end of the world as it was once known, Romantic drama casts into relief both the crisis of that doomed world and the various historical forces struggling to establish themselves in its place.

"In That New World"

Samuel Taylor Coleridge's *Osorio*

In March 1797, when he began writing *Osorio,* Coleridge had not yet retreated from radical politics, as is evidenced by his powerful denunciation of England in "Ode to the Departing Year," written only months earlier.[1] His approach to politics, however, had begun to change by this time. The failure of *The Watchman* in May 1796 convinced him that he was unsuited for the sort of active and public political life he hitherto had pursued. Thus in December of that year he removed to Nether Stowey, leaving the public world of politics to be attended by such people as his radical friend John Thelwall, while Coleridge himself set about channeling his political energies into poetry. Despite reservations about the direction that the French Revolution had begun to take, his commitment to the rebel cause, and his efforts to advance that cause through poetry, remained more or less firm until 1798, when France invaded the republic of Switzerland.[2]

These well-known details have long provided a helpful frame of reference for discussion of *Osorio,* a work of questionable literary merit but of tremendous intellectual importance for what it tells us about Coleridge's politics in the 1790s.[3] Written at the suggestion of Richard Brinsley Sheridan for possible production at Drury Lane,[4] *Osorio* effectively illustrates the sort of radical thinking with which Coleridge wished to invest his poetry. The drama contains strong anti-Catholic, antimilitary, and antiaristocratic sentiments, going so far as to project the ultimate triumph of the lower orders over aristocratic tyranny.[5] Such details forcefully represent Coleridge's unwavering radicalism and illustrate his self-conscious effort to elaborate and disseminate his political ideas in works of the imagination.

Emphasis on local detail alone, however, while perhaps a necessary starting point for investigating such a drama as *Osorio,* at the same time risks limiting what can be said about its political and social dimensions, for most often such emphasis uncritically accepts the explanatory authority of empirical data, leaving larger historical considerations unexamined. Put differently, data alone—whether drawn from plot or biography—cannot satisfactorily explain the complex historical and structural issues that become visible in Coleridge's efforts to formulate and elaborate his politics through poetry. Investigation of biographical information and plot issues can effectively locate the drama at the level of historical conjuncture—that is, it helps us to know better Coleridge's individual hopes and fears at a specific moment in the 1790s—but says nothing about the place of the drama within the frame of much longer and slower historical changes, or to illuminate the relation of Coleridge's political imagination to those changes. The result is that, in addition to eliding, or obscuring, a potentially rich area of inquiry, critical activity has locked itself into a position of paraphrasing the political theme of the drama and of collecting additional biographical details to elucidate that theme. Such efforts, which perhaps embrace too readily the individualist problematic from which Coleridge himself begins, risk unintentionally duplicating the ideological commitments—and predicament—of the writer and work that they would explain.[6]

If historical investigation of *Osorio* is to overcome these kinds of limitations, it must, in my view, develop a critical perspective that would acknowledge the categories of biography, authorial intention, and historical detail, but would at the same time decenter them by placing them within the larger category of what Robert Weimann calls the historical genesis of a text, thereby creating the possibility of gaining critical distance on the political and historical values assigned to the drama by Coleridge himself. According to Weimann, genesis transcends local detail to embrace "that complex of historical origins by which the temporal complication of literary images, themes, genres, modes, and functions can be understood." It is "a more objective category" than authorial intention, "referring to the total context of which the individual 'generative intention' is only a factor": "The artist's private world is not the opposite of society, any more than the recognition of the public world precludes a consideration of the creations of men as individuals."[7] According to this view, biographical information and expressive intention are not transparent categories but rather emerge from within already present historical and social structures, which alone are capable of explaining them.

To investigate *Osorio* from the perspective of its historical genesis is to place critical emphasis on the social (rather than only literary) history within which the drama was written, as well as on the political unconscious of the story being dramatized. One way (among others) of developing this emphasis is to investigate the drama as both a product of the structural change within society required by the transition in England from an aristocratic to a bourgeois worldview, and as a register of the sensibilities and consciousness accompanying that change. At this level of investigation, historical anxiety and ideological confusion become visible in Coleridge's story, illuminating some of the historical limits within which his imagination was forced to operate and some of the cultural allurements that drew him into their influence, even as he directed his energies to other, sometimes even contradictory, goals. In other words, this deeper level of textual activity discloses the dialectical tensions that shaped Coleridge's poetic imagination, allowing us to see how his expressed desire for liberty and human integrity was occasionally and unwittingly betrayed by historical pressures that controlled that desire. In short, the drama does more than provide a gloss on Coleridge's mind or even on his expressed political views: it offers a narrative of the complexity, political stakes, and depth of structural-historical change.

The presence and operation of these historical matters in *Osorio* can be glimpsed by initially considering the probable political significance that Coleridge attached to the setting. For the setting, perhaps more readily than any other single feature, allows us to see the relationship between certain positive details on the textual surface—that is, details under the control of authorial intention—and the larger historical frames of reference that embrace, enliven, and (occasionally) subvert the values traditionally attached to those details.

The setting of *Osorio*—the Spain of Philip II shortly after "the civil wars against the Moors, and during the heat of the persecution which raged against them"[8]—seems particularly well suited to Coleridge's immediate political and poetic interests. The world of Philip II had long held a prominent place in the British imagination, as it is filled with important figures from British history, not least among them Sir Francis Drake and "Bloody" Mary Tudor, the latter of whom was briefly married to Philip and who, before her death, seemed willing to help Philip bring England under Spanish rule. It was, moreover, a world where the Catholic church ruled supreme—often by force, in the form of the Inquisition—and threatened to reclaim its authority over England. Finally, it was a world in which actual war between Spain and England erupted, with the famous failed attack of Philip's Armada in 1588 effectively shifting world historical momentum from Spain to England. In writing about sixteenth-century Spain, then, Coleridge was describing a familiar and exotic past world that his audience could comfortably condemn, while at the same time taking pride in the successes of their own nation against an imperialist and religiously dogmatic enemy.

Even while the setting plays to long-standing British biases against Spain, Coleridge interestingly undermines those biases by using the setting as the basis for a displaced commentary on the British government of the 1790s. His characterization of Philip's world strikingly resembles the England of his own day, which was marked by a repressive and often violent government that sought to crush all resistance— especially the popular opposition to the war with France—and to allay the fears of a ruling elite who felt the threat of a revolutionary uprising within its own borders. Further, the imperialistic exploits of Spain in the sixteenth century were not radically different from those of England in the eighteenth, as exemplified most readily by the hugely profitable (and hotly debated) slave trade that England conducted until the early part of the nineteenth century. If the immediate effect of the drama is to display the political and social failures of Spain, clearly a deeper intention is to warn that England in the 1790s could run the same risk of failure. In these respects, at least, as Coleridge's sophisticated irony insists, the anti-Spanish sentiments voiced in the drama are also anti-British sentiments.

Although the setting is doubtless intended by Coleridge both to appeal to a projected Drury Lane audience and to provide a context for exposing the political naiveté of that audience, at the same time it calls into play certain historical crosscurrents that politicize the text in still different, often complex, ways that would seem at odds with the more obvious political message just described. By setting his story in the sixteenth century—at the time of the struggles between England and Spain—while at the same time drawing historical parallels to his own day, Coleridge broadens the historical scope of the drama to embrace the formative era of the making of the middle class, and it is at this level that political and historical reality slips out of authorial control. This era—with its moments of creative brilliance in the Renaissance and the Romantic periods—entailed not only the obvious destruction of an aristocratic worldview but also—what was more difficult to see in the later eighteenth century—the replacement of this worldview by bourgeois structures of feeling and value. While the specific tensions between old and new worlds never manifest themselves in the plot of the drama (for instance, none of the characters is from the middle class), they nevertheless energize and shape its deep structure; indeed, they are the necessary material condition for the actions portrayed—appearing in a multitude of features and details that make little sense except in terms of far-reaching social and historical change. At this deeper level of textual activity, authorial intention is of little help to critical investigation—except insofar as it provides a guide to Coleridge's particular understanding of historical process—for Coleridge himself is implicated in (his work and imagination are products of) the very sort of turmoil and change that are presented in the drama. The particular dramatic details, the particular emphases on conflict, and the authorial insistence on what is historically and dramatically decisive are themselves historically determined, even as Coleridge chooses them for and enlivens them in the text of the play.

What I am suggesting here is that the radical political stress of the drama—particularly the anti-Catholic, antiaristocratic interests—develops within a specifically bourgeois set of values that are implicitly endorsed by Coleridge and assumed finally to transcend history itself in permanent victory. One simple detail will help to illustrate the nature and extent of Coleridge's ideological blindness in his appropriation of historical detail for dramatic purposes. According to the stage note introducing the play, Philip persecuted the Moors who lived in Spain in the sixteenth century. The dramatic action that follows allows an audience to assume that, because the forces supporting Alhadra expose and promise to punish the villainy of Osorio, the Moors are successful in their resistance to this persecution. In fact, however, as Coleridge himself knew, the Moors—whose presence in the drama constitutes its major plot-level public event—were brutally crushed by Philip II. The omission of this historical fact, accompanied by the implicit conclusion that Alhadra and her followers win justice, allows and perhaps encourages a misreading of history by hinting that social stability follows directly on the fall of the house of Velez, though of course further social misery—at least for the Moors, who are lower-class people of color—is what in fact follows.[9] Such misrepresentation—or, at the very least, incomplete representation—of history arises, as I shall argue in detail momentarily, not from Coleridge's desire to withhold information but rather from his own deep-seated desire for stability in the face of certain and extreme instability. The social contours of this desire become visible, in this instance, only after we learn what Coleridge's text has not shown us. A historical detail that lies entirely outside both textual and thematic grounds, once brought to the surface, forces a different sort of reading of Coleridge's presentation of history and of the characters in the drama who participate in that history.

I want now to turn directly to the drama itself in an attempt to sketch the workings of its political unconscious. While I do not provide an exhaustive analysis of the many layers of social life registered in the drama, my general critique shows that, whatever its expressed intention and despite the nature of its plot-level episodes, the drama's unifying ideology is class specific, advancing a bourgeois position not only against aristocratic authority but also against lower-class needs, desires, and claims. The personal crises that are presented, the commentary on religion and the aristocracy, the handling of race and class—all are historically significant insofar as they are presented and defined by middle-class structures of feeling and desire that in the 1790s were struggling to be born.

The central feature of *Osorio* is historical anxiety, specifically anxiety among an aristocracy whose social authority is seriously disintegrating even as the drama opens. Aristocratic daughters refuse to do what is expected of them by aristocratic fathers; aristocratic brothers attempt to kill their brothers; aristocratic religion is far removed from the Christian love and charity that are its ostensible center, instead supporting the commands of blind power and justifying the enforcement of law by physical force. These events, attitudes, and practices, while in the beginning seeming entirely personal in nature, ultimately constitute a rupture within aristocratic society, infecting the entire aristocratic state apparatus, challenging its underlying structures of value, eroding its integrity, and destroying its ability to rule. The ideas of the ruling class, at least in the particular moment of pervasive social turmoil described in the play, are not the ideas of all society, and in the anxiety issuing from this fact many social relations and ideological claims are laid bare.

One of the most obvious relations of aristocratic social life brought into question in the drama involves gender. From the beginning Lord Velez, father of Osorio and the individual of highest social rank portrayed in the drama, is depicted in paternalistic terms, as one who takes for granted the sacred authority of aristocratic patriarchy and who understands his patriarchal integrity in terms of his ability to give gifts to those women over whom he holds power. In the opening scene, for instance, when he attempts to persuade Maria to marry Osorio (whom she does not love), his warm and fatherly treatment of his adopted daughter (I.7–11) is accompanied by a gentle reminder that her well-being has always depended upon his kindness. From his point of view, Maria's very life has been preserved, protected, and nurtured by the gift of his love and strength; when she was "a powerless babe" (I.12), and her "mother with a mute entreaty / Fix'd her faint eyes on mine [Lord Velez's]" (I.13–14), Lord Velez rescued and reared her as his own child.

That the seeming warmth and benevolence of this patriarchal attitude in reality mask a hatred of women is shown later in the drama, when it becomes obvious that Maria will not budge from her position regarding Osorio. Lord Velez, once convinced of his adopted daughter's immovable loyalty to Albert, turns absolutely and violently against her, displaying explicitly the ugly power that had been hidden by his seeming benevolence. He sneers at her, calls her a "thoughtless woman" (IV.ii.247), an "Ungrateful woman" (IV.ii.268), and ultimately sends her from his house (IV.ii.274–76). The gift of protection that he had bestowed upon Maria, as his blunt and authoritarian withdrawal of that gift makes plain, is at the same time a powerful expression of domination. Maria's human worth is measured directly in terms of her subservience to him; once she refuses to occupy a subservient position, she is despised and rejected.

The relation between Lord Velez and Maria, however, serves as more than a sign of patriarchal villainy. The violence of Lord Velez's response to Maria, by exposing the real hatred behind his patriarchal authority, signals as well a weakening of that authority, suggesting that more socially palatable exercises of power have become ineffective. That is, while his treatment of Maria is a sign of real power—he *can* dismiss her from his house—it is at the same time an act of desperation in that it can produce no satisfactory solution within the frame of the existing aristocratic patriarchal estate. It reflects an authority that can only manifest itself negatively, an authority that thus fails in its more important constructive capacity of enriching and extending aristocratic masculine power and property, and thus it marks an opening for challenging that authority.

The particular psychological landscape upon which the challenge to aristocratic patriarchy unfolds can be glimpsed in the consequences of Maria's conduct and attitudes that have called Lord Velez's tyrannical authority into action. Her refusal to conform her thoughts and actions to the accepted social codes that minimize personal feminine love and that uphold masculine decisionmaking, as I shall explain below, does not constitute in any way a feminist move toward autonomy. Nonetheless, her passive resistance does help to illuminate a remarkable moment of change in relations of gender, for it both erodes aristocratic patriarchy and makes room for the construction of an alternative arrangement for gender and social relations. She avoids marriage to Osorio; she finds and wins the ostensibly dead Albert, whom she has loved all along; and she triumphantly attaches herself to an emerging authority that is certain to replace the demise of Osorio and Lord Velez: these plot-level developments describe a radical disruption of social life and redirection of social energy toward a world defined by its possibilities for women rather than by its limitations. The psychological healing that accompanies this giant restructuring of personal and social arrangements is seen in the fact that it is not alienation but rather personal and social wholeness that flow to Maria from the crisis that she has helped to precipitate.

To put the matter this way, however, risks distorting the portrayal of gender relations in the drama, for it suggests that Maria is more materially engaged in changing the world than she really is. The actual deeds that produce social change are most often performed not by Maria but by Alhadra, the Arab woman of color who, unlike Maria, is outspoken, active, a leader of rebels, and willing to shed blood to further her cause.[10] Never a model of the new woman—the feminine values of the drama do not center around her character—she nonetheless exemplifies explicitly the antiaristocratic energy necessary for social change. Her active resistance to established authority and her bold exercise of her own authority (seen most powerfully in her command that Osorio be executed) point toward the inevitable termination of aristocratic patriarchal rule and the new possibilities for women in a transformed world. In fact, her final speech courageously dares to imagine the overthrow of "the kingdoms of this world; / The deep foundations of iniquity" (V.ii.313–14). Though her imaginings here are, arguably, sadly out of touch with the actual direction of social change described in the drama—at least with those changes involving issues of gender—they declare the promise of a new world and of the changed position of women in that world.

Alhadra's activist response to aristocratic patriarchal authority helps to clear the political and ideological ground for the more positive values associated with Maria, whose character shows something of the real shape and direction of the new (and acceptable) femininity described in the drama. Never dirtied by the actual struggles against patriarchy—as Alhadra is through her association with political conspiracy and political violence—Maria is consistently shown in idealized and humane terms, as a woman who embodies absolute integrity. Her triumph over adversity, and the happiness she eventually finds through unwavering commitment to her beliefs, are a sign of an emerging new world and of her secure place in that world.

The characterization of Maria, though positively drawn as a beneficiary of the social changes taking place, is fraught with difficulties of its own, as it suggests that the new self-satisfied femininity is less than independent. The sympathetic portrayal of Maria, in fact, is to a large degree a description of a new kind of patriarchy and an endorsement of the structures of value and authority undergirding that patriarchy. Though she successfully resists the authoritarian threats of Lord Velez and Francesco, she nonetheless remains entirely dependent upon masculine strength or masculine presence; and thus even in her triumph over her oppressors she does not discover the freedom that Alhadra is so bold to imagine. The persistence of Maria's dependent mind-set even at that moment when she rejects prevailing authority (that is, Lord Velez and Francesco) can be seen in her absolute constancy in matters of love. One need not suggest that she is wrong to love, and to love sincerely, to recognize that in the extremity of her commitment to Albert she entirely negates herself, even to the point of imagining her own death and imagining Albert, finding that she has died, "listening to my constancy" (I.i.39), "hover[ing] round, as he at midnight ever / Sits on my grave and gazes at the moon" (I.i.40–41). She describes her worth here entirely in terms of her own belittlement, her power in terms of her nonbeing. Though this passage relates only a lover's dream, it nonetheless contains within it a commentary on a very real hierarchy of relations, a hierarchy that subordinates women to men. Feminine desire, at least as it is here expressed by Maria, is incapable of imagining feminine autonomy.

The negation of Maria's autonomy and her own approval of that negation suggest one of the means by which an inchoate bourgeois patriarchy establishes its control over women. The beliefs and needs that energize her commitment to Albert are signs of a new world in which sexual love replaces arranged marriage; dreams and nostalgia replace real social exchange; and the isolated self develops an identity over against that assigned to it by the state apparatus. All of this clearly marks the decline of aristocratic social authority, and it does so in ways that directly involve gender relations: as the characters of both Alhadra and Maria attest, women can no longer be controlled absolutely by the father or the church, for other claims determine the choices that women make. And yet these claims are often characterized and given meaning by women's own self-abnegation. Maria never has autonomy or public authority and integrity; she never wishes for more than to be released from the power of Lord Velez and allowed to live in dreams of Albert. And her self-worth is always determined either by those dreams or by Albert's actual protective presence. In short, Maria carries within her character the values of a new world, but clearly it is not a world in which women are equal to men: it is a world in which women's imaginations and desires are entirely privatized and in which women themselves valorize that privatization.[11]

The changing relations of gender, as aristocratic patriarchy gives way to bourgeois patriarchy, involve new roles for men as well as for women, as is seen most readily in the differences between Osorio, the cold, strong man who stands to inherit the old estate, and Albert, the sensitive individual whose actions are motivated by compassion and subjective desire. As with the depiction of a new kind of woman, the portrayal of the new bourgeois male is invested with integrity and sincerity, surpassing the stock callousness of the aristocratic characters whose social authority is threatened. Indeed, the simple presence of a disguised Albert is sufficient to elicit from Maria feelings of sympathetic identification and to make the austere Osorio uncomfortable.

Numerous passing details help to situate Albert, despite his aristocratic birth, among an emergent bourgeoisie and to establish him as a carrier of modern attitudes and values. Early on, for instance, it is alleged that he has been kidnapped by a merchant ship (I.66); later too, after having returned in disguise to his homeland, and when the evil of his brother and father has become disturbingly apparent, he contemplates permanent self-exile to the Netherlands (II.184)—a strong trading nation and perhaps the foremost challenger for economic supremacy in the sixteenth century—where he is certain he will be protected by "the heroic Prince of Orange" (II.185). In addition to such small details that distance him from the aristocracy and attach him symbolically to the middle class, his disguise as an Arab situates him socially. When he comes home after a three-year absence, he abandons his native aristocratic dress for the dress of the Moors, thereby rejecting not only his inherited social class but also the (Catholic) Christian values that historically have underwritten that class. By taking on the dress of a people violently at odds with Spanish aristocracy, he creates an important emotional and personal space for the development of an independent identity—an identity that draws energy from the Arab resistance without actually becoming a part of that resistance and without becoming ideologically associated with the Arabs.

Two important and related features of Albert's inchoate bourgeois sensibility include the reformulation of patriarchy and Christian belief along new social lines. With respect to patriarchy, Albert clearly is never harsh or cold in the way that Lord Velez and Osorio are; quite the reverse, he displays great sensitivity and compassion throughout, even to the point of telling his brother, whose villainy has been thoroughly exposed, that "We will invent some tale to save your honour" (V.244; see also II.168–77 for an example of the compassion of which he is capable even in moments of great distress). Despite such shows of human regard, however, his character is implicated in a patriarchal structure of values, as it is through his eyes—not Maria's or Alhadra's—that the major issues of the crisis-ridden world come to be seen. The authority with which his character is invested is evident in the very first exchange between him (in Moorish disguise) and Maria. Here he relates to Maria and Alhadra a dream, which in fact is the story of the wrong he has suffered at the hands of Osorio and (he believes)

Maria. After recounting the dream, and when Alhadra asks whether he also dreamt of revenge, he remarks of the woman in his dreams (that is, Maria):

> She would have died
> Died in her sins—perchance, by her own hands!
> And bending o'er her self-inflicted wounds
> I might have met the evil glance of frenzy
> And leapt myself into an unblest grave!
> I pray'ed for the punishment that cleanses hearts,
> For still I loved her! (I. 323–29)

While such a comment may honestly reflect his deep love for Maria, it also displays masculine supremacy, for it uncritically assumes the integrity and purity of Albert himself, as well as the guilt of Maria.

Even when he comes to doubt her guilt, as he does almost immediately (I. 351–74), Albert remains the measure of guilt and innocence and specifically the measure of feminine guilt and innocence. His authority is seen most emphatically in the conjuring scene of Act III, where he subverts Osorio's scheme to prove his own death. The effect of this episode is to leave Maria both utterly confused about the fate of Albert, whom she now believes may in fact be alive, and helplessly looking to the mysterious Moor (Albert in disguise) for guidance and explanation, which he does not at this point provide, and in fact does not provide until near the end of the final act. Two important developments follow from this scene: first, Maria must wait until Albert chooses to disclose his identity before she can overcome her alienation and hardship, a fact that suggests her constant dependency on masculine decisionmaking and conduct; and second, Albert, through his disguise, is provided with the opportunity to observe Maria from a position of secrecy and to establish the authority of his own character.

Viewed in this way, Albert's disguise and Maria's helplessness are much more than necessary ingredients in the plot-level machinations set in motion by Osorio. They are a representation of a new set of gender relations under construction. The emergence of Albert from his disguise, in the presence of both Maria and Osorio, marks the triumph of these gender relations over aristocratic patriarchy. Following upon Maria's vicious treatment at the hands of Lord Velez and at the moment of Osorio's greatest weakness, Albert's unveiling points toward a new masculine authority: he is the dream come true of Maria and the compassionate superior of his brother.

The spiritual-ideological side of the masculinity associated with Albert can be seen in the portrayal of religion. While the many extremely negative descriptions of Francesco, as noted above, establish a strong anti-Catholic sentiment in drama, they cannot be equated absolutely with antireligious sentiment. They are rather part of a larger ideological shift involving the subversion of church authority and its replacement by a more personal religious sensibility. This shift necessarily involves dislodging Maria and Albert's self-identities from church authority, as can be seen in Maria's comment to Francesco:

> [I]t is a horrid thing to know
> That each pale wretch, who sits and drops her beads
> Had once a mind, which might have given her wings
> Such as the angels wear. (IV. 302–5)

Rejecting Francesco's specific claim on them, as well as the more general claim of Catholic structures of authority, Albert and Maria become dreamers committed to constancy and idealism in matters of love, personalizing religious devotion.

The religious-spiritual dimension of their devotion is made explicit in a brief scene in Act II, where Albert, having been asked by Osorio to prove (by means of the mysterious conjuring ceremony described above) his own death, describes a portrait of Maria in the following way: "Dear image! rescued from a traitor's keeping, / I will not now prophane thee, holy image! / To a dark trick!" (II. 321–23). Here Maria appears as the new Mary, a secularized and personalized version of the feminine principle idealized by Francesco's Catholicism. She is the repository of Albert's most sincere spiritual longings, her appeal deriving at least partly from the fact that her spiritual worth is created and appropriated by Albert alone. Sexual love is integral to the new spiritual love, and it is governed by private masculine desire.

The relationship between Albert and Maria raises yet another complex issue, one governed not so much by patriarchy as by taboo. Incest is never made an explicit issue in the drama but, as in much Romantic literature, it hovers in the margins enticingly, even as it threatens to dissolve upon close inspection. Albert and Maria are not blood brother and sister, and yet they describe themselves—and are described by others—as siblings. As she puts it to Lord Velez, "Were we [Maria and Albert] not / Born on one day, like twins of the same parent? / Nursed in one cradle?" (I.97–99). In addition, she commonly refers to Lord Velez as "father" (for example, I.61), further confusing the nature of her relationship to Albert. These details, in fact, suggest that her mature sexual attraction to him derives, at least in part, from their youthful brotherly and sisterly love, which seems to represent an innocent and permanent affection—so much so that she cannot think of marrying Osorio, Albert's brother, toward whom she has never felt close, and bearing his children without feeling that *this* would be incestuous:

> . . . O my sire!
> My Albert's sire! if this be wretchedness
> That eats away the life, what were it, think you,
> If in a most assur'd reality
> He [Albert] should return, and see a brother's infant
> Smile at him from *my* arms? (I.45–50)

The incestuous suggestiveness of Maria's relationship with Albert, and the curious feelings of sexual taboo bound up with her rejection of Osorio, indicate the charged significance of sexual arrangements in the world of the drama. The estate—represented in the characters of Lord Velez and Osorio—cannot see where Maria's marriage to Osorio would constitute a violation of a social-sexual taboo, while Maria cannot see marriage to Albert, whom she describes as a brother, as a violation of this same taboo. The contradictions evident in these attitudes are part of the difficult psychological landscape shaped by the competing forces of social authority and personal desire. The values attached to both domestic scenarios presented in the drama—a Maria-Albert marriage; a Maria-Osorio marriage—reflect the particular needs of the individuals involved. Maria's desperate, undying love for Albert, for instance, suggests the extent to which her life has become privatized, alienated from the mainstream of a world that would make her most intimate decisions for her; in such a world, intensely personal commitment—even sexual attachment to an individual whose relationship with her has always been that of a sibling—holds the only possibility of meaning for her, and any threat to that commitment is a threat to life itself. For Osorio, on the other hand, marriage to Maria stands as clear evidence of the stability and continuing authority of aristocratic privilege; similarly, his failure to control Maria's youth and beauty, as the drama bears out in the fall and then the death of Osorio, points toward the demise of that authority. In short, incest and sexual love are both a resource of hope and a sign of social debilitation.

Questions of sexual taboo and love are intimately connected to the issue of family life, an issue that carries within it the anxieties and weakening value structures of aristocracy. Two major plot threads define family life in the drama and can be sketched briefly. The first involves the question of a child's responsibility to the father, and is seen most emphatically in the actions of Maria, who refuses to obey Lord Velez's command that she marry Osorio. For her disobedience she is decried as mad and then banished from the house of Lord Velez (IV.235–329). The second involves Osorio's attempted murder of his brother, Albert, an effort that leads to the death of Osorio and the disgrace of the house of Velez. These plot-level matters point toward opposite kinds of pressure on the family. Lord Velez's intervention into Maria's personal life shows the father's attempt to stabilize the family through the exercise of his traditional authority over children. Ugly though his actions may be, especially when we consider them from the point of view of gender, they are culturally acceptable and even necessary within his world and are meant, quite simply, to secure aristocratic family relations. Osorio's attempt on Albert's life, however, violently denies the assumptions and possibility of family stability upon which Lord Velez's actions are based; indeed, Osorio's actions signal the inevitable decline of aristocratic family life. That Lord Velez does not see this decline suggests the extent to which he remains ideologically trapped within aristocratic structures of authority; that Osorio is moved to fratricide suggests the desperation to which he is driven in trying to control a shifting world that threatens to exclude him from the authority he believes rightly belongs to him.

The death rattle of the aristocracy that has been sketched thus far is accompanied by repeated references to and instances of extreme violence. The abusive treatment of Maria by Lord Velez, and seconded by Father Francesco, the Inquisitor; the murder of Ferdinand by Osorio, who is euphoric after committing his vile deed (IV.150–51); and Francesco's vicious persecution of Alhadra, Ferdinand, and other Muslims: in the context of Osorio's demise and the triumph of Albert and Maria, these all amount to class anxiety verging on paranoia, as the various stalwarts of aristocratic patriarchy and class privilege maneuver desperately to stabilize a world moving out of their control. The violence to which all three are driven, however, cannot resolve the contradictions within public and personal life that are manifested in the antiaristocratic solidarity developed among the Muslims and in the uncompromising personal commitments of Maria and Albert; violence in this context, indeed, appears not as strength but as weakness, as the last desperate efforts of a class unable to claim the authority it once knew. The extent to which their authority has diminished and to which their violence shows weakness is suggested in the final scene of the play, where Alhadra, having led her people successfully against the house of Velez, announces that none of that house will be executed, except Osorio. The power of those who were once dispossessed is in the ascendancy at the end of the drama and—once ideological authority has shifted out of the hands of Velez—does not require violent action to secure the political and ideological ground that has been earned.

I want to turn finally to a consideration of the problematic foster-mother scene in Act IV, which has appeared to some scholars to be out of place in the drama. Despite its apparent awkwardness, this scene in some respects ties together all other issues and points toward the structure of values and beliefs that triumph with the happy union of Albert and Maria.

At the suggestion of the disguised Albert, Maria visits her foster mother (III. 139–43) to learn what she can about Albert. During their conversation, Maria remarks on a mysterious entrance into the castle of Velez, which the foster mother proceeds to explain by relating "a perilous tale" (IV. 170) of a foundling who is raised by Leoni, a woodsman and the father-in-law of the foster mother. The story of this foundling, simply put, is the story of the birth, struggle, and eventual freedom of the individual from the constraints of both aristocratic political control and aristocratic religion; it is a nostalgic story celebrating primitivism—which was popular during the Romantic period—and at the same time it illustrates that the cult of primitivism was a distinctively modern and bourgeois phenomenon. As a young boy, the foundling is both unteachable and resistant to orthodox religion (IV. 182–83). Eventually he is taught to read and write by a friar, gaining a knowledge and intellectual ability that turn him against all accepted structures of authority, including religion. Still he is loved by Lord Velez under whose protection he lives, until a natural disaster convinces Lord Velez that the foundling's unorthodox thought and behavior must be punished.

Thrown into the castle dungeon, the foundling occupies his time in solitary song until Leoni, the woodsman, hears him and, risking death, digs a secret escape for the boy, who leaves the castle—which has become his prison—joining a group of voyagers who discover "golden lands" (IV.226) in a "new world" (IV.229). Once in this new world, the foundling lives out his days "among the savage men" (IV.234).

Given life by a worker, supported within the walls of aristocracy by traditional authority and values until these become confining, and finally liberated through the hard labors once again of a worker, the foundling discovers perfect freedom in a radically new world, one enriched by money, voyages of discovery, and individual independence from institutional codes and definitions of individual and social life. This is the birth of the bourgeoisie, and it finds its corollary in the story of Albert and Maria, who are confined and alienated by aristocracy (the story of Albert) while at the same time having been nurtured by aristocracy (the story of Maria), until the labors of the lower orders (Alhadra and the Muslims) make possible an escape from the world that holds and threatens them. While they do not move literally to new "golden lands," certainly they are associated with such lands through Albert's affection for the prince of Orange and through his alleged experience on a merchant ship; and, at least ideologically, they do indeed move into a new world, one characterized not by aristocratic privilege and expectation but rather by personal need and desire.

Osorio is a remarkable, progressive story of the struggle for freedom, powerfully capturing the political energy with which Coleridge invested his poetry in the 1790s. But the progressiveness of the story is not unmarked by the specific class warfare that characterized both the 1790s and the much larger transition period from the sixteenth to the nineteenth centuries. What the drama depicts as an abstract and absolute struggle for freedom is in fact a struggle involving its own particular middle-class agenda. The lower-class Muslims who make the happiness of Albert and Maria possible, while treated sympathetically, remain throughout on the margins of the text, entering the action only to further the aims and to help construct the values of other—that is, white—characters. While Alhadra is given the final speech of the drama—a speech that is quite noble in its desire for justice and freedom and in its condemnation of oppressive state and religious institutions[12]—her remarks only provide the necessary hard edge behind the softer and more appealing characters of Maria and Albert, who are shown not in politically violent terms, as Alhadra is, but rather always as figures of compassion and forgiveness. In other words, here, as throughout the story, people of color and people of the lower classes perform the unappealing, often ugly, task of clearing away the debris of a crumbling social order that makes possible the emergence and apparently unreproachable integrity and sincerity of the new order.

The surge of bourgeois feeling coursing through *Osorio,* moreover, helps to explain why the title character is perhaps the least interesting in the drama. Following the traditions of literary history, Coleridge constructs the story around an aristocratic figure whose actions lead to tragedy. And yet that tragedy produces little if any sympathy for Osorio—who is drawn consistently in cold, callous terms—and still less for the aristocratic world whose values he is meant to embody. The story is his in title only; the real interest lies in Albert and Maria and in the swelling tide of new possibilities that displace Osorio while carrying the two lovers to happiness and security. While Coleridge's inability to create an effective hero doubtless damages the dramatic integrity of the work, it nonetheless enriches it historically by allowing us to glimpse the conflicting social energies competing for his imaginative allegiance.

To argue in this way about the relative significance of the various characters and actions is not to insist that the drama—against Coleridge's own intentions—is in fact politically conservative, but rather to insist that it is marked by a particular class reality: what Coleridge presents as absolute is historically specific; the triumph of the bourgeoisie is not the end of history and ideology but rather their transformation into new class terms. Only when we recognize and begin to excavate the historically specific nature of the drama, particularly the deep ideological structures of value, feeling, and authority that define an emergent bourgeoisie, can we begin to understand the often oppressive power relations undergirding bourgeois social life—relations registered in the drama even as it endorses the bourgeois dismantling of aristocracy.

"The Gait Disturb'd of Wealthy, Honour'd Men"

Joanna Baillie's *DeMonfort*

Recent scholarly work in the area of Romanticism and feminism has begun to bring Joanna Baillie back from the dead in literary history. We now have been reminded that, as Stuart Curran states, "two years before Wordsworth's celebrated preface, [Joanna Baillie] had published her own seventy-two-page argument for naturalness of language and situation across all the literary genres," and that, in her capacity as dramatist, she was often compared to Shakespeare.[1] Despite the efforts of Curran and a few other notable scholars, however, the hard labor of reviving and critically investigating Baillie's literary accomplishment, particularly her dramas, has barely begun. While the reason for this no doubt can be found among the masculine biases that continue to dominate Romantic scholarship and criticism, Baillie herself has contributed to the difficulty of the critical task by writing plays that were utter failures on stage in her own day and that continue to baffle (and often bore) would-be sympathizers today. Her plots are frequently embarrassingly simple, her characterizations subordinated to a fixed idea, and her handling of emotion compromised by her commitment to cold logic. Such matters, not surprisingly, overwhelm critical efforts to place her alongside Coleridge and Wordsworth as one of the great Romantic writers.[2]

These apparent weaknesses notwithstanding, Joanna Baillie is one of the extremely important (and perhaps great) writers of the Romantic period. For one thing, she powerfully displays what Curran, in speaking of women's poetry generally in the period, calls an "alienated sensibility,"[3] which gives her critical imagination considerable leverage in treating certain social structures of value and belief. For example, while her major dramatic effort is suggested in the title of her *Series of Plays: in which it is attempted to delineate the stronger passions of the mind,* she does not treat human passion in the abstract but rather situates it among social and historical pressures of immense complexity, focusing a range of highly specific details and material situations that disclose the inner workings of social life during the Romantic period. Further, her genre of choice in exploring and articulating these pressures (that is, drama)—despite her awareness of the limitations of theater in her day—reveals, in ways that lyric poetry cannot, the ideological conflicts disturbing and shaping the passions that constitute her primary thematic and psychological interest. As a genre in decline, drama in the Romantic age is at once weighted with nostalgia and desire for the once powerful social world that had brought it to prominence, and also—at the same time—pressured by the confidence, individualism, and sheer defiance of the social energies struggling (like Keats's Apollo) to assert their newfound power and authority. Baillie's imagination intervenes powerfully in this social, historical, *and* formal-generic crisis, tracking the complex intersections of psychological, social, and imaginative motion at an especially intense moment of historical—specifically class and gender—anxiety, when one structure of authority and belief is on the verge of displacement by another.

DeMonfort (1798) provides an excellent introduction to the historical richness of Baillie's work, for it depicts in astonishing detail many of the specific social problems and issues—ranging from class and domestic life to gender and law—caught in the cross fire of this certain and radical transformation of society. Written as a psychological drama about the workings of the passion of hatred, it is in fact much more than this, as its psychological interests necessarily draw upon deeper and broader social, historical, and cultural realities that determine the specific contours of individual psychological turmoil. In Baillie's hands, hatred is more than a purely psychological, private, self-generating, or autonomous passion; it is rather an *effect* of larger, if submerged, social forces and conditions, ranging most immediately, for instance, from the Counter-Revolutionary War that began in 1798, to the fear of a

French invasion of England. Nor is it a sign of the essential character of DeMonfort, the protagonist of the drama, but rather a symptom of a radically splintered self—a self that presumes social privilege and autonomy while at the same time suffering from claustrophobic social transformations that overwhelm, and are utterly unresponsive to, that presumed privilege and autonomy. Thus even as DeMonfort *claims* to be the personal measure of human value in the world of the drama, he *experiences* displacement of his personal and psychological authority. In exploring the deep turmoil and confusion that are seen between these two extremes, the drama discloses the contingent nature of the passion of hatred, illuminating its dependence; that is, upon antecedent material conditions (set down in the text of the drama itself) that constitute the ontological ground upon which psychological issues— however powerful, or expressive—must be situated.

The following pages investigate some of the social conditions that undergird the psychological interests of DeMonfort's character. While the logical and historical connections between these conditions are not fully elaborated in my argument, they are shown to be part of a common social reality within which characterization and dramatic action are situated, and from which these take their life and draw their credibility. After sketching these concerns, I will return to a consideration of the psychological dimension of DeMonfort's character, in an effort to historicize his isolation, alienation, and violence, and to show thereby that his troubles are not his alone but also those of his social class.

The largest and most severe crisis described in the drama, and the one within which all other issues and interests must be situated, is the transition from an aristocratic to a bourgeois social structure. The primary spokespersons for these worlds in conflict are DeMonfort and Rezenvelt, respectively; in them can be seen, on the one hand, the anxieties and despair resulting from the loss of aristocratic social authority and, on the other, the energy and defiance arising from the acquisition of bourgeois energy and authority.[4] DeMonfort himself recognizes this social dimension of his personal affliction, as he describes for his sister how mere contempt for one of a lower social order transmogrifies over time into obsessive hatred when the lower-class individual begins to advance socially:

> . . . As we [DeMonfort and Rezenvelt] onward pass'd
> From youth to man's estate, his narrow art,
> And envious gibing malice, poorly veil'd
> In the affected carelessness of mirth,
> Still more detestable and odious grew.
> There is no living being on this earth
> Who can conceive the malice of his soul,
> With all his gay and damned merriment,
> To those, by fortune, or by merit plac'd
> Above his paltry self. When, low in fortune,
> He look'd upon the state of prosp'rous men,
> As nightly birds, rous'd from their murky holes,
> Do scowl and chatter at the light of day,
> I could endure it: even as we bear
> Th' impotent bite of some half-trodden worm,
> I could endure it. But when honours came,
> And wealth, and new got titles, fed his pride;
> Whilst flatt'ring knaves did trumpet forth his praise,
> And grov'ling idiots grinn'd applauses on him;
> Oh! then I could no longer suffer it!
> It drove me frantic—What, what would I give!
> What would I give to crush the bloated toad,
> So rankly do I loath him! (II.ii)[5]

Later in the drama this same story is related from the opposite perspective by Rezenvelt, who explains to Count Freberg that

> . . . Though poor in fortune
> I still would smile at vain-assuming wealth:
> But when unlook'd for fate on me bestow'd
> Riches and splendour equal to his own,
> Tho' I, in truth, despise such poor distinction,
> Feeling inclin'd to be at peace with him,
> And with all men beside, I curb'd my spirit,
> And sought to soothe him. (III.ii)

The tension evident in these descriptions twice erupts in physical confrontation between the two men, with Rezenvelt each time disarming DeMonfort and then sparing his life, a fact which both personally humiliates DeMonfort and reverses the social order of privilege, as DeMonfort comes to owe his life to Rezenvelt.

This purely personal dimension of the transformation of social life is given social significance by developing public responses to individual life, as is seen, for instance, in the fact that it is Rezenvelt rather than DeMonfort who is respected and lauded for social benevolence. While even DeMonfort's own servant, Manuel, is unhappy with his increasingly unpredictable master—"for many times is he / So difficult, capricious, and distrustful, / He galls my nature" (I.i)—and while DeMonfort's peers and even his sister scold him for his personal conduct, the social elite commend and celebrate the character, virtue, and generosity of Rezenvelt. As Count Freberg remarks to DeMonfort:

> This knight is near a kin to Rezenvelt,
> To whom an old relation, short while dead,
> Bequeath'd a good estate, some leagues distant.
> But Rezenvelt, now rich in fortune's store,
> Disdain'd the sordid love of further gain,
> And, gen'rously the rich bequest resign'd
> To this young man, blood of the same degree
> To the deceas'd, and low in fortune's gifts,
> Who is from hence to take possession of it. (II.ii)

Such generosity inspires public celebration and respect among the aristocracy itself (excepting DeMonfort)—"For, on my honest, faith," Count Freberg says, "of living men / I know not one, for talents, honour, worth, / That I should rank superior to Rezenvelt" (II.ii)—creating a social space of privilege and authority for an individual who was once on the margins of society. DeMonfort knows that his own aristocratic privilege weakens as this social space enlarges.

The class conflict exemplified in the tension between DeMonfort and Rezenvelt provides the structural center of the play. It is a conflict, as has been suggested, that depicts the inevitable demise of aristocracy and probable triumph (despite Rezenvelt's eventual death by murder) of the bourgeoisie. As such, it is a conflict that is constitutive of the social reality depicted in the drama, embracing and conditioning every characterization, thematic issue, episode, action, and expression of belief or value used to construct the dramatic action.

The pervasive and uneasy deep rumblings in the social world of the drama can be glimpsed initially in two seemingly minor matters relating to the tone of the drama: anxiety and claustrophobia. Despite their immediate plot-level function as tonal details that deepen the psychological interest of DeMonfort's character, they connect interestingly to the class issues just sketched as signals of the social threat under which DeMonfort's character is drawn. For DeMonfort the world is unstable, and that instability extends outward even to a small, isolated town in Germany where he has sought escape; it no longer possesses a proper center. At the same time, the world is closing in on him, denying him even air to breathe, as friends and foes alike pressure him to conduct himself according to their expectations.

The most visible sign of anxiety in the plot is the recurrent (real or imagined) knocking on doors to rooms inhabited by DeMonfort (a knocking that unsettles and distracts him to the point where peace of mind is impossible), and on doors behind which the most pious and spiritually pure segment of society is to be found. This knocking begins almost immediately in Act I, after DeMonfort has arrived at old Jerome's apartments. At a serious moment, when DeMonfort is commiserating with his host whose wife has died two years previously, there is a loud knocking on the door that so unsettles DeMonfort that he loses all composure: "What fool comes here, at such untimely hours, / To make this cursed noise?" (I.i). Knocking occurs again in the following scene at a moment when DeMonfort is not in a mood of deep sympathy but rather intense rage after a servant has announced that Rezenvelt has been seen nearby. In the middle of vehemently denouncing his archenemy (calling him such names as "cursed reptile" [I.ii]), DeMonfort hears a knocking at his door, jolting him from his frenzy. Much later too, after DeMonfort has murdered Rezenvelt and the action of the drama has shifted to a convent, nuns and monks are interrupted twice from their prayers and conversation by loud knocking, which brings news of Rezenvelt's murder.

This frenetic knocking is complemented at various moments by DeMonfort's intense listening for activities just beyond his actual notice, or for events that he believes are about to occur. This activity is seen, for instance, at one of the soirees he attends where, in the middle of a lighthearted conversation, he stops abruptly, distracted by a noise that the others do not hear:

> *Lady Freberg:* Praise us not rashly, 'tis not always so.
> *DeMonfort:* He does not rashly praise, who praises you;
>   For he were dull indeed—
> *[Stopping short, as if he heard something.]*

Lady Freberg: How dull, indeed?
DeMonfort: I should have said—It has escap'd me now.—
[Listening again, as if he heard something.]
Jane: What, hear you aught?
DeMonfort [Hastily]: 'Tis nothing. (II.ii)

What he hears—or imagines that he hears—of course, is the approach of Rezenvelt, whose real or imagined presence haunts him at every moment. The anxiety of this scene is repeated in a more pathological manner later, just before DeMonfort murders Rezenvelt. Alone after dark on the barren path where Rezenvelt will soon pass, DeMonfort is described in a stage direction as "looking behind him, and bending his Ear to the Ground, as if he listened to something" (IV.i). When Rezenvelt comes on stage, he too is described by the stage direction as wary, anxiety-ridden, listening: "Enter *Rezenvelt,* and continues his way slowly across the Stage, but just as he is going off, the Owl screams, he stops and listens, and the Owl screams again" (IV.i).

These details are doubtless meant to create suspense or tension on-stage, though it is arguable that Baillie does not handle them as effectively as she might for this purpose. But whatever their success as devices of suspenseful theater, they effectively signal social-psychological instability. In the various scenes and exchanges just described we are reminded that retreat from one's community assures no protection from the troublesome crosscurrents of daily life; that the home itself is not safe from those crosscurrents; that public and festive exchange is burdened by external pressures; that nature is alive with the energies of human struggle and violence; and that religious seclusion cannot keep the world at bay. In short, the personal anxiety seen on the surface of these details is deeply saturated in the institutions and conduct of society itself, constituting a troubled stream that runs through a world that wants to be—and assumes that it can be—secure in its values, beliefs, and daily practices.

If the details of anxiety course through the many settings of the drama in a way that suggests the largeness of the world and the severity of its troubles, images of claustrophobia pull the opposite direction, suggesting that the world is not large enough to allow even a single individual comfortable breathing space. It is worth noting a few of these images: near the beginning of the play, after learning of Rezenvelt's presence in the community, DeMonfort remarks to Freberg,

"Come, let us move: / This chamber is confin'd and airless grown" (I.ii). One act later, after agreeing to confess the cause of his mental anguish to his sister, Jane, DeMonfort comments:

> I'll tell thee all—but oh! thou wilt despise me,
> For in my breast, a raging passion burns,
> To which thy soul no sympathy will own.
> A passion, which hath made my nightly couch
> A place of torment; and the light of day,
> With the gay intercourse of social man,
> Feel like th' oppressive airless pestilence. (II.ii)

Still later, he responds to Freberg's story of Rezenvelt's enormous generosity with the comment that "This morning is oppressive, warm, and heavy: / There hangs a foggy closeness in the air; / Dost thou not feel it?" (II.ii). Finally, upon being informed by Grimald that Rezenvelt is in love with Jane, DeMonfort responds: "'Tis false! 'tis basely false! / What wretch could drop from his envenom'd tongue / A tale so damn'd?—It chokes my breath" (III.iii). These statements are accompanied by less direct remarks that nonetheless suggest the stifling nature of DeMonfort's social environment. He tells Jane that Rezenvelt "presses me" (II.ii); in describing his hatred for Rezenvelt, he likens himself to a plant "whose closing leaves do shrink / At hostile touch" (II.ii); and in promising to maintain a noble countenance in Rezenvelt's presence, he tell his sister: "The crooked curving lip, by instinct taught, / In imitation of disgustful things, / To pout and swell, I strictly will repress" (II.ii).

The obvious social and psychological point here is that because Rezenvelt is everywhere in society—from DeMonfort's home town to Amberg, where he has sought refuge; from DeMonfort's apartments to public gatherings; and from the garden outside DeMonfort's window to the barren areas outside Amberg—there is literally nowhere for DeMonfort to situate himself that is free from his enemy's presence. The two, finally, are even laid side by side in death, a grimly ironic reminder of the extent to which Rezenvelt presses upon and helps to define every aspect of DeMonfort's existence. DeMonfort's claustrophobia is a psychological response to his particular situation, to be sure, but it nonetheless clearly reflects at the same time the literally shrinking world of his social class, at least as that class is represented in its presumed superiority and autonomy by DeMonfort. As DeMonfort's world grows smaller, Rezenvelt's grows larger, as Rezenvelt is literally everywhere that DeMonfort turns, a fact that ultimately produces a crisis subject to resolution only by passing through the tragic territories (DeMonfort believes) of violence and death.

If anxiety and claustrophobia are signs of tense psychological pressure produced by antagonistic class relations, the feasts and parties described through much of the early part of the drama suggest one way that the aristocracy deals with that tension. These decadent pastimes constitute, moreover, an arena of social exchange in which both the downward negotiation of aristocratic social life and the upward motion of bourgeois respect and authority become visible.

In the opening scene, shortly after DeMonfort has arrived at Jerome's, Count and Lady Freberg enter unannounced, and at an extremely late hour, to welcome him to town. The Frebergs, DeMonfort is told, are on their return "from a midnight mask" (I.i). During their conversation, Count Freberg, sensing DeMonfort's melancholy humor, promises to "reestablish" his friend by making available to him the highest pleasure in life, partying: "Little time so spent, / Doth far outvalue all our life beside. / This is indeed our life, our waking life, / The rest dull breathing sleep" (I.i). Before the Frebergs leave, they make good their promise, inviting the morose DeMonfort to a party already set for the very next evening that they themselves will host. The anticipated pleasure of the evening is expressed confidently by Lady Freberg: "To-morrow night I open wide my doors / To all the fair and gay; beneath my roof / Music, and dance, and revelry shall reign" (I.i). Still later in the drama, only shortly after the Freberg party, DeMonfort is invited to yet another festivity by Count Freberg, this one to be hosted by old Count Waterlan in honor of Rezenvelt (see II.ii).

The repeated extravagant parties and planning of future parties define the public activity of the aristocracy depicted in the drama, and thus they are a key to its values and direction of social meaning. Two social realities are fundamentally connected to the enthusiastic embrace of decadence as a way of life. First, in the conduct of the Frebergs is seen the predictable last fling of a social class that has lost its commanding position in society. If DeMonfort's extreme sullenness represents the dark, reactive personal side of class erosion, the Frebergs' party fever represents its cynically indulgent side. While Count Freberg's hedonistic commitments are in no way cold or malicious, neither are they attuned to social realities outside the scope of his personal pleasure. For him a party, at its most serious and ambitious, marks an opportunity to manipulate small events within his personal sphere of experience, as is evidenced by his good-hearted yet dismally failed efforts to bring Rezenvelt and DeMonfort (who, in his view, possess "two minds so much refin'd" [III.ii]) together in friendship. At their most common level of occurrence, the parties and festivities that seem to constitute the central portion of Freberg's life are a public display of obscene wealth and conspicuous consumption, an ugly gesture refusing all claims of the world beyond aristocratic self-gratification.

Second, the never ending stream of parties and plans for more parties provides interesting insight into the actual social and political compromises that necessarily accompany social transformation. The difficulty and complexity of these compromises are glimpsed most readily in the fact that one major difference between DeMonfort and Count Freberg is that the latter has accepted the rising Rezenvelt as an equal, and perhaps even as a superior, while the former detests Rezenvelt literally more than death itself. While the aristocratic DeMonfort denies completely the social position that has been accorded to Rezenvelt—thus assuring DeMonfort's increasingly intense alienation from society—the aristocratic Freberg embraces it enthusiastically and publicly, displaying his acceptance of a new social arrangement in the many parties and social gatherings around which he has organized his life.

But Freberg's regard for Rezenvelt signals more than acceptance; it signals a far-reaching social compromise with presumed social payoffs for both the aristocracy and the inchoate bourgeoisie. The environment of the party is socially significant in this regard because in it the newly rich Rezenvelt finds public support and applause from a social class whose historical position has been the very definition of cultural credibility and political authority; that is, he finds himself meeting the approval not merely of individuals but of a long tradition of social and cultural privilege, as his leisure is their leisure, his pleasure is their pleasure. The expensively clad and ostentatiously privileged aristocracy, on the other hand, welcome Rezenvelt into their company both because of what they perceive as his individual merit and because of his newly acquired wealth, wealth which (according to the much-impressed Count Freberg) he displays with all proper decorum and modesty (see III.i). The fact is, of course, that in honoring Rezenvelt, Count Freberg and his fellow aristocratic partygoers attach themselves to and gain renewed social identity from one whose privilege and recognition have surpassed their own. As Count Freberg says bluntly to DeMonfort: "I know not one, for talents, honour, worth, / That I should rank superior to Rezenvelt" (III.i).

The tensions, compromises, and negotiations caught up in radical transformation are seen at other levels of social life as well. One site where they receive their most compelling depiction is the female body. The social significance attached to women, and specifically to their physical features, begins to be glimpsed in the comments of Lady Freberg's page about Lady Jane, who has just arrived at the Freberg residence but who has not yet been introduced or even identified. In this young man's eyes, the woman who turns out to be Lady Jane is a veritable goddess, one who is "So queenly, so commanding, and so noble, / I shrunk at first, in awe" (II.i). Such descriptions continue from the page's mouth with no sign of abating until Lady Freberg at last, in exasperation, interrupts him to say, "Thine eyes deceive thee, boy, / It is an apparition thou has seen" (II.i). When Count Freberg interjects that perhaps the page has not seen an apparition but rather Lady Jane, Lady Freberg coldly responds, "No; such description surely suits not her" (II.i). Lady Freberg's unease with Jane's presence is seen again moments later in Count Freberg's admiring comments about Lady Jane after she has left the room, which prompt Lady Freberg's cold response that what Count Freberg admires in Jane is in fact her "pride" (II.i).

This small, lightly humorous scene most obviously discloses competition between women for the attention of men. But the competition is by no means only personal, nor is it socially innocent. While Jane is "no doting mistress," and "No fond, distracted wife" (II.i) of DeMonfort, she is nonetheless a competitor for his attention and affection and for the attention and affection of other men; and thus she threatens Lady Freberg's (ostensibly) secure position as a preferred object of masculine desire, a fact that raises the issue of the cultural value attached to the female body. Unlike the social position of men, which is determined largely in terms of class in the world of drama (as can be seen in the conflict between Rezenvelt and DeMonfort), that of women is determined in terms of patriarchy, largely irrespective of class. This means that both bourgeois and aristocratic men stand in positions of power with respect to women; and thus women in the world of the drama—as is most clearly seen in the various actions and comments

of Lady Freberg—self-consciously transform themselves so that they
might be objects of choice, and thereby attach themselves to some sort
of social authority, be it bourgeois or aristocratic. One sign of the ongoing and shaping power of patriarchy in the midst of class struggle
can be found in Rezenvelt's lengthy, self-satisfied survey of the women
at the Freberg's party:

> . . . [M]en of ev'ry mind
> May in that moving crowd some fair one find,
> To suit their taste, though whimsical and strange,
> As ever fancy own'd.
> Beauty of every cast and shade is there,
> From the perfection of a faultless form,
> Down to the common, brown, unnoted maid,
> Who looks but pretty in her Sunday gown.
> . . .
> And if the liberality of nature
> Suffices not, there's store of grafted charms,
> Blending in one, the sweets of many plants,
> So obstinately, strangely opposite,
> As would have well defy'd all other art
> But female cultivation. Aged youth,
> With borrow'd locks in rosy chaplets bound,
> Clothes her dim eye, parch'd lip, and skinny cheek
> In most unlovely softness.
> And youthful age, with fat, round, trackless face,
> The downcast look of contemplation deep,
> Most pensively assumes.
> Is it not even so? The native prude,
> With forced laugh, and merriment uncouth,
> Plays off the wild coquet's successful charms
> With most unskilful pains; and the coquet,
> In temporary crust of cold reserve,
> Fixes her studied looks upon the ground
> Forbiddingly demure.
> . . .
> I' faith, the very dwarfs attempt to charm,
> With lofty airs of puny majesty,
> Whilst potent damsels, of a portly make,

Totter like nurslings, and demand the aid
Of gentle sympathy.
From all those diverse modes of dire assault,
He owns a heart of hardest adamant,
Who shall escape to-night. (II.i)

According to this cynical view, women are objects to be chosen like produce by desiring men, and their value as objects is not in the least class specific, but rather form specific. From native prudes to coquets to damsels of a portly make, the women of whom Rezenvelt here speaks are varieties of Lady Freberg—women who seek to place themselves in the arena of social value, and to hold their place in that arena through the use of their bodies. In such a world, friendship and trust between women are impossible—as they are impossible between Lady Freberg and Lady Jane—as every woman is a threat to every other woman.[6]

The most illuminating insight into the social and cultural significance of the female body and into the workings of patriarchy can be found in the scene describing Lady Jane's appearance in disguise at the Freberg party. In denying even a glimpse of her face, the disguise both focuses attention on her physical form and inspires masculine fantasy to create a dream face for that form. As the drooling comments of Rezenvelt describe the situation: "this way lies attraction" (II.i). Refused access to her face, he (like DeMonfort) quickly constructs in his imagination a vision of her as far superior to other women in her presence: "We bid you welcome, and our beauties here, / Will welcome you the more for such concealment" (II.i).

Beyond the obvious masculine erotic fantasies about the faceless (dehumanized) female body, however, is another, more delicate, matter of sexual politics, one still related to the cultural value of the female body but charged with a combined class and erotic interest: incest. The conversation between DeMonfort and his disguised sister approaches sexual longing, as Jane speaks freely (protected by the veil that she wears) of one "who has, alas! forsaken me" (II.i), and of one who shared his life with her entirely: "Within our op'ning minds, with riper years / The love of praise, and gen'rous virtue sprung: / Through varied life our pride, our joys, were one" (II.i). DeMonfort, for his part, responds in kind, remarking first upon his sister's "virtuous worth," and then celebrating her unusual beauty, which, he says, is at least as great as that which he imagines lies behind the veil of his unknown companion: "And though behind those sable folds were hid / As fair a face as ever woman own'd, / Still would I say she is as fair as thee" (II.i). Furthermore, he remarks with considerable pride that his sister, in her younger years, declined the offers of many suitors, preferring to remain devoted to her brother (II.i).

Their relationship, as it is manifested in this exchange, is distinguished by DeMonfort's admiration for Jane's beauty and virtue; by his recognition of her undying love for him; by Jane's view of the two of them (at least in earlier days) as soul mates with a single identity; and by their mutual sense of an absolute faithfulness to one another that overwhelms all other potential love interests.[7] The details of this relationship develop within a complicated web of psychological and historical interest that charges incest with social significance. Perhaps most important to an understanding of the larger and determining contexts of the relationship is the fact that DeMonfort and Jane were left orphaned very early in life, compelling Jane not only toward close companionship with her brother but also toward a role as mother to him. As DeMonfort puts it:

> [W]ithin her house,
> The virgin mother of an orphan race
> Her dying parents left, this noble woman
> Did, like a Roman matron, proudly sit,
> Despising all the blandishments of love. (II.i)

In purely psychological terms, the relationship may thus be seen as reflecting oedipal and pre-oedipal desires that were shocked by the death of the parents and then transferred to the sister, where they were allowed to flourish, as the law of the father had been effectively removed. This view is reinforced by the descriptions of guilt that De-Monfort experiences ("My heart upbraids me with a crime like his" [II.i]), even as his love for Jane expands.

But their love is also socially formed, as the death of the parents is also, in the larger context of the drama, the death of the parent class. DeMonfort and Jane are an "orphan race," marginalized from the main flow of social life, as is evidenced in DeMonfort's extreme alienation and in Jane's disguise. Their love is a kind of mutual support, a desperate defense against a changing world that has begun to displace their parents' authority and even to isolate the orphaned children from one another. The move to isolate and divide Jane and DeMonfort from one another is suggested near the end of the disguise scene, when Rezenvelt steps between Jane and DeMonfort as the latter moves to unveil his sister; and it is more emphatically depicted in subsequent scenes, where rumors abound that Rezenvelt and Jane are planning to marry, which of course would sever the Jane-DeMonfort relationship entirely. In these ways the psychological explanations of the mutual affection between Jane and DeMonfort become mediated by historical and social considerations; the ostensibly self-generating and local oedipal conflict modulates from an example of purely private psychological phenomena into an *effect* of public turmoil and pressure: the determinants of personal life in this view are to be found not only in the individual psyche but also in social and historical reality.[8]

It should be clear from the cast of this argument that even at this level of personal and social life the female body, or at least the female person, is one important site upon which the drama of masculine need, desire, and demand gets played out. Even as the relationship between Jane and DeMonfort is characterized by mutual affection, it is Jane's body and person—as ideal beauty and as mother—that are the repository of DeMonfort's desire. Her role as "other" to a masculine "subject" is consistent throughout the drama.[9] Whether she appears disguised (as in this scene) or plainly dressed (as in the scene, described above, involving Lady Freberg's page) or troubled by deep grief (as in the final scenes following DeMonfort's death), she is made to bear the weight of masculine circumstance; she is defined and valued at the pleasure of both aristocratic and bourgeois patriarchy. Even in the final scene, when she appears to display her greatest nobility of character, she fulfills the role of "Roman matron" described much earlier by DeMonfort; virtually all of the principal male characters gather around her (along with the abbess and nuns), one supporting her, one embracing her knees, one holding her robe—her body is literally the focal point for the expression of collective emotion.

Two additional issues that are raised only briefly, religion and law, help to illuminate the social anxiety and historical crisis at the center of the dramatic action. Both of these issues appear only very late in the story—after the murder of Rezenvelt—and, in the context of that murder, they function as markers of the direction of social meaning, pointing up the social and ideological transformations symbolized by DeMonfort's tragic deeds.

Immediately after the murder of Rezenvelt in Act IV, the scene shifts to the inside of a convent chapel, providing the first clear glimpse of religion in the world of the drama. And, as will be the case nearly twenty years later in Charles Robert Maturin's *Bertram,* the world of the monks and nuns is initially portrayed as suffering from the severe shock of a storm that "howls along the cloisters" (IV.ii). Amid the seething and tumultuous energies of nature, the nuns and monks attempt to preserve the integrity of their religious practice, carrying out a solemn ritual for someone recently deceased. The ritual, however, is interrupted, first by a hysterical lay sister who has heard a piercing human cry above the storm blast, and then by frantic knocking at the chapel door by a monk who has seen the murdered corpse of Rezenvelt just beyond the chapel. These disturbances are further compounded by the arrival of yet another shocked monk who has seen the greatest horror of all: the person of DeMonfort who, following his murderous deed, has come, like Coleridge's Ancient Mariner, to resemble the living dead.

These frantic developments in the plot, shifted as they are into the territory of institutional religion, suggest the threat under which traditional faith operates in a world marked increasingly by alienation, decadence, severe class conflict, and tragic violence. The anxiety that is felt by religious people themselves is indicated by the fact that one nun sees revenge as the only proper response to the murder: "The good Saint Francis will direct their search; / The blood so near his holy convent shed, / For threefold vengeance calls" (IV.iii). This anxiety gradually modulates through the final scenes of the play into a morbid fascination with death and dying, as various nuns and monks gather outside DeMonfort's holding room in the convent, listening intently as the life of the despair-ridden murderer slowly slips away. Indeed, the sound of death echoes with growing resonance through the entire convent, disturbing the inhabitants with its nightmarish rumblings. As one lay sister, unable to sleep and wandering the halls of the convent, remarks to the monk Bernard and several nuns who also cannot sleep and who have positioned themselves just outside DeMonfort's room:

> I cannot rest. I hear such dismal sounds,
> Such wailings in the air, such shrilly shrieks,
> As though the cry of murder rose again
> From the deep gloom of night. I cannot rest:
> I pray you let me stay with you, good sisters. (V.iv)

The literal storm that so disturbed the nuns and monks when they were first introduced into the dramatic action here modulates into a psychological storm that disturbs their rest with even greater horror and threatens their very faith.

The turmoil into which institutional religion has been thrown is set against the confident authority of the institution of law, which also appears in the final portions of the story. Though only briefly present, the officers of the law serve a clear and important function: they provide a stabilizing presence at a moment of growing instability, asserting firm control of a situation that is but confusingly handled by an uncertain and anxious religious authority. Their power, as they themselves describe it, is absolute, a secular equivalent of—and replacement for—the divine law that is under siege. As one officer states, in the very first pronouncement by a representative of law, "we are servants of the law, / And bear with us a power, which doth constrain / To bind with fetters this our prisoner" (V.ii). The power of which he speaks is never identified in practical social terms, except insofar as it is said to be bolstered by sacred custom, and yet this power is real, and an unmistakable sign that the world has changed; it is a sign of a world in which the aristocracy has been overthrown and its religion paralyzed, both replaced by a firmer and more vibrant authority.

DeMonfort, at least on some level, recognizing the change signaled by the presence of a secular authority representing civil life, is grimly and sarcastically shown in his submission to his accusers:

> Here, officers of law, bind on those shackles,
> And, if they are too light, bring heavier chains.
> Add iron to iron, load, crush me to the ground;
> Nay, heap ten thousand weights upon my breast,
> For that were best of all. (V.ii)

DeMonfort's last best resistance, he knows, is a Manfred-like assertion of will and integrity that will be followed shortly by death. Whatever triumph might be enjoyed by his adversaries and their representatives of social authority must be understood within this purely negative context. When the officers of the law return in the final scene of the drama to bear DeMonfort away to punishment, they are told that he has died, and this news leaves them powerless and looking foolish: "I am an officer on duty call'd, / And have authority to say, how died?" (V.iv). DeMonfort's death in the convent marks a personal victory and at the same time points to the much larger social defeat of the aristocracy and the institution of religion that once represented its highest values and strongest authority.

Before turning to a final set of comments about the social significance of DeMonfort's character, I want to touch glancingly, once more, upon the important role of Lady Jane, this time considering her character in terms of class as well as of patriarchy. It would seem, with the death of Rezenvelt and the ensuing despair of DeMonfort, that the bourgeois elements in the drama are successfully contained, and that aristocratic values, despite the actions of DeMonfort, come to be restabilized and presented nostalgically in DeMonfort's final anguishing days as signs of personal and social integrity. The descriptions of DeMonfort's death, however, are followed by an interesting portrayal of Jane, which suggests that her character has changed through the course of the drama in ways that keep a bourgeois sensibility alive. Indeed, after Rezenvelt's murder and DeMonfort's death, Jane's character gradually begins to represent, in idealized form, an individualism and subjectivity over against aristocratic and religious structures of value—to display bourgeois sensibilities shorn of the ugliness associated with Rezenvelt's character. Rezenvelt, as one of the newly rich rubbing shoulders with the landed aristocracy through much of the play, must of course be seen as the public example of the ugly *embourgeoisment* of society. But Jane comes to embody its personal integrity, its intensity of personal commitment, and its impeccable personal values. Rather than Count Freberg or the abbess, it is Jane who becomes the focal point of social life near the end of the drama; Count Freberg, the monks and nuns, and even the servants Jerome and Manuel defer to her. She is one whose "simple word" (V.iv) carries the weight of truth, and whose simple conduct expresses respect for the long history of aristocratic hegemony, acceptance of a changed world, and recognition of the course that individual conduct must now take.

It is fitting that Jane becomes an example of bourgeois value because in the drama women are one primary locus of masculine power and desire, and hence of social meaning. If in the earlier scenes women were shown to be malleable, transformed in ways that reflected the direction of an essentially masculine reality, in the final scenes Jane is transformed once again, this time moving to the foreground of the dramatic action, not as a primary agent of social change or social authority but rather as an idealized projection of change that has already occurred, symbolized in the ugly and physical struggles between Rezen-velt and DeMonfort. With such a view, the integrity evident in her final speeches is certainly her own, but the meaning of her comments and actions belongs as well to social currents that, historically, have positioned and valued women in quite specific ways.

Finally, I want now to consider briefly Baillie's portrayal of De-Monfort and to suggest, specifically, that the deep psychological passions seen in his character are best understood against the trajectory of social transformation that has been sketched thus far. The psychological confusion and the passion of hatred seen in DeMonfort are, in the larger context of the dramatic action, signs of a radically divided subject. From the beginning DeMonfort unyieldingly—and desperately—asserts the authority of an autonomous, stable subject, and he seeks a reflection of that stability and autonomy in the world around him. At both the biological and social levels, however, stability has been denied, as his parents' early death has left him orphaned and an emergent bourgeoisie has left him socially marginalized. Unable to discover the stability he desires, either in social life or in the personal world inhabited by himself and his sister (he fears that she plans to marry Rezenvelt), he is cast loose upon a stream of ever changing personal and social events within which he, as subject, is repeatedly displaced and reconstituted—as generous master, as cold tyrant, as dignified aristocrat, as old friend, as archenemy, as caring brother, as betraying brother, as superior noble, and as murderer. The chain of this movement is suggested in DeMonfort's many literal changes of scene: upon arriving in Amberg, he is seen at various times in the meager apartments of old Jerome; in the ostentatious surroundings of the Freberg estate; in the barren wilderness outside Amberg; and in the convent. With each new location his character modulates, changing according to the demands and possibilities of the world within which he moves.

Amid these fluctuations, DeMonfort's character never approaches wholeness or autonomy, despite his repeated claims that his life is under his command. One of the bleakest and clearest examples of the contradictions tearing at his character appears in the final scene, in which he gives himself over, as if by choice, to be placed in chains by the officers of the law. Even at this moment of absolute physical defeat he speaks from a position of apparent superiority, explicitly revealing what has been the case from the beginning: personal desire notwithstanding, his is a character entirely subject to social forces—Rezenvelt's money, the rumored pending marriage of Rezenvelt and Jane, and Count Freberg's regard for Rezenvelt—that he has all along attempted to repress but which always return to haunt him, and with ever increasing severity, until he finally believes that the only way to free himself is through a definitive act of extreme violence.

As this brief explanation makes clear, DeMonfort's troubles are involved with matters of passion and psychology. But passion and psychology are always socially mediated. What might appear to be pure oedipal and pre-oedipal confusion is connected vitally to DeMonfort's overwhelming sense of alienation from the specific social configuration of the world around him; what one might prefer to see only as one man's personal quarrel with another derives fundamentally from the changing direction of wealth and power in society; what might be described in pathological terms as one lunatic's violent ambush of an innocent individual occurs necessarily alongside the demise of an entire social class. Thus DeMonfort's movements are never his alone; his is "the gait disturb'd of wealthy, honour'd men" (I.ii) generally in his world. While his specific actions are unique to his character, the passion of hatred that energizes those actions is fired in the oven of rapidly increasing social change whose flames are felt not only by DeMonfort but by everyone—Count Freberg, Rezenvelt, Lady Jane, the various servants, and the nuns and monks in the convent.

That *DeMonfort* has been all but forgotten by literary history is no doubt partly attributable to shortcomings in the play itself—it is long, melodramatic, and ill-suited for the popular stage. But the fate of the drama (and of Baillie's work generally) is also attributable to the inability—or unwillingness—of scholarship to probe the deeper structures of a work whose significance is barely glimpsed on its surface. Like many of Byron's dramas (which have hardly fared much better), *DeMonfort* works not so much through action and dialogue as through ideological disclosure, which Baillie achieves by focusing on social relations rather than individual events. This focus necessarily slows the pace of dramatic action—and thus damages stageability—but the payoff is an astonishingly comprehensive and profound picture of personal life drenched in the many currents of social circumstance.

More than forty years ago, Bertrand Evans called for a complete reevaluation of Joanna Baillie's works.[10] When that reevaluation comes—

and the present discussion is meant to encourage it—it will best serve Baillie by recognizing and emphasizing that the strength of her dramatic imagination lies not only in her probings of individual psychology—or in any narrowly defined poetic beauties that she may have achieved—but also in her wide and deep historical vision. Only through an exploration of the historical dimensions of her imagination can the considerable achievement of her dramatic works be recovered.

"These Have Eat into My Old Estates"

Charles Lamb's *John Woodvil*

It is perhaps true, as some scholars have dismissively remarked, that Charles Lamb's verse drama *John Woodvil,* despite its subtitle to the contrary, is not a tragedy, but rather an embarrassing exercise in "silly sentimentalism," hardly worth critical mention.[1] Recent Romantic scholarship and criticism, indeed, have eagerly avoided the work as though even to acknowledge its existence would be a breach of good taste. Over the past fifty years scholars have often noted—and have come increasingly to study—the importance of Lamb's essays and criticism to Romantic literature, history, and thought, and yet virtually no critical commentaries on *John Woodvil* of any real seriousness or length have appeared.[2] The charge of silly sentimentalism has been absorbed so completely and uncritically that, like Baillie's *DeMonfort,* the drama has been almost entirely erased from literary historical memory.

While I do not here wish to argue against conventional wisdom that Lamb's drama is in fact a tragedy, and a good one at that, I do want to suggest that literary and aesthetic criteria, at least in their narrow formalist definitions, cannot effectively measure the historical importance of the work. That importance is great, for, like much Romantic drama, *John Woodvil* interestingly engages the material conditions under which it was produced and therefore provides us with a specific and at times compelling articulation of the historical moment of Romantic culture and society. Not at the level of plot and theme, which admittedly are handled clumsily, but rather at the level of its political unconscious the drama discloses an array of historical tensions and anxieties in the Romantic period that paralyzed a once powerful literary genre—drama—denying it the voice that, during the Renaissance, had spoken the values and beliefs of an entire age. At this deeper level, Lamb's work provides both an example of and an avenue into social and historical crisis, enabling us to glimpse the deep structural shifts that helped to shape the literature and culture of the period. Whatever its literary and dramatic shortcomings, *John Woodvil* provides an opportunity for understanding that genres in decline (such as drama during the Romantic period) no less than genres in ascent (such as lyric during the same period) are important areas of historical and critical investigation.[3]

Because Lamb was an avid student of Renaissance literature, and particularly of the drama of that period,[4] it is tempting to view *John Woodvil* in narrow literary historical terms as the author's unsuccessful effort to recreate the drama of an earlier age, an effort allegedly marked by "over-imitation of the antique in plot, characterisation and style."[5] But Lamb's personal literary aspirations are much less significant— and certainly less productive of serious critical commentary—than the historical anxiety and ideological complexity within which the drama itself is saturated, and which investigation of literary history, authorial intention, and formal features alone is incapable of explaining. From a historical perspective the most immediate critical questions involve not so much the success or failure of Lamb's attempt to rewrite the old drama but rather the social and cultural pressures shaping and determining that attempt. Investigation of these pressures in the work reveals, among other things, tense and problematic relations between past history and the imaginative reception and representation of that history in the present.

W. L. Renwick remarks that the failure of *John Woodvil* is attributable largely to the fact that Lamb was unable to balance his general subject matter—England during the early days of the Restoration—with the contemporary demands on drama imposed by Drury Lane.[6] While Renwick does not pursue this insight, and indeed seems unaware of its larger historical significance, his comment in raising the issue of past and present points toward precisely the historical dilemma through which the meanings of the drama are filtered. *John Woodvil* was written during a period of severe national and international political turmoil

(1798–1802) about a period in the past when turmoil ostensibly has just ended (the Restoration). Not surprisingly, then, it is marked by conflicting imaginative tendencies: nostalgia for a time of relative peace, and a realistic social vision of hardship, struggle, and instability. It displays at once an intense desire to move back in time to a world of wholeness and possibility and a disconcerting recognition of pressures in the historical present that block that desire. Unable to avoid or to find a workable voice for containing or expressing this conflict—for example, as Matthew Lewis had done by casting history as spectacle or as Shelley would do by casting history as psychodrama[7]—Lamb's dramatic imagination was left paralyzed, incapable of satisfying the demands of the theatergoing public or of producing a work that his age (or ours) would judge to be of real literary quality. *John Woodvil* is, in short, a virtual parody of Renaissance drama and, for the most part, an inept expression of Romantic desire.

If the limitations of *John Woodvil* as drama are best understood in terms of the disabling historical double bind just described, so too is its importance. *John Woodvil* has a claim on historical scholarship and criticism today precisely because of its peculiar entanglement in history. Its desperate effort to escape (or, at the very least, to account for) present history through the door of past history—that is, to construct a nontranscendental vision of redemption and positive human meaning—as well as the direction it takes when this effort fails, create an intellectual space for examining certain important structures of authority and belief, historical determinations of desire, and the developing and changing relations of social life and personal identity during the Romantic period.

The opening act, by introducing a variety of characters whose significance, explicitly, is socially and ideologically grounded, establishes some of the national political issues and social values that help to shape and promote the personal turmoil at the center of the dramatic action. Beginning with a portrait of the Woodvil estate servants at a moment shortly after Charles II's restoration—the servants are singing "When the King enjoys his own again" as the play opens—this act portrays, on the surface at least, a celebration of Charles's return to England. As one servant remarks, summarizing the thoughts of his peers: "I think everything be altered for the better since His Majesty's blessed restoration" (I.i).[8] Under Charles the restrictions that had been placed on society by the Commonwealth are loosened, especially those relating to personal conduct, and the servants commend the king for promoting greater individual freedom, while at the same time exercising their newfound freedoms by getting drunk.

The levity of this scene, with its praise of Charles and its celebration of an apparent return of social harmony, is obviously an awkward and simplistic foil for the real conflict and instability which follow, when John Woodvil is forced to confront the weaknesses of his character. Despite its inept dramatic presentation, however, it is not entirely a transparent picture of happiness to be set against a later picture of tragedy; in fact, the servants' various comments cut across a difficult ideological landscape of personal and social life, displaying traces of uncertainty and anxiety even at a moment of celebrating an apparent national triumph. Tangled in the nets of radical social change, the servants readily embrace the views of the state while drinking themselves into a stupor—a fact in itself that ironically undercuts expressions of social harmony and social possibility. Worse, their views, while presented loudly and in song, are not at all authentic but rather follow the lead of the master who provides their employment. The servant Daniel states this point explicitly, when he remarks that he has learned his loyalist song about Charles's return to England "where thou learnest thy oaths and thy politics—at our master's table.—Where else should a serving-man pick up his poor accomplishments?" (I.i). Even as he sings Charles's praises, he knows that political support is bought with the promise of employment; in such a world, a logical corollary is that (as his conduct emphatically attests) social goals or ideals are measured in terms of the availability of liquor. From a servant's point of view, the Restoration is good inasmuch as it promises an opportunity, through drink and easy labor, to become oblivious to real politics.

The powerful impact of changes at the national level on domestic life evident here is seen as well in the servant's comments on the Woodvil estate. The rightful master, Sir Walter Woodvil, a longtime supporter of Cromwell, is said to have gone into hiding to avoid prosecution by the recently returned Charles II, leaving the everyday affairs of the estate to his eldest son, John, who is (at least ostensibly) a loyalist. While much needs to be said about Sir Walter's unswerving support for Cromwell and his son's support for Charles, we should note first that this information, following as it does upon the celebration of Charles's restoration, calls attention to inextricable connections between the various and multiple threads of social life, from royalty to aristocracy to the serving class. Displaying a consistent interest in questions, issues, and gossip bearing on those individuals who control society, the servants' conversation is given coherence by its understanding that John Woodvil's newfound authority is equivalent to Charles's new-found authority, just as Walter's exile finds its political equivalent in the collapse of the Commonwealth. Amid these radical political changes are smaller but no less significant domestic changes, suggested above, as the serving people nervously shift their allegiances and celebrate the latest rulers—both Charles II and John Woodvil, in this case—in an effort to assure themselves material security; that debauchery fuels their political songs and that cynicism marks their political attitudes are clear signs that social stability, for them, is more a dream (or hollow rhetoric) than reality, for they are at the mercy of a world that itself has been severely shaken.

The politics of Sir Walter and John Woodvil, as described by the drunken but politically attuned servants, point toward yet another social complexity in the world of the drama. That the progressive, antimonarchist spokesperson—Sir Walter—is exiled while the loyalist spokesperson—John—is triumphant, produces the appearance of a world at ease with monarchist or absolutist politics. Indeed, one complaint that the servants have against the way Sir Walter governed his estate is that he was too puritanical, not allowing servants to get drunk before 2 P.M.; John is the preferred master because he allows servants to begin drinking as soon as they arise in the morning. At the same time, however, the servants are pleased that Sir Walter has eluded his political enemies, and in fact they retain a curious sense of loyalty to him. Though there is a £200 reward for their old master, though they know his place of exile, and though they suspect that they are subject to penalty under the treason act for withholding this information, they nonetheless drink a toast to his safety.[9] If their loyalty to Charles (and John) is coated with cynicism, their memory of Sir Walter is tinged with nostalgia. No political element of Restoration society, at least as the servants see it, is easily compartmentalized or characterized, though all elements are politically intertwined: they recognize that the various structures of authority and belief embrace a single social reality.

The servants' drunken political analysis of monarchy, aristocracy, and labor is interestingly complicated by Sandford, the old steward of Sir Walter. Coming upon the servants as they discuss the whereabouts

of Sir Walter, Sandford bitterly lashes out at them for their drunken-
ness and political wavering, claiming that their expressions of political
loyalty are merely occasions to drink, as is evidenced, he says, by their
earlier expressions of loyalty to Sir Walter: "How often in old times /
Your drunken mirths have stunn'd day's sober ears, / Carousing full
cups to Sir Walter's health?" (I.i). In his view, their political spineless-
ness is combined with a complete ignorance of and disregard for true
social and personal integrity. Once bound to the loom and plough for
their livelihood, Sandford reminds them, they were brought by Sir
Walter into a better world where they were fed, clothed, and entertained "in a worthy service, / Where your best wages was the world's
repute" (I.i). This benevolent paternalism is repaid with debauchery
that threatens society at its core, as worthwhile labor is replaced by
empty expressions of personal satisfaction. As Sandford puts it, these
opportunistic servants are little more than

> Well-fed and unprofitable grooms,
> Maintain'd for state, not use;
> You lazy feasters at another's cost,
> . . . [E]at like maggots into an estate. (I.i)

Besides offering a powerful example of absolute loyalty, Sandford's
scathing comments (which entirely break the drunken confidence of
the servants) point to one of the central social problems in the drama,
namely the relative stability of the estate and the importance of that
stability to social and human value. The conduct and statements of
the drunken servants, the exile of Sir Walter, and the restoration of
Charles II all mark for Sandford the moment of social collapse, the
destruction of "a well-order'd family" (I.i). What for others is an opportunity for personal advancement, or at least for personal leisure
and self-indulgence, is for him the eruption of chaos into the world,
a chaos characterized by treachery, villainy, and loss of commitment.
The absolute quality of his loyalty to Sir Walter focuses the social issues
at stake in the changing world of the Restoration and thus helps to
clarify the extremity and multiplicity of response to those changes.

The introduction of one additional character in the opening act
helps to elucidate the social anxiety and the direction of social meaning
in the world of the drama. As the servants depart, breaking up what
Sandford calls their "atheist riot and profane excess" (I.i), Sir Walter's
orphan ward, Margaret, enters. In many respects she is a stereotypi-

cal female character in Romantic literature, particularly the drama. We see very similar characters, for instance, in Coleridge's *Osorio* (Maria), in Matthew Lewis's *Castle Spectre* (Angela), in Mary Shelley's novel *Frankenstein* (Elizabeth), and elsewhere. Like the female characters in these works, Margaret is an orphan who depends entirely upon the charity of men for her well-being and social status; she is character-ized in highly sentimental terms; her primary role in the plot is as a love interest and as a supporter of a man in distress (as she puts it, she has always been John Woodvil's "conscience, his religion" [I.i]); her sexual desires have a quasi-incestuous dimension to them ("I was his favourite once, his playfellow in infancy" [I.i]).

Despite the derivative or stock nature of her character, however, Margaret is an example of real alienation experienced at a moment de-scribed by those loyal to the existing social authority as a triumph of justice and human possibility. That she would rather "trust for food to the earth and Providence" (I.i) than to the Woodvil estate in its current condition—that is, in its celebration of debauchery by everyone from John Woodvil to the servants—suggests the extent of that alienation, as well as the instability, or inadequacy, of the world of the Restora-tion. More importantly, in her decision to leave the Woodvil estate for the purpose of searching out Sir Walter Woodvil, and in the manner she designs to do this (by disguising herself as a boy), she brings the issue of gender into prominence. John Woodvil has become a "cold protector" (I.i), and in leaving him to search for Sir Walter, she knows she will pass along a dangerous way; thus she dons "boy's apparel" (I.i). With this scheme she focuses two kinds of escape that are neces-sary and, for her, desirable: from a morally hollow social situation and from a gender that is the first to be compromised by that situation. Her character is never developed along what might be called feminist lines, and yet her actions and comments encourage a feminist critique of her world. For her, liberty is not possible under John Woodvil nor under Charles II, but is possible only, if at all, in Sherwood Forest, to which Sir Walter has fled.

The introduction of characters in Act I, clearly, is at the same time an introduction to a variety of social issues that provide the drama with its primary intellectual unity; these issues range from political struggle at the national level, to family disputes at the domestic level, to personal hardship at the level of gender, and to security questions at the level of the serving class. While they are distinguished by their association with specific characters or sets of characters, they are ultimately linked as parts of a single social reality that pressures and shapes each. And while that social reality is awkwardly handled, it is nonetheless identifiable, its underlying features compressed into a father-son conflict between John and Sir Walter. In this conflict, presented most directly and compellingly in Act II, can be seen the crisis of social class that stands behind both the English civil wars (which the Restoration unsuccessfully attempted to put to rest) and the England of Lamb's day. The drama shows in its final acts that out of this conflict emerged a set of social values and a structure of authority and belief that came to maturation during the Romantic period.

To understand the direction of social change that is being suggested here, it is necessary to understand first that Lamb assigns social value to his principal characters in an odd and confusing manner. Put simply, John Woodvil, as a loyalist and supporter of Charles II, would seem most appropriately to be associated with a retrogressive set of social values, while Sir Walter, a staunch Cromwellian, would seem to be most suitably aligned with progressive politics. In fact, however, the characters display slightly different, more complex, values, which cannot be easily or reductively assigned to the political allegiance that each character expresses.

The social realities underlying the political and domestic conflicts can be glimpsed in John Woodvil's long, drunken soliloquy, spoken after he learns that Margaret has left him, and after observing the dissipated gentry who remain as his only company, surrounding him as permanent but worthless fixtures on his estate.[10] In this speech John Woodvil's character is shown to be formed neither by his father nor by the politics of Charles II but rather by the isolating and alienating struggles of the age, struggles that have ruined all possibilities and destroyed all dreams of social stability and that have thus deadened his regard for political authority and his desire to be socially responsible. Because this speech is the most socially revealing in the drama, I want to quote it at length:

> Now Universal England getteth drunk
> For joy, that Charles, her monarch, is restored:
> And she, that sometime wore a saintly mask,
> The stale-grown vizor from her face doth pluck,
> And weareth now a suit of morris bells,

With which she jingling goes through all her towns and villages.
The baffled factions in their houses skulk;
The commonwealthsman, and state machinist,
The cropt fanatic, and fifth-monarchy-man,
Who heareth of these visionaries now?
They and their dreams have ended. Fools do sing,
Where good men yield God thanks; but politic spirits,
Who live by observation, note these changes
Of the popular mind, and thereby serve their ends.
Then why not I? What's Charles to me, or Oliver,
But as my own advancement hangs on one of them?
I to myself am chief.—I know,
Some shallow mouths cry out, that I am smit
With the gauds and show of state, the point of place,
And trick of precedence, the ducks, and nods
Which weak minds pay to rank. 'Tis not to sit
In place of worship at the royal masques,
Their pastimes, plays, and Whitehall banquetings,
For none of these,
Nor yet to be seen whispering with some great one,
Do I affect the favours of the court.
I would be great, for greatness hath great *power,*
And that's the fruit I reach at.—
Great spirits ask great play-room. Who could sit,
With these prophetic swellings in my breast,
That prick and goad me on, and never cease,
To the fortunes something tells me I was born to?
Who, with such monitors within to stir him,
Would sit him down, with lazy arms across,
A unit, a thing without a name in the state,
A something to be govern'd, not to govern,
A fishing, hawking, hunting, country gentleman? (II.i)

In this speech John Woodvil reveals fully not only his alienation and loneliness, which he has tried to hide through debauchery, but also an inchoate bourgeois sensibility. At this early point in the drama that sensibility is portrayed in rather ugly and selfish terms. Woodvil avows allegiance to no authority greater than himself—"I to myself am chief"—and claims to support the return of Charles II only because that support will enable him to advance socially and politically. His only real interest, he confesses, is in power, and power in its most personal form; all of his actions and activities revolve around this single concern. Disdainful of "Universal England," of Charles II, and of the state—at least in their *social* definition—he sees only himself, and uses his personal ambitions and desires as the single measure of the worth of the world.

Ideologically, this passage displays the dislodgment of the individual from all frames of social reference, replacing these with private interest. This is the necessary first step of an emergent bourgeois sensibility or identity. Father, king, lover, friends: all become insignificant in the face of Woodvil's personal ambition, an ambition to avoid being just another nameless "country gentleman," "A something to be govern'd." The power he seeks is the power to establish an identity over—and against—society. All other goals, in his view, are foolish, whether they are in the cause of Charles, Cromwell, the fifth-monarchy-men, or even God. The extremity of his commitment to himself is seen in his willingness, ultimately, to reveal the hiding place of Sir Walter to Lovel, effectively sentencing his own father to certain death, apparently in a cynical effort to assure his own absolute personal control over the Woodvil estate.

After this violent and ugly dislodgment of John Woodvil from every conventional social tie, all that has been cut away gets recovered and reestablished through subsequent scenes, but in bourgeois rather than aristocratic terms. Having remarked, in his most cynical moment, that his father remains in England out of "A child-like cleaving to the land that gave him birth" (III.i), John Woodvil comes to love and respect "my native village / In the sweet shire of Devon" (V.ii); having lost Margaret during the days of his drunken self-indulgence, he welcomes her return as though she were a virtual angel, "Whose suit hath drawn this softness from my eyes" (V.ii); having doomed his own father to death through his own malice and self-interest, he recovers his father in memory, entering the family church, recalling "Where I so oft had kneel'd, / A docile infant by Sir Walter's side" (V.ii); and having denied the promise of religious comfort, he meekly attends church to find "the guilt of blood was passing from me, / Even in the act of agony of tears, / And all my sins forgiven" (V.ii). John is a changed person at the end of the drama, and yet the frames of reference are the same, only defined in more palatable terms than in the long confes-

sional speech, presented above: personal life—or individual desire—
still takes precedence over social life.

To put this issue in somewhat different and more abstract terms,
we might say that the drama traces the growth of a bourgeois structure of values and feelings through the portrayal of a single character.
The emergence of those values on the social scene is at first cynical
and violent, as they are values that attempt to carve a social space for
themselves by denying absolutely the claims that any segment of the
existing social structure may try to make on the individual. As the old
order dies—in this instance, in the form of Sir Walter—the new order,
no longer threatened, begins to manifest itself in more positive terms.
Indeed, this new order, in the form of John Woodvil, attempts to re-
trieve the *memory* of the old order, in the form of tradition, as a necessary ballast for the present. After Sir Walter's death, for instance, John
Woodvil is described looking nostalgically upon the historical paintings in the Woodvil estate (at portraits "of our most ancient family"
[V.i]), using them as a prod to his memory of Sir Walter's stories about
the "worthy histories" (V.i) contained in the paintings. But, as John
Woodvil's musings here show, the reference point for history itself is
personal rather than public and, like the religion described in the final
act of the drama, is intended to reflect individual desire rather than
social good or social responsibility.

One additional question bears consideration here: namely, if the
character of John Woodvil is to be associated with the emergence of
the bourgeoisie in British history, then why is he presented as a supporter of Charles II and, more broadly, why is the dramatic action
set at the moment of the Restoration rather than, for example, during
the English Civil Wars? The answer to this question is contained, at
least partly, in John Woodvil's comment to Lovel, after Lovel has been
disarmed in a fight with Woodvil:

> Stay, sir.
> I hope you have made your will.
> If not, 'tis no great matter.
> A broken cavalier has seldom much
> He can bequeath: an old worn peruke,
> A snuff-box with a picture of Prince Rupert,
> A rusty sword he'll swear was used at Naseby,

Though it ne'er came within ten miles of the place,
And, if he's very rich,
A cheap edition of the *Icon Basilike,*
Is mostly all the wealth he dies possest of. (III.i)

Woodvil's comments here show that his values, as well as his actions, are not at all those of the loyalist, but rather those of one violently opposed to monarchy. He knows the old order has little wealth, though much in the way of fond memories of past greatness (Woodvil himself, on the other hand, has acquired money, as is evidenced in "the Vandyke I have purchased" [II.i]), and his every effort is to deny the claim of that empty order on his life. In this view, the Restoration is no restoration at all but rather a desperate last effort to assert the authority of a hollow and dying order. John's presence in the midst of that order, as a loyalist only insofar as loyalty provides him with control of the Woodvil estate, demonstrates the aggressive and cynical denial of it.

Just as the references to Charles II do not accurately reflect the direction of social value in the world of the drama, the depiction of Sir Walter does not constitute a viable alternative to the world that Charles would rule. While the lives of the loyalists in the drama are characterized by debauchery and self-indulgence, Walter's character is defined by a nostalgic regard for domestic stability, by commitment to a public cause, and, most of all, by respect for land. These values are not marked by movement toward a future world of private interest but toward a past world of public responsibility and action, and therefore they too are denied by John Woodvil. The actions against the loyalist Lovel lead to the demise of the traditionalist Sir Walter, leaving John Woodvil in a position to reconstruct his own character along independent and, for him, positive lines.

I want now to turn briefly to a consideration of Sir Walter, in an attempt to establish his place and significance in the changing social world that this chapter describes. Like his old steward, Sandford, Sir Walter knows that the domestic world he once governed has been irreparably damaged by a new order of "riotous men," who "have eat into my old estates" (II.ii). These men owe their positions to a "jealous court" (II.ii) that extorts loyalty by both threat and promise of advancement. Sir Walter's personal integrity recoils from such cold political maneuverings, which, he says, are entirely ignorant of "what free grace or mercy mean" (II.ii), and for this reason he refuses "To beg or bargain with the court for my life" (II.ii), preferring exile and isolation to subservience and hypocrisy.

It is interesting that the place of Sir Walter's exile is a stereotypically Romantic setting: the Sherwood Forest once inhabited by the noble outlaw, Robert, Earl of Huntington (Robin Hood). In this setting Sir Walter and his younger son, Simon, idealize the past, speak nostalgically of Robin Hood as an earlier outlaw aristocrat, and generally commend the beautiful, natural landscape that they inhabit. If the servants in the opening act welcomed the changes that Charles's restoration promised, Sir Walter and Simon celebrate a primitive Rousseauistic and Godwinian world oblivious to change:

> *Sir Walter:* How quietly we live here,
> Unread in the world's business,
> And take no note of all its slippery changes.
> 'Twere best we make a world among ourselves,
> A little world,
> Without the ills and falsehoods of the greater;
> We too being all the inhabitants of ours,
> And kings and subjects both in one.
> *Simon:* Only the dangerous errors, fond conceits,
> Which make the business of that greater world,
> Must have no place in ours. (II.ii)

The small commune, individually governed and inspired by the natural beauties within which it is situated, marks a radical alternative to what Margaret will later call "the politics of state revenge" (II.ii). It offers a world of integrity, personal freedom, and (ostensibly) security; it offers a world limited only by the individual imagination.

Margaret's discovery of Sir Walter's hiding place reinforces the ideology of Romantic escape just described. After speaking at some length of Simon and Sir Walter's exile, which has cost them their personal wealth, as well as the "manners, laws, . . . [and] customs" (II.ii) of their homeland, Margaret (who until now has been disguised as a boy) reveals her true identity and requests to join them amid the "Free liberty of Sherwood" (II.ii). As a member of this primitive band of outlaws, she not only happily abandons the customs of her world, which have become abhorrent to her, but even her "Sweet mother-tongue, old English speech"—"Margaret has got new name and language new"

(II.ii)—and, as Sir Walter puts it, prepares to spend her days in the forest, "expecting better times" (II.ii).

The rejection of the world, where fortune is but "A light-hell'd strumpet" (II.ii), where "young men's flatteries cozen young maids' beauty" (II.ii), and where "sweet humility withers" (II.ii), is accompanied by the imaginative construction of a new set of values, which revolve not around the court, ambition, and politics but rather around nature. Love, for example, is not narrowly defined in terms of selfish and aggressive pursuit of the opposite sex, but is seen as love of "all things that live, / From the crook'd worm to man's imperial form" (II.ii): the "sunbeam," the "feeble bird," the "fish," and the "tall and elegant stag" (II.ii)—all of nature is an object of human love. Similarly, the sports and customs of a primitive society are radically different from the narrow pursuits of court life. Time is happily passed seeing "the sun to bed" and watching it rise; observing the moon rest on soft clouds; idly watching the leaves dance in the wind, or the birds eat corn in the fields, or the deer passing by; or noting the structure of plants and trees (II.ii).

Human conduct in Sir Walter's adopted world is modeled perfectly on Wordsworth's philosophy of "wise passiveness"—that is, on the patient willingness and ability to absorb nature into one's being—and as such it tells us a great deal about human society. For the nature that is idealized by the alienated and exiled individual is not a positive value; rather, it is a refuge from society, and as such receives its particular definition in opposition to the world that is being denied. As the world of Charles II becomes increasingly cold and impersonal, the idyllic world of Sherwood Forest becomes ever more warm and inviting; as love and daily activities come to be defined by deception in Charles's world, they come to be seen as wholesome in Sir Walter's; as life inside the court consumes the supporters of Charles, life in the out-of-doors takes on absolute value for Sir Walter and his compatriots. Nature, in other words, is, as Raymond Williams describes it (writing in a different context), "a place of healing, a solace, a retreat," [11] and as such its value is contingent rather than essential, determined in significant ways by the direction of change in Restoration England.

Clearly, what I have been describing here is what Marxists from Caudwell to Fekete have identified as the explicit bourgeois dimension of Romanticism.[12] Sir Walter's primitivism, his rejection of a sordid social life, and his embracement of natural beauty constitute a structure of values that are essential to the bourgeois sensibility that comes to be embodied in John Woodvil. From this perspective it might seem contradictory that Sir Walter dies and that his compatriots abandon Sherwood Forest, apparently having lost their bid to construct an alternative world. In fact, however, these plot-level actions are not signs of the destruction of bourgeois life but rather are a necessary step toward their incorporation into society. Sherwood Forest is an idealization, or projection, of bourgeois life, not a manifestation of its social reality; it is a device that lays bare certain underlying values that get fed into the social world inhabited by John Woodvil. As such, its values are not abandoned but simply brought, primarily in the character of Margaret, into John's world, where he embraces them wholly, transforming them into their social definitions: his love is directed to Margaret; his spiritual needs are met by the institution of religion; and his family is reconstructed in memory as he observes pictures of family history and then occupies the family pew in church. Like Coleridge's Ancient Mariner, John Woodvil comes to believe that the greatest social act is "To go to church and pray with Christian people" (V.ii), which washes "the guilt of blood" (V.ii) from his soul and leaves him prepared for life in "my native village / In the sweet shire of Devon" (V.ii).

I want now to touch glancingly, once more, upon the character of Margaret, who plays an important role in the changing class and social relations depicted in the drama, and whose portrayal helps to elucidate the vital connections between class and gender in the transition from an aristocratic to a bourgeois world. First, as noted above, that she is an orphaned female places her in a position of absolute dependence on men, who hold all real social power and wealth in the drama. But the significance of her orphan status extends much farther than this. By making Margaret an orphan, Lamb cuts her loose from a fixed social location, enabling her to serve as a carrier of values from one world to another: from the Woodvil estate to Sherwood Forest and back again. In this way she serves a major unifying function in the drama, connecting the world of John Woodvil to that of his father, hence enabling Lamb to ground John Woodvil's character within a continuous tradition of domestic and social life, without compromising the social dimension of the bourgeois values that John Woodvil embodies.

While serving as a central unifying device, the characterization of Margaret at the same time allows us to see the continuation and modu-

lation of patriarchy from one social order to another. In her first appearance (in Act I) she is clearly a marginal figure, physically pursued
by the drunken companions of John Woodvil and ignored by John, to
whom she is betrothed. As a woman, an orphan, and dependent, she is
at the mercy of an aristocratic patriarchy incapable of seeing her, except
perhaps as a nuisance or as an object of sexual desire. With John's transformation and her return to the Woodvil estate, her situation changes
radically, and yet patriarchal relations are not overthrown. Rather,
they are redefined in such a way that Margaret becomes now angelic—
as opposed to the whore role she was identified with earlier[13]—the
repository of John Woodvil's highest spiritual imaginings. He lowers
himself—"These your submissions to my low estate" (V.i)—and exalts
her; and yet she still serves him, only now as a personal and idealized
love whose supporting presence affords him the opportunity to carve
out his personal identity. Her presence in the final scene of the play
gives substance to an essentially protestant formulation of personal life,
guilt, and redemption, and as such it focuses the continuing subservient role of women within bourgeois social relations: the world remains
a masculine construction and the role of women, though changed from
what it once was, remains defined by masculine need.

Although it is weakened by poor dialogue, characterization, and
plot construction, *John Woodvil* is, with *The Borderers, Osorio,* and *De-
Monfort,* a historically revealing drama, for it provides a glimpse of
the complexity of social life during the 1790s and during the larger
period embracing the decline of aristocracy and the gradual, ineluctable emergence of the bourgeoisie. While at certain points the drama
appears destined to collapse under the weight of historical and ideological contradictions—and expository ineptitude—it finally negoti-
ates successfully the various threads of social interest that direct it. The
Restoration was not a period marking a return to feudalism and aristocracy but rather, as the drama correctly shows, a period of realignment
for the bourgeoisie; further, the valorization of nature so common
in the Romantic period does not constitute an absolute alternative to
a sordid social world, but rather an imaginative means of expressing certain social values; finally, the class conflict tearing at England
and at the creative imagination from the seventeenth to the nineteenth
centuries involved important questions about gender relations. The
drama discloses the social significance of all of these matters, and it dis-

plays as well their central shaping influence on the poetic imagination. Though *John Woodvil* is less successful than we might wish as drama, it is nonetheless more than silly sentimentalism. It is a document of considerable social historical significance that must be accounted for in any historical definition and description of Romanticism.

"In These Degenerate Days"

Henry Hart Milman's *Fazio*

In the prefaces to his lengthy histories of the Jews (1830) and Latin Christianity (1854–55) that he wrote in his mature years, Henry Hart Milman describes his desire to avoid all bias and to present, as accurately and objectively as possible, the actual events of history.[1] He believed this goal could be accomplished only if he refused to become embroiled in questionable points of interpretation debated by other historians and, instead, offered a single historical narrative of clearly connected and readily verifiable facts. That he felt compelled to state this common objective in the prefaces to works written twenty-five years apart says something about Milman's admirable respect for historical accuracy; but it also says something about his sensitivity to the problems of historical writing in the nineteenth century. Despite his expressed desire for objectivity, he seems to have understood what other historians of the period had learned: that matters of historical circumstance and situation were not settled, and that selections of details and descriptions of events constituted not only a record but also a judgment.[2] For someone of Milman's temperament, recognition of an elusive, complex, and apparently unstable past generated considerable personal anxiety that seems to have been compensated for by explicit statements of allegiance to the objective and neutral recording of events in his historical writings.

In a much earlier and very different work, the verse drama *Fazio*

(1815), Milman interestingly displays—perhaps more vividly than he would have known—some of the kinds of unstable historical and social details that might cause the later historian moments of anxiety. Set in Italy, presumably at the time of the Renaissance, the drama registers certain broad and deep structural changes wrought by the emergence of money as capital onto the stage of Western culture. While the focus of the dramatic action is on purely personal and domestic affairs, those affairs are shown to unfold within quite specific contexts of social life that are, almost without exception, shaped by the pervasive influence of new money and by the individual desire, approaching obsession, to possess that money. Marriage, law, family life, the state, mothering, class position, and religion: these social relations are at every turn energized or besieged by the fact of invested money, and in them can be seen the turbulence, anxiety, and desires that defined not only the early emergence of capitalism during the Italian Renaissance but also, and more pressingly, the bourgeois structures of social life that were radically redefining English culture during the early nineteenth century.

The single most important plot detail, which governs the political significance of all other actions in the drama, concerns Fazio's obsession with alchemy as a means of overcoming his poverty. That obsession appears to be rewarded when Fazio's miserly neighbor, Bartolo, is murdered by unknown assailants, who are then unable to discover the whereabouts of the old miser's money. Fazio, who knows where it is hidden, suddenly finds himself with access to considerable wealth, which, after very little soul-searching, he steals. He then proclaims to a believing public that he has successfully transformed iron into gold, giving the impression that through his own initiative he has become a wealthy man. By his own account, the stark and utter isolation into which his alchemical researches have directed him is repaid with material security, public status, and respect.

Fazio's dedication to alchemy, and the public's willingness to believe in the great rewards of that dedication, cut across the personal and social landscape of the drama in interesting ways. Most obviously, alchemy is an expression of Fazio's desire to relieve his straitened circumstances and to overcome his alienation, which is produced by his poverty. But, while the expression of that desire by someone in Fazio's situation is perfectly sensible, its formulation is contradictory, calculated finally to intensify rather than relieve alienation and hardship. For alchemy is emphatically a nonsocial solution to a social difficulty; that is, Fazio's poverty is both a product and a sign of the structures of social life in his world, while alchemy is a narrowly scientific or philosophical pursuit that would alter the natural order. While Fazio believes that changes in the natural order will automatically bring positive changes in the social order, the reverse in fact is the case, as is seen not only in the direction that the dramatic action takes—Fazio is ultimately executed—but also in more local or specific episodes, such as Fazio's refusal every evening to accompany his wife to bed, for fear that time spent with her is time lost in his pursuit of pure happiness. The desire for nonsocial solutions to hardships that are fundamentally social leads Fazio ever farther into a dark world of alienation, isolation, and ultimately death.

But the tragedy that arises from Fazio's wrongheaded dedication to alchemy is not merely the result of his personal shortcomings, nor is it only the result of his belief that social reality is controlled on some deep level by natural phenomena, which can be personally mastered. For in an important respect the values associated with alchemy are simply a sign of the larger structures of value governing the world depicted in the drama. That the public, for instance, readily believes Fazio's lie that he has found the magical key to wealth and that that key lies on a path outside society, suggests that his personal desires are also the desires of his world: everyone wants to believe that untold wealth is within individual reach. The drama suggests that such an attitude is a sign of social ill health, as is clearly seen in the actions of various characters—from Aldabella to the sycophantic Philario, Falsetto, and Dandello—all of whom jockey shamelessly to get closer to money that has magically appeared and thereby (they believe) get closer to true human happiness.

To recognize the larger social significance of Fazio's personal desires and tribulations is to understand that his tragedy is not reduced to his fascination with alchemy, but rather involves the structures and relations of social life within which that fascination emerges and takes shape. Alchemy is but one particular sign of a more elusive, but no less determining, set of social concerns, and in fact it helps to specify, and finds a crucially important social corollary in, a different magical key to wealth, namely usury or capitalism. To put the matter bluntly, the money in Fazio's possession that appears to derive from alchemy in fact derives from usury by means of theft. That is, it derives from specific economic relations of social life.

Following the money trail backward to its source for the purpose of explaining the social meaning of alchemy requires at the same time that the explanation be explained. For just as the apparent magic of alchemy is in fact dependent upon real social relations—usury—those relations are subject to specific determinations that are not transparent. We can begin to penetrate the mystery of usury—and thereby the mystery and tragedy of Fazio's character—by considering the important role of Bartolo in the dramatic action. Bartolo, of course, is the real immediate source of wealth behind Fazio and, as a source of wealth, holds the key to the economic dynamic of social life in the world that Fazio inhabits.

The most important and emphatically drawn feature of Bartolo's character is that he is not only defined in the stereotypical terms of squint-eyed, nasty miserliness—though certainly these details are readily present in Bartolo—but he is also drawn in terms of the larger economic relations of society. If the friendless and hermit-like Bartolo "looks as he were stain'd / with watching his own gold" (I.i),[3] at the same time that gold derives from Bartolo's very real interactions with his world. As Fazio tells Bianca,

> There's not a galliot on the sea, but bears
> A venture of Bartolo's; not an acre,
> Nay, not a villa of our proudest princes,
> But he hath cramp'd it with a mortgage; he,
> He only stocks our prisons with his debtors. (I.i)

In his dying moments the fatally wounded Bartolo, who has stumbled onto Fazio's premises, reveals even more explicitly one of the sources of his money, lamenting that "My ducats and my ingots [are] scarcely cold / From the hot Indies" (I.i). And much later, as state authorities sort out the circumstances of Bartolo's disappearance, one of the duke's council remarks that all that was found in Bartolo's apartments were "piles indeed of parchments, / Mortgages, deeds, and lawsuits heaped to the roof" (III.ii). The duke also notes that Bartolo's

> . . . argosies encumber all our ports,
> His unsold bales rot in the crowded wharfs;

The interest of a hundred usuries
Lieth Unclaim'd. (III.ii)

Not just any miser, Bartolo is a usurer, and specifically a capitalist with national and international investments and returns. His wealth and influence, indeed, are so great that they have direct claims upon state authority and even upon the international economic scene. His is the kind of money that is changing the world and that, however ugly it may be in Bartolo's possession, defines personal power and personal worth and makes social prestige possible in the world of Florence. That he keeps entirely to himself, therefore, is not a sign of his denial of society but rather of his extreme self-interest in his many financial dealings with society. This self-interest, moreover, is not entirely a matter of Bartolo's personality but also of social necessity. That is, his particular character and conduct are constituent features of the push for economic power defining his world, and they find corollaries in other individuals seeking wealth and power. Bartolo's self-interest, in other words, derives in large measure from an encompassing structure of values that enliven and shape the whole social fabric.

The socially pervasive nature of self-interest is seen everywhere, both in Aldabella's obsessive drive to attach herself to big money and prestigious social position and in the spineless, self-serving characters of Dandello, Philario, and Falsetto. But the smothering grip of self-interest on individuals is seen most emphatically in Fazio's conversation with himself about whether to take the dead Bartolo's money. With the rare opportunity for untold wealth immediately before him, Fazio remarks:

'Tis a bad deed to rob—and whom? the dead!
Ay, of their winding-sheets and coffin nails.
'Tis but a quit-rent for the land I sold him,
Almost two yards to house him and his worms:
Somewhat usurious in the main, but that
Is honest thrift to your keen usurer.
Had he a kinsman, nay a friend, 'twere devilish.
But now whom rob I? why the state—In sooth
Marvellous little owe I this same state,
That I should be so dainty of its welfare.
Methinks our Duke hath pomp enough. (I.ii)

This passage reveals the extent to which human values can become transformed by economic drive. Fazio is a man of individual integrity who cannot conceive of robbery as an acceptable means of relieving his poverty. And yet the temptation of Bartolo's money is too great to be avoided. He thus rationalizes taking the money by viewing it as payment, with exorbitant interest, for burying his murdered neighbor, reminding himself that in his world usury is not theft but rather honest financial dealing. As for his obligation to turn the money over to the state, Fazio surmises first that the state has no need for additional wealth and second, that, in the state's hands, the money would be dispersed among many individuals and its brilliance thus destroyed. The just response to found money, in his view, is thus to take it for himself, and in so doing to liberate it so that it may achieve its full greatness:

> With a deliverer's, not a tyrant's hand
> Invade I thus your dull and peaceful slumbers
> And give ye light and liberty. Ye shall not
> Moulder and rust in pale and pitiful darkness,
> But front the sun with light bright as his own. (I.ii)

Before moving to other matters, I want to pause here briefly to make several concluding assertions about the nature and role of alchemy, usury, and money in the drama. First, as the above passage makes clear, the reification of money explains an important dimension of its authority in Fazio's world. In literally burying Bartolo and asserting the magical creation of gold through the devices of alchemy, Fazio gives to his money an apparently transhuman status; it is an object, a thing, that is ostensibly free of human relations. This reification both gives money added authority and greatness and hides the human activity that determines its real significance. Second, and relatedly, just as Fazio conceals the source of his money, so does Bartolo conceal from public view the full scope of his public economic life. Apparently a filthy, isolated, and mean-spirited miser, Bartolo in fact is a shrewd businessman with large international investments and high-stake deals with figures and organizations in government. The gaping disparity between his personal appearance and his public investments has the effect of obscuring the real relations that govern the world and people's lives, so that his money, no less than Fazio's, seems to come from nowhere and to be unattached to the extremely public activities, for example, of the state.

Viewing the plot-level details in this way helps to elucidate the drama's emphasis on the distance between the apparent innocence of money and the very real relations of social life that charge it with significance. Money is a social hieroglyphic, containing within it the secret of social life in Fazio's world.[4] Never innocent, it derives from thievery of one sort or another, whether of the dead Bartolo or of the people of the Indies. And yet it would escape these guilty associations by drawing together and eliding the contradictions of social life, both by its alignment with public displays of greatness and by its less glamorous behind-the-scenes financial machinations—represented by the character of Bartolo—that control the quality and nature of everyday human life. Not a power in itself, though Fazio mistakes it for power, money is a sign within which are enfolded the complex relations of social power and personal life that touch upon every action in the drama.

The pervasive and controlling social authority of money, and the anxieties that often are associated with that authority, are seen most immediately in the relationship between Fazio and Bianca who are described in the drama's opening lines as enjoying a blissful, entirely harmonious marriage. As Fazio tells his wife of two years, his love for her has never diminished, nor has he ever been tempted to stray from the domestic arena; all stories claiming that a husband must ultimately grow tired of marriage, he says, are utterly false: "My own Bianca, / With what delicious scorn we laugh away / Such sorry satire!" (I.i). Immediately, however, Bianca corrects his idealizing statements, reminding him that he leaves their bed every evening to pore over his alchemical texts and to experiment with "Drugs and elixirs" (I.i). Alchemy, in Bianca's eyes, is Fazio's "mistress" (I.i), tempting him away from her and thus threatening to destroy the real domestic relation that stands behind his idealized description of it. Far from being the key to human happiness, alchemy is a "wondrous secret" (I.i) of a world apart, a world unknown to Bianca except insofar as it tears at her daily life with Fazio.

The more explicitly social side of the money-generated troubles in the Fazio-Bianca marriage is seen in Fazio's continuing infatuation with Aldabella, the high-society woman who once spurned him be-

cause he lacked wealth. Aldabella, in fact, is the human representation
of the range of personal and sexual issues caught up with alchemy,
much as Bartolo is the human representation of the range of economic
issues associated with alchemy. This connection is suggested in the odd
exchange between Fazio and Bianca in which Fazio lauds his former
lover and chastises his wife for speaking ill of her. Like the gold that
he would produce from his secret investigations, for him, Aldabella is
absolutely pure: "If she be spotted, oh, unholiness / Hath never been
so delicately lodged / Since that bad devil walk'd fair Paradise" (I.i).
Like alchemy itself, in Fazio's mind Aldabella is a pure edenic world
of superior beauty and worth, and it is precisely this dream of a transhuman redemptive power, Bianca fears, that constitutes the greatest
threat to her daily existence.

The plot-level jealousy that Bianca articulates and the seductive
power of Aldabella's beauty and social position are connected to a
much larger social issue, namely patriarchy.[5] While on the level of plot,
Bianca and Aldabella play very clear roles—Bianca is the poor but virtuous wife, while Aldabella is the beautiful but evil, family threatening
temptress—within the larger structures of social life their significance
becomes more complex. Despite very real differences of social position
and personal character, they share a similar relation to the capitalist
power structure. Not only do both women lack real social authority;
in various ways they are objects of that authority as well as vehicles for
its extension and stability. As wife and mother, for instance, Bianca is a
public example of Fazio's personal accomplishment and responsibility
as a citizen; her virtues are in large measure idealizations presented by
Fazio himself. Similarly, as a mistress of the richest and most prominent men in Florence and as a hostess of lavish feasts for various people
of social importance and political authority—she hosts an extravagant
party for the duke even as Fazio is being executed—Aldabella stands
as a public example of the prestige of money and government.

That these roles do not allow Aldabella and Bianca individual authority is seen in the facts that both women are finally objects of
exchange within the prevailing relations of economic and ideological
life, and that, as objects of exchange, both are ultimately dispensable:
once he has gained wealth, Fazio would exchange Bianca for Aldabella,
hence winning (in his view) social status by publicly demonstrating
his newly won power; and in the final scenes of the drama, when
she is no longer useful to any men with public power, Aldabella is

swiftly and mercilessly relegated from her high-profile position as state beauty. Both women, as is borne out in these two plot-level matters, are useful and socially acceptable only within the constraints of commodity exchange and patriarchal power politics. When Fazio advances economically to the point where he is able to purchase a high-prestige love relation, he does so, quickly and without guilt abandoning his wife and children; when the state reaches the point where one of its symbols of success and stability (that is, Aldabella) has become socially compromised, it discards her without hesitation. The differences between Bianca and Aldabella, in terms of patriarchy at least, are only apparent, as both have social credibility only in terms that are set down for them by a masculine power structure, and both are individually expendable within the workings of that power structure.

I am not suggesting here, of course, that there are no *personal* differences between Aldabella and Bianca—Milman very clearly draws one as villainous and the other as virtuous—but rather that personal differences do not determine the social significance of the characters. That significance derives from capitalist patriarchal relations that not only subordinate women to men (Bianca to Fazio; Aldabella to the duke) but also transforms them into objects of consumption and objects of exchange. The particular details of their subordinate roles cannot be separated from capitalist exploitation generally (represented obliquely, as I have shown, in Bartolo's usury). To cite only one additional example of the way exploitation of women works in the drama: in the Fazio-Aldabella relationship, Aldabella clearly appears to control her situation; Fazio is driven by lust and seems to shape his every action around his desire for Aldabella, who repeatedly toys with his affections. In fact, however, Aldabella's responses to Fazio are not a sign of her authority but rather of her lack of authority. Once Fazio has money, for instance, she sets about making herself desirable to him in an effort to attach herself to his newly acquired wealth and power; she converts herself into an object to be consumed, for only her consumability can give her social identity.

In this view, patriarchy cuts across class lines, as both the lower-class Bianca and the upper-class Aldabella are subordinate to and oppressed by men. But, although it does not discriminate along class lines, patriarchy is nevertheless socially situated in quite specific ways: it does not escape the determining economic authority of capitalism. Lower and upper classes alike, as seen in the characters of Bianca and

Aldabella, function within a common economic constraint, one which also controls relations of gender. That is, within the capitalist world depicted in the drama, relations of gender are formulated along patriarchal lines that not only serve men but, more to the point, serve the prevailing structures of social life, structures that reduce neither to men nor to classes but rather answer the needs of capital. For this reason, it matters socially that Bianca feels the need to preserve her family and her relationship with Fazio, just as it matters socially that Aldabella attaches herself to men of power and position and publicly displays herself as an object of their desire: while meeting deeply personal needs, these desires at the same time serve the cause of social stability by providing both a nucleus for its growth and a public image of its pleasures and greatness.

That these different roles ultimately come into conflict, producing violence and tragedy, is not only a sign of character difference but also of deep-seated social contradictions. As suggested by the elaborate parties attended by the duke, by the self-interested maneuverings of Dandello, Falsetto, and Philario, by the shrewd financial dealings of Bartolo, and by the obsession of Fazio with alchemy, the absolute key to human meaning in the Florence of the play is money. But, as becomes emphatically clear, money follows its own path and will not be harnessed by personal virtue or by public expressions of stability and happiness. In fact, the domestic stability upon which Florence would build its public life inevitably collides with the unquestioned equation of financial value with human value. Bianca and Aldabella are enemies; but more importantly they embrace mutually exclusive values within a single structure of social life, and as their respective situations unfold they bring into clear view the dilemma with which the entire culture of Florence is faced.

The general point I am making here may become clearer by reference to the one encounter between Bianca and Aldabella, after Fazio has been sentenced by the duke to be executed. In a desperate effort to save her husband, Bianca visits Aldabella in the mistaken belief that Aldabella can (and would want to) intervene with the duke on Fazio's behalf. In an act of complete self-abnegation that, she believes, might save her husband's life and thus create the possibility of resolving the contradictions that are on the brink of destroying her, she offers not only to "give" Fazio to Aldabella but, in addition, to become Aldabella's "handmaid." Moreover, she remarks:

> . . . [I]f ye see a pale or envious motion
> Upon my cheek, a quivering on my lips,
> Like to complaint—then strike him dead before me.
> Thou shalt enjoy all—all that I enjoy'd:
> His love, his life, his sense, his soul be thine;
> And I will bless thee, in my misery bless thee. (IV.iii)

Completely deaf to these desperate pleadings, Aldabella sees only the great social distance between herself and Bianca—as she asks chidingly of Bianca, "Know'st thou to whom and where thou play'st the raver?" (IV.iii)—and the more Bianca pleads from personal hardship the more Aldabella insists that her world is untouched by the tribulations of poor individuals: "I but debase myself to lend free hearing / To such coarse fancies—I must hence: tonight / I feast the lords of Florence" (IV.iii). It is precisely the world of the lords and the world of feasting that lured Fazio into alchemy and then theft, and then Fazio's money that lured Aldabella to him; yet she adamantly refuses the personal baggage that these facts bring with them, just as Bianca, in the passage quoted above, refuses to see that her personal integrity or life could not be salvaged by her groveling subservience to Aldabella. In this awkward, painful scene it becomes clear that both characters stand on a common, determining social ground—one shaped by the authority of money and social position—and yet that ground is so torn with contradiction and has hammered individual life into such privatized particles that neither character can do more than press on doggedly toward further isolation, an isolation which means madness and death in Bianca's case, and, in Aldabella's case, public ridicule and relegation to a convent.

One final gender-related issue can be briefly noted, and it involves Bianca's descent into madness. During her conversation with Aldabella, Bianca becomes increasingly distraught and desperate, to the point where Aldabella finally states that she should be taken "to th' hospital for the lunatics" (IV.iii). Later, when Bianca interrupts the feast to tell the duke of Aldabella's destructive affair with Fazio, Aldabella pleads with the duke not to listen "to the tale / Of a mad woman, venting her sick fancies / Upon a lady of my state and honour!" (V.iii). Whether Bianca is actually mad, of course, is a difficult matter to determine—she insists that "I am not mad" (V.iii)—but certainly the madness associated with her character is revealing for at least two very different reasons. On one level her ostensible madness is the one moment in the play of absolute sanity; in her desperate situation she describes clearly and in no uncertain terms the actual social relations governing her world that have compromised her personal happiness and domestic stability. As she says to the duke:

> I'll tell my tale
> Simply and clearly.—Fazio, my poor Fazio—
> He murder'd not—he found Bartolo dead.
> The wealth did shine in his eyes, and he was dazzled.
> And when that he was gaily gilded up,
> She, she, I say (nay, keep away from her,
> For she hath witchcraft all around her), she
> Did take him to her chamber—Fie, my liege!
> What should my husband in her chamber? (V.iii)

The thread of this sad story begins with the lure of money and trails upward toward social prestige and purchased pleasure, the exchange and consumption of objects gradually replacing human sharing and responsibility. Aldabella's alleged witchcraft, like Fazio's alchemy, is the magic lure (in Bianca's mind) that equates self-gratification, the acquisition of money, and individual worth.

On another level the madness associated with Bianca's individual character is actually the madness of society that becomes crystallized in her tragic situation; much like Ludolph in Keats's *Otho the Great*, Bianca's inability to hold her life together is a reflection of the contradictions within the state that have destabilized it to the point where even the ruling elite become alarmed for its security. Once convinced of the truth of Bianca's story, the duke turns angrily to Aldabella, seeing in her very character these debilitating contradictions. She is, he says, "high-born baseness! beautiful deformity! / Dishonour'd honour!" (V.iii), and her character and actions feed "this world's misery, this world's sin" (V.iii).

Although the interesting exchanges between Aldabella and Bianca help to illuminate the structures and relations of social life, they do not change them, and in fact one significant effect of concentrating the social analysis of the drama so heavily in the characters of women is to leave the state and patriarchy just as they are. Both women, despite their class differences, are expendable—Bianca dies and Aldabella is relegated to a convent—and their removal from the growing social tensions depicted in the world of the play helps to restabilize prevailing social authority. At the end of the drama the duke emerges with absolute command over his world, and this command is given credibility both by his swift and strong punishment of Aldabella, a woman of rank, and by his sympathetic attitude toward to the poor and victimized, but dying, Bianca. Although nothing has changed with respect to the economic relations that have produced the specific tragedy—in fact, in punishing Fazio with death earlier in the drama the duke moves mercilessly (and within the law) to protect those relations—the duke gives the appearance of rectifying a specific human wrong and in so doing he leaves the relations of gender, law, and capital unexamined and unchanged. In fact, one of his final promises to Bianca, which passes for compassion, actually assures that her children will always be poor (V.iii).

I want briefly to consider now a slightly different matter involving Fazio's response to the crisis-ridden world of Florence. Fazio's driving desire is to possess wealth and thereby to possess happiness and social prestige. His motivating concern is to overcome or to allay the contradictions of daily life that besiege him. From his alienated position, however, the society that has assigned him a life of poverty cannot be trusted, and thus the only way that he can fully realize his desires is to anchor his identity within a completely private domain of individual freedom even as he seeks social advancement. For this reason, even the money necessary to social advancement should be independent of social definition, and for this reason he studies alchemy. That such money, in fact, is never to be found intensifies his desire for individual autonomy, even as he uses Bartolo's money to purchase the recognition and respect of society. Like Byron's Manfred, Fazio never loses sight of the challenges and threats posed by his world, and he seeks to master them completely through philosophy or some other means (I.i). At the same time, however, he is deeply anxious about his prospects for success, and therefore desires a pure, contextless, alternative world of individual freedom alongside the world of social exchange, challenge, and hardship.

Put differently, Fazio's pursuit of "This wondrous secret" (as Bianca describes his obsession with alchemy) must be seen on one level as a means of giving him position in the world and at the same time should be perceived as an activity that would deny the claims of the world, even the claims of domestic life. Further, once he secures wealth for himself and redirects his affections from Bianca to Aldabella, he laments the social codes that would prevent fulfillment of his personal desire by remarking: "Why should that pale and clinging consequence / Thrust itself ever 'twixt us and our joys?" (II.iv). He needs and desires domestic responsibility, and yet is driven to distraction by a greater need for secret knowledge beyond that responsibility; he dedicates himself to the quest for social recognition and yet rejects the codes of conduct and value that accompany that recognition. He is, in short, a near perfect example of the Romantic divided subject: alienated from the world, he seeks social integration; at the same time, his loneliness and desperation are a product of that very world into which he seeks integration, and for this reason he denies its claim on him even as he voices his need for it.

Such mutually exclusive desires are not far removed from the plot-level conflict between Aldabella and Bianca—between the socially prominent aristocrat and the sentimental, isolated, and poor individual. And just as the Aldabella-Bianca relationship is defined fundamentally by a single, contradictory structure of social values, so are Fazio's confusing, opposing articulations of his situation. The values of Aldabella and the duke control society, among other ways, through their presentation of the world as an arena of self-gratification; at the same time, however, the real ugliness and degrading character of that world (as seen, for instance, in the lechery of Aldabella, the conspicuous consumption of the aristocrats attending the feast in Act V, and in the toadyism of Philario, Falsetto, and Dandello) encourage individuals to hope for private, nonsocial spaces where human fulfillment is possible. But no private world exists, either above or outside society, as is emphatically and tragically seen in the execution of Fazio, the death of Bianca, and even in the punishment of Aldabella, all of which leave the duke and the state in complete control of all personal, economic, and social relations.

A final set of general remarks about the state, and particularly about the role of the duke, may help to draw the foregoing discussion together. In virtually all of the characters depicted as inhabitants of Florence, two mutually exclusive tendencies are seen: a desire for wholeness or fullness of being, and the fact of social contradiction that prevents that wholeness. Bianca desires domestic stability but experiences personal tragedy; Aldabella desires social prestige but ultimately finds public disgrace; Fazio desires individual autonomy but is sentenced to public execution. These portrayals of character suggest the irreconcilability of certain wide-ranging elements within Florentine society. That these elements seem never to pose a serious threat to Florence is attributable not only to the commonly shared structures of value binding culture but also to the state apparatus—particularly its legal mechanisms—that provides both ideological and practical control over daily life. The contradictions that manifest themselves in the actions of the characters are drawn up and at least ostensibly settled at the level of the state, even as the state adamantly protects the economic and property relations that, as I have shown, are largely responsible for those contradictions.

The workings of state authority are seen clearly in the duke's investigation of Bartolo's disappearance. His purpose in the investigation is to discover what has happened to the old miser and, what proves to be of more pressing concern, to account for the "Mortgages, deeds, and lawsuits" (III.ii) that, he knows, Bartolo must control. Once he discovers that Fazio has taken Bartolo's money, the duke then unleashes "The bloodhounds of the law upon his track" (III.ii) and condemns him to death for "thy evil-gotten wealth" (III.ii). And even when the duke learns that Fazio is not responsible for Bartolo's murder, the sentence is not lifted or even modified. As the duke tells Fazio:

> Robbery, by the laws of Florence,
> Is sternly coded as a deadly crime:
> Therefore, I say again, Giraldi Fazio,
> The Lord have mercy on thy sinful soul! (III.ii)

With the money accounted for and confiscated by the state (III.ii), the murder is entirely forgotten, not to be mentioned again by the duke. From the state's point of view, the financial and property rights of Florence have been entirely vindicated, with the punishment of Fazio offered as a public example of both state authority and integrity in protecting individual rights.

A second example of state authority occurs at the very end of the drama, when the duke learns that Aldabella has lured Fazio to her bed and thus condemns her, "by the warrant / Of this my ducal diadem, to put on thee / The rigid convent vows" (V.iii). The duke's judgment here is politically significant, for it is a protection of personal rights— in this case the right of Bianca to sole enjoyment of her husband's person. Further, it suggests that the poor, no less than the wealthy, possess absolute rights that warrant protection by the state, even against assaults by those of the privileged classes. Finally, the duke's harsh judgment of Aldabella complements his earlier judgment against Fazio; that is, the earlier judgment was made in defense of economic and property rights, while this judgment is made in defense of personal, individual rights. Together, these judgments, while in fact protecting the specific structures of social life under its control—structures that, as the dramatic action vividly illustrates, are torn with contradiction and viciously destroy individual potential and social harmony—appear to represent the best interests of individual and society alike. All contradictions are apparently resolved and human tragedy reconciled by the strong hand of the state. That the real concerns of the state are with the protection of property and money, and with keeping the disenfranchised segment of the population in its place, is entirely elided by its forceful rhetoric of justice and display of absolute authority.[6]

Fazio interestingly presents an array of issues and concerns that elucidate the structures of social life in the modern world. First, it emphasizes that wealth is never socially pure but arises from a complex and often unjust arrangement of social relations; relatedly, it shows that wealth necessarily is connected to a specific economic system, in this case capitalism, whose internal operations are often hidden from society. Further, it portrays the alienation and contradictions in social and personal life that are associated, often in vitally significant ways, with the driving economic interests of capitalism. Finally, it suggests, at least in passing, some of the roles of the state in mediating the often conflicting interests, needs, and desires of the individual on the one hand, and of economic and social privilege on the other. In short, the world of Fazio's Florence desires stability and certainty but is in fact defined in fundamental ways by conflict and hardship.

If in his later historical writings Milman felt compelled to announce his respect for objectivity in his narratives of the past, at least one of his earlier works of the imagination shows how scarce real objectivity can be, as both the past and the writing about the past are ineluctably bound to operations of power that always, and disturbingly, seek to advance specific interests. In *Fazio* the very subject matter defies objectivity, for inherent in it are the strange contradictions of an entire world. These contradictions generate extreme anxiety among the characters of the drama—most notably Bianca and Fazio—and also promote an even deeper anxiety associated with the writing of the story, as Milman seems committed to transforming certain economic issues into purely personal issues, even as economic issues repeatedly raise their ugly head as necessary components of the story: in the portrayal of alchemy; in the portrayal of usury; in the portrayal of Aldabella's conspicuous consumption; in the portrayal of the state's vicious effort to claim loose wealth for itself; and in the portrayal of the hardships and desires arising from poverty and low prestige. That the later Milman, much like the later Coleridge, sought ways to contain such matters in his writing of history is one indication of the difficulty of writing history—and of writing imaginative works about historically significant subjects—during the nineteenth century.

CHAPTER

✣

6

"Tenants of a Blasted World"

Charles Robert Maturin's *Bertram*

Despite the fact that literary historians have always acknowledged Charles Maturin's *Bertram* (1816) as "a document of the taste of the Byronic period,"[1] very few serious attempts have been made to explain and elaborate its critical importance to English Romanticism. The few discussions of the play to appear during this century have been brief and usually descriptive rather than interpretive and critical. Bertrand Evans has situated it within a tradition of Gothic drama dating from the eighteenth century, helpfully cataloguing its themes, plots, character types, and so on, and paying particular attention to what have been called its Byronic elements in order to assert that Byronism itself is part of Gothic tradition.[2] Joseph W. Donohue, Jr., follows Evans's strategy of placing *Bertram* in Gothic tradition, but goes farther than Evans in describing the development of Bertram as a character type. As Donohue states, "the predisposition of the age was such that, as the agonies of the villain became more obvious and more detailed, greater sympathy was elicited for him. So by degrees the villain turned a hero who, through circumstances beyond his control, had become possessed by some evil force which drew him on to sin and despair, a force against which his conscience struggled valiantly but ineffectually."[3] Dale Kramer also acknowledges the importance of Evans's work, but departs from the explanation of Bertram as merely a type, arguing instead that the hero of the play has a psychological complexity that distinguishes him "from his ancestors in the Gothic drama."[4] While these and a few other commentaries have helped to keep alive our awareness of the play's existence,[5] they have done little more than this because they rely primarily on plot summary, description of literary tradition, and character sketch as an expository strategy, leaving unconsidered many conceptual matters that are central to the meaning of the drama. Thus *Bertram* remains little more than a literary curiosity, an example of a work that was tremendously popular in its day but that seems to possess no real literary merit, intellectual substance, or critical interest.

Even if critical investigations of *Bertram* have been lacking in our own day, at least one contemporary of Maturin saw the importance of the work and produced a serious and sustained commentary upon it that gives us a clue to its profound significance for Romantic studies. In *Biographia Literaria* Coleridge gives an entire chapter of vilification to Maturin's drama because, in his view, it was an extreme example of certain British literary sensibilities—"bloated style," "strained thoughts," "figurative metaphysics," and "horrific incidents, and mysterious villains"—that had traveled to Germany, been reformulated in dramatic form, and then returned to England to the embarrassment and detriment of all that was good and proper in British culture. The works in this tradition, Coleridge pronounced, were "the mere cramps of weakness, and orgasms of a sickly imagination, on the part of the author, and the lowest provocation of torpid feeling on that of the readers."[6]

For Coleridge the problem with such works as *Bertram* was not simply that they were examples of bad literature (which seems to be our reason for excluding the drama from critical consideration) but rather that they were an exceptionally dangerous kind of literature, a literature reflective of a commitment to "godless nature, as the sole ground and efficient cause not only of all things, events, and appearances, but likewise of all our thoughts, sensations, impulses, and actions. Obedience to nature is the only virtue: the gratification of the passions and appetites her only dictate: each individual's self-will the sole organ through which nature utters her commands" (213). Coleridge feared that such materialism "may influence the characters and actions of individuals, and even of communities, to a degree that almost does away [with] the distinction between men and devils, and will make the page of the future historian resemble the narration of a madman's dreams" (214). In *Bertram,* Coleridge found a perfect and, in his view, particularly ugly example of such madness, for it was a play that combined "robbery, adultery, murder, and cowardly assassination" (233) into a general, misanthropic portrayal of human experience. It displayed "confusion and subversion of the natural order of things" (221), threatening all "law, reason, and religion" (221). It was, in short, a "jacobinical drama" (221), without "moral sense" (225), providing "melancholy proof of the depravation of the public mind. The shocking spirit of jacobinism seemed [in *Bertram*] no longer confined to politics" (229).

The importance of Coleridge's denunciation of the play resides not so much in his personal moral outrage—though this in itself is interesting—as in his correct recognition of a literature entangled in quite specific historical crises. The moral stance that Coleridge takes is deeply situated in a nostalgic vision of history as stable, ordered, and hierarchical, and the thrust of his moral argument is on behalf of this historical vision. The "Satanic hatred of Imogine's lord" that he condemns in the drama, as well as his condemnation of Maturin's failure to bring his characters before "the just vengeance of the law" (227) are condemnations of a literary imagination capable of displacing lords from the center of social life; such an imagination subverts human order and purpose (as Coleridge would define them) and thus must be described as mad. Coleridge's large and serious critical effort in discussing *Bertram,* in short, is nothing less than an effort to define the proper bounds of historical and social order, and to ward off all threats (such as *Bertram*) to that order.

In the analysis of *Bertram* that follows, I assume that Coleridge was correct in arguing that the play's importance extends beyond literary history into social history and beyond character portrayal into ideology. This is not to say, however, that I wish to endorse Coleridge's plea for a return to a preindustrial, pre-Jacobinical, Burkean past of chivalry and aristocratic rule, or that I believe the play to represent a species of madness. Rather, I want to provide an explanation that unfolds in historical terms the ideological forces behind Coleridge's denunciations of the play, his desire to retreat to a past (imagined), edenical world and his blunt accusation that literary imaginings of the demise of that world are simply mad. Such an explanation takes for granted that the popular excitement and moral revulsion inspired by *Bertram* arise from the play's distillation and articulation of powerful, contradictory historical forces. The various shocks, desires, fears, social relations, and structures of authority presented in the drama are inscriptions of the Romantic historical moment, both of the immediate post-Waterloo situation and of the larger historical crisis involving the transition of British society from an aristocratic to a bourgeois ruling class and worldview. It is the play's historical imagination that provides its particular power and claim to our critical attention.

The central historical feature of the drama is derivative, borrowing a stock plot device that had become commonplace to the Gothic imagination in the eighteenth and nineteenth centuries—the use of cross-class marriage as a basis for psychological tension and unrest.[7] In this case, Imogine, a woman "of humble birth" (I.v),[8] marries Saint Aldobrand, a wealthy, bold, and powerful lord, against her will to save her destitute father:

> . . . What could I do but wed—
> Hast seen the sinking fortunes of thy house—
> Hast felt the gripe of bitter shameful want—
> Hast seen a father on the cold cold earth,
> Hast read his eye of silent agony,
> That asked relief, but would not look reproach
> Upon his child unkind—
> I would have wed disease, deformity. (I.v)

This detail, more than Bertram's Byronic character, provides the key to the dramatic action. As a plot device, it explains Imogine's loneliness and Bertram's alienation, and also provides stimulus for the various atrocities in the play that were so popular in its staging. Married against her will to someone she does not love, Imogine is emotionally distracted and driven to the point of violating at a fundamental level the authority represented by her aristocratic husband (that is, she succumbs to Bertram's advances), thus making possible everything that follows in the way of psychological turmoil, physical violence, and, ultimately, social collapse.

But the detail is more than a plot device. It takes on broad historical significance when it is viewed as a sign of weakening aristocratic authority. Imogine's marriage to Saint Aldobrand is presented in such a way that it must be regarded not so much as an extension of aristocratic power, or as a show of aristocratic generosity, or even as just another aristocratic action; rather, the blatantly unjust conduct surrounding

the marriage (the poverty of Imogine's father is held over her to force
her hand) is one sign that aristocracy, however personally generous
and admirable Saint Aldobrand may be, needs desperately to rejuve-
nate itself, and hence looks to outside human resources (Imogine) for
renewed energy and meaning. From the perspective of social class, the
marriage stands at the center of the drama as a sign of social instability,
representing a fracture in the structure of aristocratic social relations,
a small break from tradition that, through the course of the play,
becomes a rupture, multiplying into violence, deceit, and madness,
promoting the decay of the aristocratic world. Traditional character
concerns—the relative goodness of Aldobrand, the amoral actions of
Bertram, and the extreme emotionalism of Imogine—are, in this view,
less significant than the social effect of the marriage, which is to satisfy
the immediate needs of aristocracy while at the same time generating
alienation and loneliness (as is seen in the characters of Bertram and
Imogine), so that the world becomes divided as individuals are thrown
out of the main flow of social life. The result is the loss of integrity
and personal regard and the refusal to accept social responsibility.[9] The
seed of social corruption is planted from the very beginning in the
marriage of Imogine and Saint Aldobrand, and the actions of Bertram
and Imogine are merely its fruits.[10]

One ideological consequence of the cross-class marriage is the privatization of human experience, the socially enforced reliance of individuals on their own personal (and ever narrowing) resources, a reliance that perpetuates and intensifies the divisions between individuals
and their social worlds. Both Imogine and (for reasons not entirely
identical with Imogine's) Bertram exemplify the loss of public life
and the concomitant construction of private values that express both
human need and human failure. Imogine, who for much of the play
functions, at least superficially, within public life as daughter, wife,
and mother, finds completeness in none of her roles, preferring the
privacy of her room to the company of people in Saint Aldobrand's
castle; treasuring the secretly kept picture of Bertram over the flesh
of her husband; and ultimately following the secret passion of a meeting with Bertram to the peril of domestic stability with her husband
and child.

More telling here than the eventual liaison with Bertram is the fact
that for all of her previous married life, and through almost the entire
play, she never crosses the lines of social responsibility, carrying out

her domestic and public role as though she were happy. As she tells
her servant:

> Mark me, Clotilda,
> And mark me well, I am no desperate wretch
> Who borrows an excuse from shameful passion
> To make its shame more vile—
> I am a wretched, but a spotless wife,
> I've been a daughter but too dutiful. (I.v)

Such a statement is remarkable for at least two reasons. First, it confesses to a hollow, pointless individual existence, whose sole function
is to support a domestic and class situation that offers little in return
that can meet Imogine's personal needs and desires. Her own spotless-
ness in such a situation reflects the vileness and smothering authority
of the class that brought her into its ranks against her will. Every compassionate gesture of her husband thus necessarily becomes "a blow
on th' heart" (I.v), for it is also a gesture of domination, a show of
compassion for a thing possessed. Even her child's love is a sign of her
oppression, for she has given birth under conditions of alienation rather
than freedom. Second, that Imogine, a woman of rank, confesses such
serious and sad realities to Clotilda, a servant, suggests that power
and class relations in her world are such that aristocracy silences oppo-
sitional or even questioning voices from within its own ranks. The
bond of confidence between Imogine and Clotilda, a woman socially
beneath her, discloses this rigid aristocratic structure of authority and
at the same time exposes the hard, unhappy conditions of sacrifice and
alienation that such authority produces.

While not class-determined in the same way as Imogine's situation,
Bertram's experiences that lead to his outlaw status are equally entangled with the machinations of an anxious and uncertain aristocracy,
and his character in this respect is the Romantic masculine equivalent
of Imogine's. Bertram is from the aristocracy and in his youth had
been a favorite of his sovereign, but, for reasons never made entirely
clear, he is turned into "an exiled outcast, houseless, nameless, abject"
(I.v). Two (apparently inconsistent) explanations of Bertram's change
in fortune—one given implicitly in Imogine's confession to Clotilda,
the other stated explicitly by Saint Aldobrand—are provided in the
drama, and both bespeak anxiety and instability among the aristocracy. Imogine's account is enigmatic, stating only that the once noble

Bertram abruptly became an enemy of the sovereign. The only possible explanation for this change of fortune, based on textual evidence, is that Bertram's sovereign opposed his union with the lower-class Imogine. As Imogine describes Bertram's situation:

> [G]lory blazed
> Around his path—yet did he smile on her [Imogine]—
> Oh then, what visions were that blessed one's!
> His sovereign's frown came next. (I.v)

The implication here is that the ruling class is absolute in its authority over *all* individuals, even those within its own ranks, obligating them to follow the dictates not of their own conscience and emotions but rather of the class that they serve. To view the situation in this way is to recognize that class authority does not reduce to individual authority—even if the individual is from the ruling class—but rather possesses a life and identity of its own that assign and define individual possibilities and limitation. In this respect Bertram's situation is qualitatively no different from Imogine's: both are denied the freedom to choose an independent life based on their own needs and desires, and both are assigned a fate by the ruling class that is radically inconsistent with those needs and desires.[11]

At least on the surface, Saint Aldobrand's account departs widely from Imogine's, offering a loyalist explanation that uncritically accepts the authority and integrity of the state and casts Bertram as an absolute villain who opposes the state. In a condescending, patriotic, and self-aggrandizing lecture to Imogine, Saint Aldobrand explains:

> Thou knowest the banished Bertram—his mad ambition
> Strove with the crown itself for sovereignty—
> The craven monarch was his subject's slave—
> In that dread hour my country's guard I stood,
> From the state's vitals tore the coiled serpent,
> First hung him writhing up to public scorn,
> Then flung him forth to ruin. (IV.ii)

Imogine does not contest this account of the past, but neither does she ask Saint Aldobrand to recall for her the cause for Bertram's "mad ambition" that led to his alleged treasonous actions, thus leaving open the possibility that her own confession to Clotilda is accurate, only emphasizing an earlier (and more immediately personal) phase of the history. To raise the possibility of compatibility between the two accounts of Bertram's exile is not to excuse what is clearly a weakness in Maturin's handling of plot and motivation but to stress that the various accounts of Bertram's past are not *necessarily* mutually exclusive, and to argue that, in either case, the political and ideological point remains the same: under aristocracy, authority ultimately resides at the level of class rather than at the level of the individual, and any challenge to this reality is punishable by absolute exclusion from the main flow of human social life. Interpretations of the past, though they emphasize different details, unfold within an identical context of class authority.

One additional question bears consideration with respect to Bertram's past and those who have had a role in it: if Bertram is punished with exile for his affection for a lower-class woman, then why has Saint Aldobrand, who marries Imogine, been exempted from the scorn of his sovereign? The answer to this question, once again, resides in the fact that actions in the drama are not depicted as being individually chosen but rather as class determined. In Bertram's case love for Imogine entailed defying his sovereign and following his own personal course of action. It is in this sense that Saint Aldobrand's remark that Bertram "strove with the crown" is accurate; Bertram did not necessarily desire—and Saint Aldobrand does not suggest this—to become the new sovereign but rather, as Imogine's remarks to Clotilda suggest, to make his own decisions about his personal life. Saint Aldobrand, on the other hand, does not move against but with the grain of aristocracy in marrying Imogine; that is, the marriage is not portrayed in terms of mutual affection but rather in terms of Saint Aldobrand's conquest over Imogine and her destitute family. Likewise, his regard for her, as noted above, derives not from love but from possession. In short, as Maturin handles it, Saint Aldobrand's marriage to Imogine, unlike Bertram's love for this same woman, is a class rather than an individual action, calculated to invigorate rather than challenge the prevailing structures of authority. That it ultimately has the reverse effect is one sign of the destabilized context within which it has taken place.

The drama, however, is not simply the story of social anxiety and decay but also of emergent social energies. Bertram's defiance and exile contain within them the seeds of an antiaristocratic ethos, even while Bertram himself retains his leadership position and posture of nobility among a group of banditti. Moreover, this antiaristocratic ethos is clearly more powerful than the aristocratic claim to authority presented in the drama. Both of these facts (stock features of the Byronic hero) certainly were as critical to the play's immediate popularity as the stock of Gothic machinery that Maturin and Drury Lane hauled before the public for twenty-one consecutive nights, for they articulate, however melodramatically and subliminally, the triumphant bourgeois defiance of aristocracy.

The inchoate bourgeois ethos attached to Bertram's character is visible most immediately in his individualism. On one level, of course, the individualism described in the drama is not bourgeois at all but rather, like the individualism presented in Byron's *Manfred,* a last extreme assertion of aristocratic authority in the face of a changing world. But behind this aristocratic assertion stand the assumption of the autonomy of the individual subject and the strong sense of self-identity that became culturally prevalent with the rise of the bourgeoisie. Rejecting absolutely the institutional expression of aristocratic codes and values (for instance, Catholic religion[12]), Bertram in exile actively subverts the world from which he has been thrown, engaging, like Byron's Corsair, in a career of invasion and robbery of the aristocracy. Giving form and definition to his defiant personality are such sentimental traits as absolute devotion to and love for Imogine (just as Byron's Corsair idealizes Medora), personal physical strength, and a moody disregard for what others think of him, regardless of the social status they carry with them. These, combined with his refusal even to submit to the punishment that has been allotted to him (he takes his own life instead), mark him as a personal identity rather than as a social figure—and this provides one context for Coleridge's condemnation of the play. In Bertram what matters are not codes and systems of belief passed down by tradition, nor even the continuing thread of lineage itself (compare, for instance, Aldobrand's dying remark, "Oh save my boy" [IV.ii], to Bertram's unflinching defiance of all socially sanctioned values), but rather the determination of life and value by one's own personal needs, desires, and experiences. Such a spirit of individualism does not die with Bertram's suicide at the end of the play but rather lives as the very spirit of the dramatic action and of the culture that made the drama tremendously popular.

Related to Bertram's individualism—and to his suicide—is another feature telling the instability and ultimate demise of aristocracy, namely Maturin's handling of forms of punishment. What is sought by the society against which Bertram has sinned, and specifically by the military and religious authorities controlling this world, are Bertram's public confession of guilt and plea for mercy, followed by public execution. Such a course of events, while doing nothing to bring Saint Aldobrand back from the dead or Imogine from madness, would effectively demonstrate the stability and continuing authority of the social order by casting Bertram's actions as an aberration from a social standard of propriety and by publicly demonstrating the sanctity and justness of the prevailing social authority. The actual course of events, however, has the reverse effect of throwing into relief the weakening of society and the changing nature of human pain and understanding of crime. When asked why he has murdered Saint Aldobrand, Bertram provides a simple, cold, and painfully narrow answer: "He wronged me, and I slew him" (V.i). This is followed immediately by Bertram's warning that public punishment cannot touch him for his crime, for his pain is immune to social judgment:

> Be most ingenious in your cruelty—
> Let rack and pincer do their full work on me—
> 'Twill rouse me from that dread unnatural sleep,
> In which my soul hath dreamt its dreams of agony—
> This is my prayer, ye'll not refuse it to me. (V.i)

At the end of the same scene, when the prior encourages him to pray for mercy, Bertram makes a similar remark: "Give me your racks and tortures, spare me words" (V.i). One major point here, of course, is clear even at the level of plot, namely that Bertram's crime and pain are so deeply personal that they cannot be publicly defined and dealt with. The ideological dimension of his comments, however, are more complex. The utter privatization of value and judgment implicit in his explanation of his conduct is staggering, rendering meaningless the authority of the prior and of the military. As Bertram himself knows, he can be executed but not conquered (V.i), and this means that the example of his conduct permanently defies authority, leaving the horror of his deeds to echo through a hollow world.[13]

The shattering significance of Bertram's actions and comments is suggested by numerous passing comments and details in the later scenes that tend to describe individual situations in a language of social or public life, so that individual fates are made to appear as the fate of aristocratic social order itself. The prior, for instance, intimates that the violence and powerful, awe-inspiring criminality of Bertram reverberate through the social order. His sense—or fear—that Bertram's deeds carry more than personal meaning is seen not only in his desperate, failed attempts to convince Bertram to accept the mercy—and hence judgment—of the church and state, but also in his several remarks identifying the immediate tragedy with the larger structure of social life. In response to Bertram's comment that

> I deemed that when I struck the final blow
> Mankind expired, and we were left alone,
> The corse and I were left alone together,
> The only tenants of a blasted world (V.i)

the prior commands the knights attending the prisoner to "Advance, and seize him, ere his voice of blasphemy / Shall pile the roof in ruins o'er our heads" (V.i). In an earlier moment he also remarks about Saint Aldobrand that "his halls are desolate—the lonely walls / Echo my single tread" (V.i). Clotilda's sad comment that, after murdering Saint Aldobrand, Bertram "sat in dread society, / The corse and murderer . . . there together" (V.i) bears testimony that the necessary vocabulary for describing the ugly situation is social rather than personal, and it is a vocabulary that echoes Bertram's own tendency to see social decay and death around him. Within such a context, where murder echoes through the "halls," "society," and the "world," even the prior's final, short, and chilling descriptions about Imogine's fatal struggle with madness ("'Tis past" [V.iii]) and about Bertram's suicide ("He dies, he dies" [V.iii]) become a description too of the larger social order. The lord of the castle, Lord Aldobrand, is dead; Imogine and her child are dead, the former from madness and the latter presumably by his mother's hand; and Bertram, a once glorious and noble youth, is dead by his own hand: the military is unable to prevent any of this, and the prior is unable to rationalize or explain it in terms of any existing codes and values.

Bertram's internalization and privatization of pain to the point where social judgment is impossible is complemented interestingly by the portrayal of Imogine's madness. Maturin's decision to thrust the heroine into madness, while giving the hero the more socially respectable conduct of defiance, noble speeches, and suicide, is a sign of the patriarchal ideology governing gender relations in the drama, and as such it provides an important insight into yet another dimension of social conflict that is borne and acted out by individuals. Imogine's

madness in the final act carries to an extreme the withdrawal and isolation that she had been identified with earlier. Caught from the beginning between the pull of her own heart and the oppressive demands of
a patriarchal society and family, she is, as a woman, powerless to act.
At various moments she is subject to a lover, a husband, a father, and
a monk—all men who make claims on her and assume responsibility
for giving her an identity, so that, even more than Bertram, she never
has a real home other than the nebulous and precarious dream world
of her own mind. As she is pushed and pulled through the world of
the drama, she finds ever fewer resources in society or within herself
to draw on.

To cite only one example of her marginalization, at a moment of
extreme crisis, when she is torn between her passion for Bertram and
her sense of obligation to her husband, Imogine confesses her anguish
to the prior:

> Last night, oh! last night told a dreadful secret—
> The moon went down, its sinking ray shut out
> The parting form of one beloved too well.—
> With nought that lov'd me, and with nought to love
> I stood upon the desart earth alone—
> I stood and wondered at my desolation—
> And in that deep and utter agony,
> Though then, than ever most unfit to die,
> I fell upon my knees, and prayed for death. (III.ii)

Her need and her plea to the prior are for human compassion and spiritual comfort, for a support, in other words, which will provide her
with an enabling basis for her identity. The response she gets from the
prior, however, is entirely deaf to these pleas, insisting instead that all
she needs to remember are her responsibilities to a situation and role
she has not chosen:

> Art thou a wife and mother, and canst speak
> Of life rejected by the desperate passion—
> These bursting tears, wrung hands, and burning words
> Are these the signs of penitence or passion?
> Thou comest to me, for to my ear alone
> May the deep secret of thy heart be told,
> And fancy riot in the luscious poison—

Fond of the misery we paint so well,
Proud of the sacrifice of broken hearts,
We pour on heaven's dread ear, what man's would shrink from—
Yea, make a merit of the impious insult,
And wrest the function of mine holy office
To the foul ministry of earthly passion. (III.ii)

The human ugliness of this speech is staggering, surpassed only by the prior's subsequent condemnations of Imogine ("Thou art a wretch"; "I do pronounce unto thy soul—despair" [V.i]). While he is respectful of, and deferential toward, Bertram, a criminal who never displays the slightest regard for religious belief, the prior refuses Imogine any possibility of integrity or even identity outside the narrow social roles that have been allotted to her, and when her own personal needs take her away from these roles he simply discards her as a blot on society. To put the matter somewhat differently and much more bluntly, the prior's handling of Imogine suggests that, under aristocratic patriarchy, a woman who needs compassion and personal support amid social and individual turmoil is worse than a man who commits murder.

The effect of the prior's accusing response, of course, is to drive Imogine farther back into the darkest regions of her own mind—rather than drawing her into the world of social exchange—and to pave the way for her eventual mad wanderings in the forest. While at this late moment in the drama the prior pleads with "all-pitying Heaven" to "release her from this misery" (V.iii) of madness, Imogine is utterly lost, voicing pain and horror that expose an opposite side of social deterioration from that which Bertram's conduct discloses. When the prior approaches the mad Imogine, for instance, and takes hold of her, she shrilly responds, "Oh, spare the torture—and I will confess" (V.iii). This statement reverses Bertram's desire for physical torture as a way of awakening his soul from an unnatural sleep, and in doing so again suggests the distance between masculine and feminine life in the world depicted in the drama. That is, Bertram's mind, like that of Milton's Satan and Byron's Manfred, is its own place, enclosing a will and spirit that are perdurable, active, and set, stone-like, against all social sensibility. Imogine's inner world, on the other hand, is entirely hollow and passive, her withdrawal into a subjective realm of desire grounded upon nothing more than dreams that have been shaped and defined by one sort or another of masculine authority. The passive

longing of the soul is all that is allowed to her. Fear of physical torture, then, naturally paralyzes her, for her inner world has long been
tortured by its very meagerness and narrowness, and only her flesh
remains relatively free of pain. In this view, her situation throughout
is more serious, more desperate, than Bertram's, though it appears
less valorous by being defined against the bold, active resistance of
Bertram to his world.

The point here is that any argument about *Bertram's* portrayal of
an inchoate bourgeois ethos of individual autonomy must be clarified
along gender lines, for the autonomy of the individual subject in a
bourgeois world—no less than the social situatedness of individuals in
that world—is discriminatory. Imogine's position as an aristocrat and
her display of subjectivity are not the same as Bertram's nobility and
individuality, for both display her apparent inferiority to her masculine counterpart. The historical transformation of individual and social
reality from aristocratic to bourgeois cultural formations, even while
destroying the ideological center of an entire way of life, retains certain hierarchies of value (in this instance, patriarchy) that enable the
bourgeoisie to secure and extend its authority and identity. Imogine's
character perfectly demonstrates this point, as it not only exemplifies—in madness and murder—aristocracy shrinking out of control
but also the emotionalism and absolute personal loyalty to the strong
individual male that are demanded of women under bourgeois patriarchal social relations.

One major feature of the drama that serves as an institutional focus
of the conflicts sketched thus far is religion, discussed briefly above in
terms of Bertram's defiance and Imogine's madness. From the beginning the monks and the prior display an odd combination of integrity,
fear, coldness, deceit, warmth, and confusion. The prior is unable to
condemn Bertram absolutely, even after Bertram's worst crimes have
been made known (see V.i), although, as mentioned above, he readily
condemns the less guilty Imogine. And throughout the play the various religious figures, who seem consistently to wish for peace and
goodness, speak of their anxiety and fear arising from actual and imagined events. Perhaps the clearest indicator of the large social significance of their various comments and attitudes is the opening scene of
the drama, which first describes several monks facing a severe storm,
followed by a description of the wreck of Bertram's ship and the
monks' desperate concern for the victims. As the storm rages and be-

fore they are aware that a ship has capsized, the monks repeatedly express their terror of the great storm besieging their convent, a storm so great, the first monk remarks, that "relic, and rosary, and crucifix, / Did rock and quiver in the bickering glare" (I.i). The immediate cause for such comments, of course, is the theatergoing public's demand for Gothic horror, and Maturin's eagerness to satisfy that demand. But narrow stage and public considerations notwithstanding, these opening scenes suggest fear and anxiety at the very center of the feudal world, articulating doubts about even the continued existence of religious authority and credibility. When Bertram's ship is spotted in the storm, religious strength and faith erode even further, as the prior first boldly commits himself to praying for the ship's members, refusing to leave the dangerous storm for the safety of the convent, and then collapses into the arms of his fellow monks who carry him away.

The distinction between this collective frenzy and Bertram's individual response to the storm is striking. Amid the monks' horror that the ravings of nature are a sign of the impending doom of all humanity, Bertram—silently, alone, and through treacherous waters—carves his own personal way to survival. And in subsequent scenes the sheer courage and will associated with this act never diminish, and the monks and prior never recover their collective self-esteem, failing even to carry out the execution of Bertram, which would display the continued authority of church and state. The various religious figures, and especially the prior, seek to follow a course of action geared to reflect and perpetuate aristocratic value, and yet at every turn they defile aristocracy and display powerlessness and awe in the face of Bertram's defiant will. Religion, however much believers try, cannot put the social order back together again once it has been invaded and disrupted by Bertram, whose mind repeatedly overwhelms all efforts to establish the controlling reality of an aristocratically defined religion and society.

Two final, related matters need to be mentioned briefly that might clarify the apparently conflicting or divergent perspectives on the inchoate bourgeois individualism that I have thus far been tracking: the separation that Bertram claims and seems to demonstrate between his body and his mind; and his suicide. It is clear throughout the drama that Bertram cares very little about the direction that his life might take, or even about whether he lives or dies. As one monk explains after watching Bertram save himself from the storm: ". . . there was

one did battle with the storm, / With careless, desperate force; full
many times / His life was won and lost, as though he recked not"
(I.iii). Once brought before the monks, he asks them to "plunge me
in the waves from which ye snatched me" (I.iii). This same disregard
for his own life is seen again later when he asks his captors to torture
him (see above, "Let rack and pincer do their full work on me"). Such
statements do not mean that Bertram lacks self-identity or self-worth
but rather that public struggle has come to be seen as pointless or impossible, so much so that Bertram retreats into the recesses of his own
inner world to establish a rigorous, defensive, and self-willed private
value system, one that is ostensibly independent of and resistant to the
sordid public world.

At this level—the level of what Eli Zaretsky (writing in a different context) calls "predetermined inner life"[14]—Bertram is confident
and strong, as is seen not only in the awe with which everyone from
Imogine to the prior approach him (despite his clearly dissipated physical appearance) but also in his suicide. While Bertram's suicide is perhaps most immediately a sign of despair, at the same time it indicates
the possibility of preventing the triumph (through trial and execution)
of aristocratic authority; thus suicide becomes a statement of the enduring defiance of Bertram's individual spirit. As he remarks in the
final lines of the drama, "I died no felon death— / A warrior's weapon
freed a warrior's soul" (V.iii). While this marks his personal demise,
it also marks the final triumph of the individual against society, and
emphatically and terribly displays the assumption of absolute division
between individual and society that is at the core of bourgeois ideology. In other words, as Maturin handles it suicide is not merely a
private act: it carries far-reaching social significance, pointing at once
to the death of nobility and to the triumph of individual will.

While Coleridge's commentary on *Bertram* does not follow the specific line of argument I have offered here, its anger and anxiety can be
traced to many of the issues I have elaborated. Coleridge knew that
Bertram and other works of the period like it (including, he feared, his
own *Rime of the Ancient Mariner,* which he spent years trying to contain within a Christian interpretive framework[15]) were products of a
changing social world and, as such, a threat to a traditional, Christian social order. It was in this respect that *Bertram* was a "Jacobinical
drama," contributing to "the confusion and subversion of the natural order of things."[16] The natural order for Coleridge in 1817, as I

noted at the outset, did not include the disruptive, changing, historical force of post-Revolutionary Europe, but the ostensibly fixed and
stable social relations found in aristocratic rule and a strong church
supporting—and supported by—the state. In this view, the demise of
aristocracy depicted in *Bertram* is also a depiction of demonic forces
that threatened to destroy all life, making humanity into "tenants of a
blasted world," into people who lacked purpose, direction, or hope.
Whether or not Coleridge was correct about the absolute demise of
culture signaled by *Bertram* and its counterparts on the public stage,
he was certainly right in recognizing that the content of the drama,
and its incredible popular reception, were both a product and sign of
marked social change during the period. For this reason the energy
behind his argument, and the areas of the play to which that energy
was directed, should remind us of the great importance of *Bertram* as a
cultural artifact, and of the importance generally of Romantic drama
to an understanding of Romanticism in its historical definition.

CHAPTER

7

"Tied unto This Wheeling Globe"

Thomas Lovell Beddoes's *The Brides' Tragedy*

Like Matthew Lewis and Mary Shelley before him, Thomas Lovell Beddoes published, before the age of twenty, a literary work of extreme horror that touches the dark underside of the Romantic imagination. Unlike *The Monk* and *Frankenstein*, however, *The Brides' Tragedy* (1822) has rarely been studied seriously, partly because it is a poetic drama and partly because it is riddled with numerous technical or expository weaknesses, especially in its handling of the motives for action and in its imbalance of dialogue and action. The few scholars who have admired and studied the drama systematically have not attempted to establish its political or social historical significance, explaining it, instead, in literary historical terms either as a throwback to Jacobean tragedy or as an example of the death of the Romantic imagination, rather than as a work produced within and shaped by the Romantic historical situation itself.[1]

But *The Brides' Tragedy* (no less than *The Monk* or *Frankenstein*), as both product and expression of the Romantic historical moment, provides an important avenue into the crises of social forms and relations that both energize and limit the Romantic imagination. In its at once naive and darkly cynical depictions of personal, domestic, and social life, it captures the paralyzing turmoil experienced by a once stable world on the verge of extinction; it painfully articulates the aloneness, fear, and dread that accompany that extinction; and, in doing so, it suggests something of the debilitating anxiety that haunts much Romantic literature, particularly after 1815, when both the apocalyptic hope for a utopian society and—at the other extreme—the nostalgic desire for a return to an aristocratic and feudal world had been irrevocably dashed.[2] Specifically and with remarkable success, the drama formulates the conflict between aristocratic authority and a bourgeois political unconscious, casting into relief not only the painful transformations of social class that haunted the Romantic period but also the connections between those transformations and relations of gender. In what follows I want to elaborate Beddoes's handling of these two social historical matters—class and gender—and to sketch as well the broader structures of feeling and belief that are revealed as class and gender come increasingly under fire in Beddoes's vision of the world.

The extreme self-consciousness of *The Brides' Tragedy* about matters of social class places it squarely in the center of Romantic bourgeois drama. Despite its plot-level attention exclusively on the aristocracy, it never escapes entirely class anxiety and even class hysteria. While class struggle is never described or even implied as the cause of the tragedy, its traces are everywhere in the action and in the network of social relations governing those actions. Changes in consciousness, crises in ordinary social institutions, and a generally increasing aristocratic vulnerability that promotes its own demise all point to turmoil larger than any individual character and larger even than the aristocracy itself.

The most immediate indicator of the class dimension of the drama is Hesperus's father, Lord Ernest, whose changing individual situation from beginning to end marks the larger social direction of change in the drama. The opening description of Lord Ernest establishes him as an aristocrat deeply in debt to another, greater aristocrat, the deceased father of Orlando. This description is followed immediately by the incarceration of Lord Ernest by Orlando, who uses the imprisonment to persuade Hesperus (Lord Ernest's son) to give up his claim on Floribel, whom Orlando loves. When Orlando achieves his purpose, Lord Ernest is released to become adopted into the Orlando estate, his outward position restored but his real power and integrity lost, as his life now depends entirely on the mercy of Orlando. In the final scenes of the drama, after Hesperus spoils the compromise of the house of Lord Ernest and the house of Orlando by murdering Floribel, Lord Ernest reappears in peasant dress, telling his doomed son that "Henceforth

I'll live / Those bitter days that Providence decrees me / In toil and poverty" (V.iv. 50–52).[3]

The decline of Lord Ernest's fortunes and the difficulties accompanying that decline may be seen as emblematic of the larger social and ideological deterioration of his world, of the ineluctable fragmentation and ultimate defeat of the aristocratic ruling class. All other actions and attitudes, though some are less explicitly class-bound than Lord Ernest's, are marked by class anxiety, by an attempt to preserve aristocratic hierarchy, order, and value, or by a desire to find some means of personal escape from certain class extinction—by the same needs and desires seen in the portrayal of Lord Ernest. The duke's legal authority, Orlando's devious legal strategies, Hesperus's deranged behavior, and Floribel's extreme sensitivity about money and social status: all of these, in ways that I hope to show, develop within and against an exhausted feudal world that claims authority as its own even while it is unable to exercise that authority fully. Like Lord Ernest, the other characters in the drama can neither arrest nor avoid the fragmentation and death of their world, nor prevent the emergence of a new network of social beliefs, values, and relations.

To implicate all other characters—many of whom seem relatively autonomous through the course of the drama—in the same process of decline and defeat seen clearly in Lord Ernest's fortunes is not to argue that every individual character is more or less a passive carrier of invisible historical energies and social structures over which he or she has no control. It is simply to make the dialectical point that individual actions and choices are made within real social situations. Thus, for instance, while Lord Ernest cannot be said to cause the peculiar course of events in which he is caught, he is not entirely innocent of them either, as his pathetic demands on his son to wed Olivia show. Nor, on the other hand, can Hesperus be viewed as the sole source of the drama's villainy (even though he certainly is not innocent) because his actions are motivated, at least in part, by the demands of his father's estate to marry Olivia. Lord Ernest and Hesperus, along with all other characters in the drama, are both agents and products; the larger social world is distilled in them even as it is partly created by them. In this view, the weight of Lord Ernest's individual history, like that of the other characters, is also the weight of social history, and it is played out both in terms of his individual needs and desires and in terms of the sweeping network of relations undergirding his situation and that of the other characters.

Some additional plot-level matters help to establish the historical bind that the drama articulates and particularly the class dimension of this historical bind. Most important among these is the fact that Floribel, whom Hesperus has secretly married, is extremely anxious about her "homely breeding" (I.i.78), and what this may mean for her relationship with her new husband. She desperately desires to have this anxiety laid to rest by public acknowledgment of her marriage and by the "blessing" (I.i.79) of Hesperus's father, acts which presumably would seal the love between Hesperus and Floribel by providing their marriage with social meaning. Much later in the drama too, after Hesperus thinks he has caught her in an adulterous situation, Floribel maintains that her difficulties have less to do with her husband's character than with her own socially inferior position, and her confused effort to think through this social difficulty leads her to desire at once more wealth for her own family and less for Hesperus's family. As she tells her mother:

> *Floribel:* Dear mother, I will strive to be at ease,
> If you desire; but melancholy thoughts
> Are poor dissemblers. How I wish we owned
> The wealth we've lost.
> *Lenora:* Why girl, I never heard
> One such regret escape your lips before;
> Has not your Hesperus enough?
> *Floribel:* Too much;
> If he were even poorer than ourselves,
> I'd almost love him better. For, methinks,
> It seemed a covetous spirit urged me on,
> Craving to be received his bride. I hope
> He did not think so; if he does, I'll tell him
> I will not share his wealth. (III.iii.28–39)

These and other comments by Floribel, though prompted and colored by intense personal anxiety, describe perfectly her understanding of the class and economic forces that both push her marriage into secrecy and drive her husband to act in unpredictable ways. And, as in the case of Lord Ernest, these forces generate (or throw into relief), without any ability to fulfill, Floribel's various personal needs and desires.

The result is even further anxiety, confusion, and finally (for Floribel) death.

The class and economic realities to which Floribel's comments call attention help to elucidate Hesperus's villainy because they provide a social framework for understanding his madness. Hesperus's socially superior position demands that he secure that position by marrying upward rather than downward, and this prevents him from publicly acknowledging his relationship to Floribel. In hiding his marriage for reasons of social class and respectability, Hesperus becomes even more a victim of class demand, to the point where his personal identity is entangled in a life-or-death struggle with the class to which he belongs. And as his personal life becomes increasingly entangled in matters of estate—or, put differently, as matters of social class increasingly overwhelm his personal life—he comes to see death as the only certain way of laying conflict to rest. Without denying his madness and villainy and without attempting to justify or defend his actions, this perspective situates Hesperus in terms of the class conflict at the center of his world and demonstrates that personal motives are never only personal; they are, on some level, a response to (or effect of) a social reality that encompasses and gives meaning to them.

Because the various elements and dimensions of class struggle presented in *Bride* are, at the level of plot, connected directly to gender relations (that is, the Hesperus-Floribel relationship and the Hesperus-Olivia relationship), they help to focus the structure and authority of patriarchy, and to illuminate some of the ways it is implicated in the transition from an aristocratic to bourgeois social formation. The connection between patriarchy and class in the drama can best be understood in terms of Eli Zaretsky's ideas on feminism and patriarchy in *Capitalism, the Family, and Personal Life*. Zaretsky argues that modes of personal life are connected directly to particular modes of production and, specifically, that the rise of the bourgeoisie entailed new ways of conceiving of personal life, the family, gender relations, and so on. Two components of his argument are particularly relevant here. First, following Engels, he argues that patriarchy is directly connected to the emergence of private property in history, a phenomenon which "spelled the downfall of women"[4] because it separated production within the home from production outside the home, relegating women to the former and giving men control of the latter. The household itself became converted into private property controlled by men, though the labor within it was carried out by women. The rise of the state coincided with the emergence of private property, sealing women's subordinate role by safeguarding these gender-specific relations of property.

While stressing the power of Engels's major thesis—that is, that "the oppression of women and the existence of the family [are tied together] with the economic organization of society"[5]—Zaretsky acknowledges that its weaknesses are its reductionism and strong antihistorical bias. He attempts to correct these deficiencies by developing a theory of personal life in terms of a particular historical moment, namely the rise of the bourgeoisie, retaining Engels's general theory of private property but specifying, in ways that Engels had not, its social dimensions and nuances. Because his explanation of bourgeois individualism is critical to understanding gender relations in *Bride*, I want to quote it at length:

> In feudal society men and women occupied a fixed position with a stratified division of labor—they owed allegiance to a particular lord and worked on a particular lot of land instead of being free to sell their labor or property. Explicit and direct relations of authority defined people's sense of individual identity. Catholicism provided them with a common purpose outside themselves.
>
> Private property freed the early bourgeoisie from a fixed social role within the feudal order. On the basis of private property, the bourgeoisie has defined individual rights throughout history. . . . The bourgeoisie has consistently defended the right of individuals to rise and fall within the marketplace through their own efforts, rather than on the basis of birth; the bourgeoisie originated the idea of a necessary contradiction between the individual and society.[6]

With this new conception of the individual emerged a new conception of gender relations, one which involved the connection for the first time in history between marriage and sexual love, and at the same time a view of the family as a refuge from the sordid conflicts of everyday public life. Both of these features of bourgeois gender relations figure prominently in *Bride*, and they conflict violently in the drama with the aristocratic world against which they are set. The complicated struggle of these new relations to achieve social authority and social form in a world where aristocratic patriarchy is not yet dead is displayed powerfully in Hesperus's different relationships with Floribel and Olivia, the two women whom he marries.

Like Orlando, who is also young and wishes to marry, Hesperus sees the impoverished Floribel in idyllic terms, telling her, for instance, in the beginning of the drama that "the veiled Moon's mild eye / Has long been seeking for her loveliest nymph" (I.i.20–21). (Orlando's comment to Claudio in the following scene is almost identical, referring to Floribel as "my goddess, / The Dian of our forests" [I.ii.18–19].) Floribel can take on this sort of pure value for the young aristocrats who desire her precisely because she does not belong to the aristocracy, which, as I have shown, is characterized almost entirely by exhaustion and decay. In fact, her desirability as an object of love and as a repository of value for Hesperus increases in proportion to his ability to imagine her as independent not only of the aristocracy but of all social relations. For him she is, as Zaretsky says of the bourgeois family, a refuge from the threat facing his social class, a threat seen most emphatically in the infighting between his family and that of Orlando, for instance, in the fact that Lord Ernest is deeply in debt to Orlando's father, and also in the fact that Orlando employs devious, legalistic strategies to win Floribel away from Hesperus. Whatever her real situation—which is explicitly revealed in her own anxieties about money and status—her constructed significance for Hesperus is that she inhabits and even constitutes a private and innocent realm more meaningful than the tangled, aristocratic world that he inhabits.

The burden of innocence that Floribel is made to carry becomes evident not only in the scene where Hesperus catches her kissing Orlando's page but also in the description of his initial mad confusion over whether or not to murder her.[7] This brilliant scene takes place in an apartment in Orlando's palace, decorated with beautiful tapestries stitched with pictures out of feudal history. Produced by female labor ("she, whose needle limned so cunningly, / Sleeps and dreams not" [II.iv.39–40]), the tapestries tell stories of men whose hands have been gloriously dipped in human blood. These stories in cloth radically divide Hesperus from himself, promoting in him a desire to shed blood, which presumably would give him a place alongside the heroes whose stories are sewn into the tapestries, while at the same time making him even more committed to preserving the vision of pure innocence that Floribel represents to him. As this fit of madness passes and he suppresses his violent urges, he states emphatically to himself, "I tell thee Floribel / Shall never bleed" (II.iv.68–69). This comment, though on the surface level expressing an abhorrence of violence, carries within it the full weight of Hesperus's confusion as well as the confusion of his world. The literal meaning here—that he will not spill Floribel's blood through jealousy—is bound up with larger cultural definitions of women as pure repositories for masculine desire, definitions which do not allow women the simple human functions of menstruating and consummating sexual relations. This contradiction between woman as an ideal and woman as a human being cannot be logically resolved, and it comes back repeatedly to haunt Hesperus, eventually overwhelming him to the point where he comes to believe that it can be laid to rest only by murder—by spilling blood despite his abhorrence of it.

The relationship between Olivia and Hesperus both duplicates and departs from the Floribel–Hesperus relationship, as it is defined first by the demands of aristocratic patriarchy while at the same time it is pressured by and ultimately responds to the challenge of bourgeois gender relations. Unlike Floribel, Olivia is of the aristocracy, and thus faces personal life quite differently from her unknown rival. Her relationship with Hesperus is determined entirely by the demands of the estate rather than by love, and within this context she cannot represent a feminine ideal, as Floribel does, but rather appears as socially real: she serves the estate rather than subjective masculine desire. The question facing her and Hesperus in marriage is not whether they love one another in the beginning but rather whether they can develop a regard for one another in a marriage intended to unite two aristocratic houses, thus preserving the power and status of their families. What that regard entails is seen clearly when Orlando tells Hesperus, in an emphatic articulation of aristocratic patriarchal values: "School her [Olivia], sir, in the arts of compliment, / You'll find her an apt learner" (II.iii.17–18). While both Hesperus and Olivia accept the responsibility placed on them by their families, neither initiates the relationship and neither is entirely comfortable with it: they do not seek out one another's company (as Hesperus and Floribel had done when they met secretly at great risk) but rather simply accept their positions within a prearranged social order.

If their marriage unites two houses of the aristocracy, it does not allay the tensions and anxieties pervading the aristocratic world nor assure survival of that world. In fact, the arranged marriage, even as it is set in motion and socially authorized, is subject to disturbing ideological and emotional pressures that suggest the demise of the aristocracy rather than its perpetuation. Those pressures are suggested not only in the early stages of the courtship, when Hesperus's reflections on marriage and love (because of his secret relationship with Floribel) are overwhelmed by thoughts of death (II.ii. 39–147), but more importantly in the fact that Hesperus, once forced into marriage to Olivia, attempts to re-create exactly the relationship that once existed between him and Floribel by converting Olivia into a repository of private emotional richness apart from society. In lines that recall Keats's *Lamia*, he remarks: "Olivia / I'll tell thee how we'll 'scape these prying eyes; / We'll build a wall between us and the world" (IV.iii.65–67). While the immediate meaning of this comment is doubtless determined by his guilt and confusion over Floribel, at the same time it carries much greater significance, expressing the emergence of a bourgeois individualist ideology within an aristocratic framework, an ideology that positions marriage against the public world and at the same time proclaims masculine authority to seek comfort in a privatized and idealized feminine world.

If Hesperus's comments display a bourgeois reconception of gender relations that marks the endurance of masculine authority in the passage of social power from the aristocracy to the bourgeoisie, the semi-lesbian exchanges between Olivia and her maidservants capture the dread, loneliness, and physical hardship that befall women as a result of that authority, and further show that, from a feminist perspective, there is relatively little difference between aristocratic patriarchy and bourgeois patriarchy. Shortly before the wedding, for instance, in describing her affection for Violet, Olivia remarks:

> Gentle maid,
> I'll not be sad; yet, little Violet,
> How long I've worn thy beauty next my heart,
> Aye, in my very thoughts, where thou hast shed
> Perpetual summer: how long shared thy being:
> Like two leaves of a bud, we've grown together,
> And needs must bleed at parting. (III.iii. 14–19)

This mournful statement of separation is also a statement of submission to masculine power and it acknowledges the sexual sacrifice that is made to that power, a sacrifice which destroys the sexual innocence that Olivia once had enjoyed in the company of other females. The blood which she knows must flow as she enters sexual union with a man is also the blood of her personal liberty. As she says to her nurse of her impending marriage:

> . . . 'tis the funeral of that Olivia
> You nursed and knew; an hour and she's no more,
> No more the mistress of her own resolves,
> The free partaker of earth's airs and pleasures. (III.iv.33–36)

Following as they do immediately upon the scene of Floribel's murder—a scene which ironically had concluded with the sound of wedding bells (III.iii. 194–97)—these exchanges disturbingly show the disempowerment of the feminine that is entailed in the sexual reality of marriage under patriarchy, whether patriarchy is aristocratic or bourgeois in construction.[8]

Another dimension of patriarchy that *Bride* captures, one that is less explicitly centered on questions of sex and gender—though it includes them—involves the relations between fathers and sons, and the struggle between them for social authority. At the level of plot alone, the importance of fathers is suggested in the frequent references to the fact that Orlando's father is dead, in the portrayal of Hesperus's father as powerless, and in the portrayal of Floribel's father as near death through most of the drama, finally dying when he learns of his daughter's murder. These references focus the demise of a once powerful social order—specifically of aristocratic patriarchy—and also describe the opening of an ideological space which allows the reconceptualization of personal life in individualist terms. With the death or disempowerment of all of the fathers in the drama, the sons and daughters seek new arrangements of power and gender relations, and these arrangements are consistently shaded by bourgeois power relations and ideological assumptions.

For instance, Orlando engages in deceptive legalistic strategies to secure the hand of Floribel, whom he describes and envisions in terms identical to Hesperus (see, for instance, I.ii.6–27), even at the very moment he would secure his public power by forcing Hesperus to wed Olivia. His plan denies the father-rights of Lord Ernest, while establishing his own personal authority. Hesperus also attempts to circumvent the authority of his father and Floribel's father by secretly marrying Floribel, thus asserting his own power against theirs. These actions of the sons are entangled both with love and private need and, at the deepest levels, with the reality of money—Lord Ernest is indebted to Orlando's father and Floribel's family is plagued by poverty, having lost the money it once had. Over against the demands of the estate, ruled by fathers, Hesperus and Orlando alike attempt to establish their individual authority, which at the same time would enable them to fulfill their personal desires.

It is clear that the transformations I am tracing here do not involve in any way the emergence of women as figures of social authority, or even as figures who enjoy real freedom. Nonetheless, Orlando and Hesperus do not represent the simple duplication of patriarchy in a new generation; rather, they represent the production and emergence of bourgeois patriarchy that displaces aristocratic patriarchy. The new social relations associated with their characters are suggested not only in the particular descriptions of their personal desires, noted above, but more importantly in the changing forms of social life charted through the drama. The aristocratic world of the fathers, for example, like the inchoate bourgeois world of the sons, recognizes public life as masculine and the private sphere as feminine, but in the world of the sons a political distinction is made between the public and private domains that is not made by the fathers. In the aristocratic world of the fathers women were simply property, and their marriages were arranged for the purpose of securing or extending the estate; in this respect there was no distinction between the home and the state. In the bourgeois world, however, the state and the family come to be conceptualized as distinctive categories, and women become part of what Zilla Eisenstein (writing in a different context) calls "a whole culture of privacy, intimacy, and individualism"[9] exemplified clearly in *Bride* in the distinction between Hesperus and Orlando's attitude toward Floribel on one hand and the attitudes of Lord Ernest and Mordred toward marriage on the other. In the world that Hesperus and Orlando would construct, in short, women are not liberated but rather are oppressed in new and different ways.

In addition to class and patriarchy, other issues in *Bride* could be sketched to elaborate the struggle of bourgeois social relations to be born. Further exploration of Orlando's use of the law, for instance, of Lenora's obsession with death, of Hesperus's madness, and of the full significance and role of money: all of these, no less than the issues considered above, point toward a deep structure of bourgeois social life at the center of the drama that destabilizes and overwhelms the aristocratic and feudal relations reflected on its surface. The ideological and political struggles surrounding such matters, more than simply Beddoes's limitations as a dramatist, help to explain the formal and aesthetic shortcomings of the work, while at the same time pointing toward its larger significance for literary and social history.

Moreover, the essential structure of ideas and assumptions in *Bride*— its expression of inchoate bourgeois needs and desires against a weakening aristocratic framework of authority—constitutes its particular Romantic significance and locates it among other dramas of the period which, for all their differences, share an inability to escape the political unconscious of bourgeois social relations. Like other dramas considered in this study, *Bride* would look to a past world and ideology for its governing values, while in fact it is shaped and vitalized by a contradictory world and ideology. The various portrayals of this contradiction within *Bride* are often aesthetically crippling, and yet they give the drama its particular and crucial importance, distilling for critical investigation the processes whereby feudal aesthetic, political, and ideological authority were destroyed by bourgeois social relations.

CHAPTER

᠊ᡃᡄᢁᢦ

8

"Where the Sires' Quarrels Descend
Upon the Son"

Sir Walter Scott's *Halidon Hill*

Sir Walter Scott's four dramas—two full-length works, and two ab-
breviated pieces—share with many of his novels a historical vision of
crisis involving figures, real and imaginary, in Scottish feudal society.[1]
MacDuff's Cross tells the story of conflict between two lords, Lindesay
and Maurice Berkeley. The long conflict has produced bloodshed and
the threat of more bloodshed until both families eventually are be-
reft of integrity and faced with destruction; the conflict is stopped
only when Berkeley "lays the title down" and, along with Lindesay's
disguised brother (thought to have been murdered by Berkeley),
withdraws from society entirely "to that last retreat" of "the sacred
cloister." *Auchindrane* offers a long-winded account of the violent,
conspiracy-driven struggles between yet another pair of lords, John
Muir of Auchindrane and Sir Thomas Kennedy of Cullayne, tracking
the atrocities committed by and the ultimate demise of the former; as
Scott notes in the preface to the drama, "The family, blackened with
the crimes of its predecessors, became extinct, and the estate passed
into other hands." *The Doom of Devorgoil* records the tribulations of
a once powerful family, capturing its anxiety and dread among what
have become "spirit-haunted ruins," and finally offering a fantasy escape from utter desolation, an escape that revolves around the interesting notion of discovering "the fated key" of untold wealth. Together,
these works sketch a grim portrait of a withering culture, and have

about them an air of great sadness, much like the sadness that afflicts Keats's fallen Titans in *Hyperion*.

Halidon Hill, written in two acts in 1822,[2] occupies a special place among Scott's dramatic efforts, not because it escapes this sadness, and not because it is dramatically superior, but rather because its vision of social crisis is historically more sharply focused. In this work multiple levels of historical and political experience and various significant ideological issues are presented with a degree of formal precision and historical urgency that are not as readily apparent in the other, more diffuse and rambling dramatic pieces. Not only does *Halidon Hill* present, as *MacDuff's Cross* had done, internal conflict among the Scottish nobility; it also presents a particular military conflict between Scotland and England, effectively calling attention to the larger historical contexts within which specific details of Scottish social life developed. Furthermore, in the particular military battle that Scott has chosen to dramatize—that of Halidon Hill on July 19, 1333—Scotland not only lost badly but also suffered the slaughter of great numbers of Scottish nobility and soldiers; from the retrospective historical point of view from which Scott was writing, the battle might be said to symbolize the ultimate triumph of the English empire and to portray vividly one means by which that empire was won. Finally, although Scott unblinkingly charts the certain defeat of his countrymen in an age long past, at the same time he bestows upon them great vigor and integrity by showing them settling among themselves their own deepest personal differences—they are militarily defeated but their national honor is intact. In this interesting ideological maneuver, Scott effects a drama of consolation; he acknowledges the demise of Scottish aristocratic social authority but finds the lasting integrity of Scottish history, thus reconciling the Scotland of his own day with its hard past. In the following pages I want to consider Scott's portrayal of these matters within a broad historical context and to touch briefly on several thematic issues of social and historical importance—including religion, money, and gender—related to them.

Several specific historical moments help to elucidate the scope and significance of *Halidon Hill*, and to give some idea of the complexity of Scott's historical imagination. Written in 1822, just after the close of the English regency, the drama describes a military conflict between England and Scotland in the fourteenth century. Sandwiched between these two moments is the important date of 1707—never mentioned

in the drama—when Scotland legally became part of the British kingdom. The imaginative turn to the distant feudal past, entirely leaping
over the most significant and transforming moment in Scottish history, can be explained, of course, in terms of personality, sentiment,
nostalgia, and the popularity, during the Romantic period, of things
medieval. But it also calls into play the historically interesting possibility that in the 1820s, with feudalism all but dead at the hands of
industrial capitalism and with no hope of future restored health, the
fact of an England-Scotland merger in 1707 would perhaps seem less
compelling and less historically urgent to Scott than the much deeper
question of the forces that led to the merger and that ultimately destroyed the way of life that had preceded it. That is, in looking to
medieval Scotland, Scott's imagination moves toward what is, for him,
the center of a far-reaching historical interest: the distantly removed
but still pressing early material conditions that significantly shaped
subsequent historical changes, including those of 1707 and 1822. The
battle of Halidon Hill, in this view, is a single, hard crystal of historical energy, a specific episode carrying within it a variety of personal
and public issues under extreme pressure. Through the optic of Scott's
imagination it becomes both an emblem of Scotland's tragic past and
a pathway into the deeper structures of history from which his own
contemporary world was formed.

One way Scott deepens the historical interest of the drama is by
focusing in the opening act on internal conflict at multiple levels of
experience—individual, familial, national—and on the consequences
and resolution of that conflict. In developing this focus he demonstrates an important historical understanding shared by other dramatists of the Romantic period:[3] societies most often suffer their greatest
debilitating blows not from hostile external forces but from weakness
and instability generated within their own borders. At that moment
when a society becomes unable to represent the interests and meet the
various needs of its own citizens, or when its citizens become driven
by private interest rather than by public good, then the social order is
most susceptible to threats from outside its borders. The Scotland of
Halidon Hill is precisely such a place, as, in Scott's hands, its ill-fated
encounter with England is shown to constitute only part of a much
larger history, a history in which Scotland defeats itself long before
the arrival of Edward III.

Scott's vision of Scotland's past draws upon several loosely related contextual issues of significant historical and critical weight. First, the dramatic emphasis on Scotland's internal conflicts creates a narrative space for imaginatively exploring certain ideological structures that have weakened to the point of collapse; for reconstructing the principles of honor and integrity central to those structures; and thus for creating a Scotland whose identity does not depend entirely on definitions supplied by English presence (as a straightforward "invasion story" might imply). Feudal traditions of family, religion, strong national leadership, and honor in servitude[4] are already attenuated as the play opens. Scott proceeds methodically from one to the next, both to trace the central features of Scottish society that have begun to decline and to specify the particular contours of that decline: to protect their personal honor, families kill members of rival families at such a pace that honor requiring retribution assures the demise of the family itself; religious piety and authority, in the character of Adam De Vipont, are relegated to the personal role of seeking peace between rival families and, in the final scene of the play, to the politically pointless task of asserting the nobility of Scotland even in defeat; leadership at the highest levels has long since evaporated, as the presence of the regent does little more than stir nostalgia among Scotchmen for the lost great leader Robert Bruce; and individual soldiers and lords squabble among themselves over their respective places in the military pecking order. With some bitterness, but with a great deal more sadness, the drama discloses the tattered seams of Scottish feudal society, capturing that society at a moment when it is so weakened that individual efforts to reunify it sufficiently to withstand outside challenge are hopeless. It is at this level of social relations—where institutions and structures of value and authority intersect—that the first act develops.

Second, and more difficult, Scott's imaginative recreation of circumstances surrounding the battle of Halidon Hill forces the issue of historical explanation. If, for instance, Scotland's initial real difficulties arose from internal conflict, then what was the nature of this conflict? Was it defined (as the drama implies) solely by the inability of various, colliding, strong personalities of the Scottish nobility to forgive any transgression? Was it a matter of a few power-hungry nobles who ingloriously sought to take power from other, more reasonable nobles? Or was internal conflict itself a product of still larger social and historical forces? No explicit answers to these questions are provided in the text of the drama; but the variety of personal and public issues, and of issues connecting the fates of Scotland and England, suggests that internal turmoil is, on some level, implicated in social and specifically economic changes that prevailing structures of Scottish authority and social life were incapable of controlling.

The economics of the Scottish situation can be glimpsed by briefly considering the personal animosities described on the surface of the dramatic action within the context of the larger world to which the drama calls attention. As the play begins, Scotland is without a ruler; the various nobles follow their personal ambitions in determining the direction of their estates and of the nation; families fight to the death with fellow families; some individuals have abandoned Scotland for England (for instance, Baliol), or have turned away from their country to religion (De Vipont). Scottish solidarity has entirely eroded, and the Scottish world appears poor, tired, and declining. In the textual margin lies a suggestion of a larger and wealthier world that both tempts and pressures Scottish social life. This world is hinted at first in the character of De Vipont, who has spent twelve years in the Near East participating in the Crusades—that is, participating in a religious venture that possessed very real economic dimensions, for the Crusades were one means by which a lucrative trade was established between Europe and the Near East and by which industry was stimulated in late medieval Europe.[5] The character of the renegade Baliol, who appears in Act II, also calls attention to the economic misfortunes of his native country by leaving Scotland[6] to find position and fortune in England, which had embraced world social and economic changes much more readily than Scotland and had accordingly benefited politically from them. While neither of these characters is central to the dramatic action, and while neither is drawn as a self-conscious agent of economic change, they both carry associations that suggest some of the world pressures contributing to the specific personal and national turmoil charted in the plot of the dramatic action.

Third, Scott's decision to place an imaginary and less than noble prince regent at the head of a declining Scotland suggests that the drama may have been written as a sort of small cautionary tale for Regency England (and for the post-Regency England of 1822), which, one could argue, suffered many of the same atrocities Scott found in medieval Scotland. This point perhaps locates the drama too snugly at the level of historical conjuncture, but it is nonetheless important, for it calls attention to the allegorical nature of some Romantic drama and, moreover, allows insight into the weight of industrial capitalism on the Romantic imagination. Without tracing the many social atrocities afflicting Regency England,[7] we might simply note that just as medieval Scotland was forced to bend to the mighty hand of mercantile capitalism that was shaping Europe in the twelfth through fourteenth centuries, so England in the early nineteenth century found itself grappling with the transformative energies of industrial capitalism. With a debauched regent at the head of state, many (including Byron, Hazlitt, Hunt, and Shelley, to name only the most famous in literary studies) wondered whether England could survive the turbulent combination of reactionary politics and radical economic development. As an allegory of the age, *Halidon Hill* seems to be one of the more bleak commentaries on England's prospects, as it insists that social survival depends in large measure upon strong leadership capable of unifying a society through the example of high principle and of representing and advancing its material interests.

All of these matters, including the allegorical reading of the Scottish regent, portray feudalism under the threat of extinction. The internal conflict that tears at the family, estate, and country and that is intensified by economic pressures and prospects from abroad, suggests a growing and far-reaching contradiction between the material and ideological structures of Scottish social life, a contradiction that cannot be laid to rest by a mere reconciliation of personal differences nor by professions of Scottish nationalism—both of which occur at the level of plot. The frames of real history encompass not only these but also deeper forces that give them significance.

The specific dilemma facing Scottish feudalism is elaborated in Act II, in the initial descriptions of the English army. Here are seen interests and issues that were relevant not only to Scottish feudalism but that also prevailed and endured well into Scott's own day. In shifting the dramatic action from Scotland to England in Act II, Scott juxtaposes the decline of feudal and aristocratic social values to the emergence of bourgeois social values. The English soldiers, like their Scottish counterparts, bicker among themselves and show little sense of cultural pride or solidarity. But they are, nonetheless, a unified and emerging social body, held together particularly by a strong leader and by confidence in individual ability. Moreover, as the character of Chandos vividly illustrates, that ability is defined entirely in secular and unsentimental terms and is motivated by a desire to preserve and expand material wealth. In his nasty argument with the abbot of Walt-hamstow, for instance, Chandos refuses to tithe before going off to battle, remarking that "I'll take my chance, / And trust my sinful soul to Heaven's mercy, / Rather than risk my worldly goods with thee" (II.i). As far as Chandos is concerned, religion is a debased and selfish institution, presumably set up to shame industrious individuals such as himself into yielding up their wealth. From his cynical perspective, one devoted to the religious enterprise (as is the abbot) lacks energy, ability, and worth, and is but "a lamb among a herd of wolves!" (II.i).

The diminishing credibility and political authority of religion seen in this personal exchange is elaborated further upon King Edward's arrival at the military camp. Continuing his abuse of the abbot, Chan-dos tells the king that, according to the abbot, one of the king's former chaplains is in purgatory for having used "secular weapons" to save the king's life. Upon hearing this, King Edward turns bitterly on the abbot, remarking: "In purgatory! thou [the abbot] shalt pray him out on't, / Or I will make thee wish thyself beside him" (II.i). While the king later asks the abbot to pray for the English soldiers in battle against Scotland, saying that "We may need good men's prayers" (II.i), the distinction between secular and religious authority is clearly drawn, as the abbot (like the beadsman in Keats's *Eve of St. Agnes*) is relegated, on the one hand, to defending the integrity of orthodox belief and, on the other, to praying for and mouthing tributes to the political authority that abuses him.

The social significance of the abbot becomes clearer when his char-acter is compared to that of De Vipont, his Scottish counterpart. De Vipont enjoys the respect of his fellow citizens, and is perceived by all as a sane and spiritual presence in a struggling, deteriorating society. For instance, when Gordon's hatred of his archenemy, Swinton, causes him to forget the immediate social cause against England, and is then reminded by the knight templar that the present national concerns do not permit "private quarrel" (I.i), the young knight adjusts his conduct accordingly, allowing himself to be guided by the greater wisdom of De Vipont. Further, through the simple piety and firm principle of his character, De Vipont gradually brings about a truce between the quar-reling Swinton and Gordon that is the basis of the integrity associated with Scotland, even as that country suffers defeat in battle. Finally, De Vipont serves his countrymen visibly and courageously throughout the bloody battle, with his spiritual presence woven fully into the social fabric of his country. These and other similar episodes firmly establish the durable connections that Scotland assumes between individual character and religious principle. The English abbot of Walthamstow, by contrast, is portrayed as little more than an unrespected servant to secular authority. To note only one example, after King Edward has slaughtered and defeated Scotland, the abbot (having been long absent from the dramatic action) is ingloriously brought onstage to proclaim, in an astonishingly brief statement, the greatness of the English victory: "Heaven grant your Majesty / Many such glorious days as this has been!" (II.iii). That De Vipont, despite his integrity, is on the losing side, and that the sympathetic but entirely helpless abbot finds himself among the militarily and politically powerful, suggest that religion is no longer the master key to social stability and power. The actions and values associated with De Vipont recall the idealized role of religion in a nearly extinct past world, while the abbot's experiences clearly demonstrate the new role of religion in an emerging secular society.

Less clearly pronounced than religion but similarly problematic in the drama are issues of gender and sexual love. Unlike almost all other Romantic dramas, *Halidon Hill* is without a single female character, thus focusing the strikingly masculine quality of the issues and themes portrayed in the dramatic action: war, politics, power, economics, and religion. But this masculine-military world is not entirely without reference to women, and these references disclose important information about social structures of authority and value. During a lull in the battle the young Gordon confides in Swinton that he loves a woman named Elizabeth, who possesses charm, grace, and honor, and who sings beautifully the songs of Scottish history and society. Faced with certain death at the hands of England, Gordon sentimentally describes this woman's many accomplishments to Swinton and at the same time proclaims his intention of providing her (assuming that he lives to see her again) with a stable and rich estate held together by their love and by a loyal and hardworking body of native Scotch. The home life that he envisions would reward him and Elizabeth with personal happiness; and that happiness would partake of a far-reaching social energy greater than that found even in the strong English system, where (according to De Vipont) "gallant yeomen" are "free as the best lord" and are therefore wholeheartedly loyal to "their King and law" (II.ii). Gordon's is a dream, in short, of a completely unalienated life of personal, domestic, and public stability.

The obvious explanation of Gordon's youthful idealism is that his dreams are materially shaped by the prospect of violent death at the hands of a hated enemy. But, nonetheless, the particular details of his dreams reflect a real social world and his deep-seated need to compensate for the shortcomings of that world, particularly for the tensions and quarrels among the Scotch themselves that have weakened the country. Elizabeth plays a central role in Gordon's dreams, anxieties, and hopes regarding his world, not only because she represents for him the possibility of personal fulfillment; she also is the key symbol of social wholeness, the voice expressing in song the integrity of the world that he, as a Scottish chieftain, has helped to create. If he imagines a postwar estate peopled with followers who "shall have portion in the good they fight for," and who "shall have his field, / His household hearth and sod-built home, as free / As ever Southron had" (II.ii), it is Elizabeth who will give that estate meaning with her smile and who will locate its value in song among the cultural richness of Scottish history. Put differently, Gordon's anxieties about the structure of Scottish society, and about his own actions that have weakened Scotland, lead him to idealize Scotland by portraying it under his authority as free, unified, and happy; that idealization is then sealed into Scottish history by Elizabeth's songs about Scottish shepherds, knights in battle, and, generally, the country's experiences of merriment and sadness.

Gordon's descriptions of Elizabeth here are peculiar. She is obviously at the center of his dreams, the individual around whom his highest ideals revolve. At the same time, however, she is the individual through whom his personal and public desires are expressed. She is portrayed as both the repository and vehicle of value, and as such she is clearly the product of masculine imagination and desire; she provides Gordon with the possibility of personal happiness, and at the same time agreeably celebrates in song the world that he and his fellow Scotchmen have created for her. She is, as it were, Gordon's religion in this moment of extremity: faith in her motivates him to go forward by holding out for him the possibility of social salvation. In this view, the chivalrous code of honor to which Gordon adheres prescribes a specific, redemptive role for women that ultimately depends upon masculine power and desire. Elizabeth's presence in the drama in name only makes this point emphatically: Gordon's world is fundamentally defined by its military character, and it uses feminine passivity, domesticity, and dependence to stabilize and articulate its dream of itself.

The idealization of social life, however, cannot preserve Scotland from the double horror of "civil discord" (II.iii) and English military power, as is shown when Gordon's dreaming is followed almost immediately by the massive slaughter of the Scottish soldiers. But, however absurd they may appear in the context of battle, the young Gordon's comments mark an important first step in the retrospective reconstruction of Scottish history that the drama pursues. His vision of personal happiness, public stability, and citizen loyalty is joined during and after the battle by the portrayal of a Scottish thief who abandons his old ways to die bravely as a soldier fighting for his country;[8] by complete reconciliation between the Gordon and Swinton families; by condemnation of the traitor Baliol, who abandoned Scotland for England; by the victorious King Edward's recognition of greatness in both Swinton and Gordon; and by De Vipont's final, noble remark to King Edward (who had criticized the knight templar for warring against England, a Christian nation) that his oath of loyalty to Scotland preceded, and therefore superseded, his oath of loyalty to his Christian order. In all of these actions and comments the defeat of Scotland by England is acknowledged, while at the same time the honor of Scotland is preserved and exalted. Just as Gordon's comments about Elizabeth describe stability and fulfillment at the level of desire, the subsequent events and comments insist that the honor of the Scottish people will endure at a level of human experience impervious to social, historical, and political change. In this respect, *Halidon Hill* is a remarkable drama of consolation, admitting military defeat and political marginalization but insisting at the same time on the permanent nobility of Scotland. Put differently, the memory of Scottish history is a source of ideal integrity, even as Scotland itself has succumbed—of necessity—to an expanding, cold, and self-interested English empire.

Written after the deaths of George III, John Keats, and Percy Shelley, and only two years prior to the death of Byron, *Halidon Hill* might appropriately be regarded as one of the literary markers of the death of the Romantic age. Its content makes it all the more important as a sign of a changing world. From one point of view, the demise of Scotland, as described in the drama, was not far removed from the demise of Scott's own world. The conflict between radical and reactionary forces within England—between laborers and the new industrial machinery, between the masses and the government, and, more broadly, between England and France—had taken their toll on British society by 1822, and it was clear to all thinking people that a new world was in the offing; indeed, as Scott seems to have understood, this new world had already claimed victory over the older forms of personal, social, economic, and religious life. For a conservative such as Scott, the last best response to this social change was to insist upon—and to articulate—a domain of permanent honor that could in no way be co-opted or subdued by transformations of society. Such a domain, as *Halidon Hill* shows, necessarily confuses nostalgia for history, but that confusion itself is historically significant to a full understanding of Romantic structures of authority and belief. For this reason alone the drama should be included in the canon of important Romantic literature.

CHAPTER

9

"Where the World Is Thickest"

The Dramas of George Gordon, Lord Byron

Lord Byron is the greatest dramatist of the Romantic period and arguably the greatest English dramatist since Shakespeare.[1] His dramas offer
an expansive historical vision, while at the same time concentrating
on the fine details of personal and social life. Running through them
are the post-Revolutionary awareness that the world had irrevocably
changed and the post-Waterloo anxiety over the narrowing possibilities of human freedom that seemed increasingly to accompany that
change. The dramas seldom resort to the nostalgia that so often informs and energizes other dramas of the period, looking instead with
a hard eye directly into the changed and changing historical circumstances of the modern world. Nor do they naively reflect or embrace
the bourgeois structures of value and belief coming to maturation in
Byron's day; rather, they interrogate those structures by casting them
within frames of historical and social reference that deny their autonomy, purity, and self-generating identity. Finally, Byron's dramas
leave no area of personal and social life untouched, as they range across
vast areas of human experience from politics and religion to gender,
identity, family, economics, art, physical deformity, and more.

The tremendous scope and sweeping power of these dramas become apparent when they are considered together, not only in terms

of their textual content but also in terms of Byron's personal efforts to develop a poetic voice suitable for expressing the contradictions, struggles, and predicament of his age. I am not suggesting that old-school biographical criticism is most appropriate to a study of Byron's dramas, but rather that certain details of his life, as well as certain ideas set down in his letters and journals, are themselves products and records of the Romantic historical situation within which the dramas were produced; thus they often help to sharpen critical investigation by providing an avenue into socially relevant issues that are deeply submerged in the dramas. While appropriation of biographical data runs the risk of reducing critical investigation to yet another set of reflections on Byronism, at the same time refusal to admit that data into a materialist critique runs the risk of limiting what can be said about the historical and social dimensions of the dramas. The challenge facing historical criticism of Byron is to find a way to use the powerful, often mesmerizing details of the poet's life without allowing these to cloud the historical significance of the dramas themselves.

Bearing these caveats in mind, I want to consider Byron's overall effort and accomplishment in drama, in an attempt to suggest the range of his social interests and the depth of his historical understanding. While I assume that his personal life, personality, and scattered comments in his letters and journals are indispensable to this consideration, at the same time I assume that critical explanation must be grounded finally in the categories of history.

I should note, by way of preface, that this discussion of Byron in some ways departs significantly from my commentaries on the other dramas of the period, especially insofar as it does not emphasize the issue of gender. I subordinate that issue here not because I question its important role in Byron's imagination,[2] but rather because I believe that it may be more immediately useful to investigate the operation of ideology and social relations in his plays. These issues are handled by Byron with greater sophistication and with a greater sense of urgency than in most of the plays examined above; therefore, their investigation may help to clarify certain nuances and dimensions of Romantic drama that heretofore I have discussed only in passing. While the turn from gender as a major point of analytic concern may appear to constitute a grating shift in the argument, in my view it constitutes rather an expansion, insofar as I attempt here to elaborate a range of social and historical dynamics that embrace at every turn the Romantic conception and articulation of gender.

Byron's correspondence after 1820 reveals his growing impatience with all criticism of his poetry. He brusquely dismissed John Murray's pleas that he boost his popularity by writing "in the old way to interest the women" (*BLJ*, 9:125)[3] and persistently steered his own artistic course. Although he alienated the fashionable reading public, outraged orthodox religious opinion, and alarmed even his closest friends, he defiantly proclaimed against all that "they shall never subdue me while I keep my senses. . . . I assure you [Kinnaird] that I will not swerve from my purpose" (*BLJ*, 9:94). His stubbornness came, at least partly, from his fear that even the smallest concession to his critics would be regressive and inevitably detrimental both to his readers and to his art. His position is stated clearly in a letter to Shelley: "[A]s long as I wrote the exaggerated nonsense which has corrupted the public taste—they applauded me to the very echo—and now that I have really written within these three or four years some things which should 'not willingly be let die'—the whole herd snort and grumble and return to wallow in their mire" (*BLJ*, 9:161).

If he was angered by the remonstrances against him, he nonetheless expected them. In fact, when he learned that *Don Juan* had been favorably received he was surprised and not particularly flattered: "[T]he work appears—with a lukewarm publisher and all the previous impressions against it—& still it succeeds.—I thought it would *not* because it's *[sic]* real qualities are not on the *surface*—but still if people will dive a little—I think it will reward them for their trouble" (*BLJ*, 9:55). He had resigned himself to the probability that his poetry would not readily find acceptance because as he put it he had adopted "a different system from the rage of the day" (*BLJ*, 9:92; see also *BLJ*, 9:84) that not even his most intelligent and supportive critics fully understood.[4] But his feeling that immediate disapproval was inevitable was matched by his strong conviction that in time his present work would be deemed his best and most durable, and indeed he believed himself to be writing more for the future than for the moment. As he remarked confidently if somewhat bitterly to Kinnaird with respect to *Heaven and Earth, Werner,* and *The Vision of Judgment*: "[M]ark what I now say—that the time will come—when *these* will be preferred to any I have before written;—it is not from the cry, or depression of a month or two that such things are decided" (*BLJ*, 9:92–93). This prediction, of course, has yet to be fulfilled, and in fact with the obvious exceptions of *The Vision of Judgment* and *Don Juan* most of the works he felt certain would endure have suffered badly at the hands of subsequent criticism. Still it would be wrong to dismiss Byron lightly as a poor judge of his own aims and accomplishments, for it is likely that when this system is at last understood he will be proven correct. I believe that this system, which has never attracted serious critical attention, both illuminates and vindicates much of his late poetry (especially the dramas) so long held in low esteem.

Although Byron never explicitly defined his poetics, he frequently described its main principles in his letters and journals. According to these, his poetry after about 1820 was written almost entirely within a context of revolutionary politics and social analysis. Refusing to play any longer the Byronic role that had made him popular, he devoted himself instead to a life that combined careful study, active literary production, and political involvement. The degree of his commitment to his new enterprise astonished even Shelley, who remarked in a letter to Mary that "Byron lives a life totally the reverse of that which he led at Venice. . . . [H]e is now quite well immersed in politics and literature" (*LPBS*, 2:317).

The perspective that Byron seems to have been developing at this time involved rejection both of the eighteenth-century view of the world as static and fallen as well as of the Romantic view of the world as organic and fallen; his position increasingly was grounded instead upon his hard-won belief that human value is historically rather than "naturally" determined, and that it is thus transformable. Moreover, he had come to understand forms of social organization—including their notions of art and genius—in the full light of what later social theory would call ideology and class struggle. Hence humanity for Byron was no longer perceived in terms of its insurmountable limitations but rather in terms of its limitless possibilities. (It is important to emphasize here, however, that Byron was no simpleminded utopian, nor was he entirely exempt from the sort of despair that characterizes much of his earlier work, as will become evident momentarily.) This revolutionary (if incompletely realized) perspective on social life represents the crux at which Byron's life and art converge into an active and unified campaign of intervention in the world's affairs.

The direction Byron's thought was taking during these years should be clear enough. Both personally and in his poetry he had long wrestled with British and European political matters ranging from the breaking of stocking frame machines by the Luddites to the Napoléonic campaigns, developing a position which was increasingly critical of the conventional institutional definitions and representations of politics and society.[5] By 1821 he could state firmly in his letters and in his *Ravenna Journal* his belief that eventual revolution was unavoidable; and it is evident that he understood both the harsh realities and the certain consequences of radical political and social change. As he put it, "Revolutions are not to be made with Rose-water" (*BLJ*, 7:77): "The king-times are fast finishing. There will be blood shed like water, and tears like mist; but the people will conquer in the end. I shall not live to see it, but I foresee it" (*BLJ*, 8:26). Keeping the prospects of extreme physical violence in close view, he devoted himself fully to promoting the revolutionary cause. He was an active supporter of the underground and militant Italian Carbonari, sufficiently committed to its goals to allow his apartments to be used as a storage depot for that group's artillery.[6] Moreover, he followed Aristotle's advice by combining his political interests with a careful study of history (note, for instance, his extensive reading during this period of such writers as Mitford, Sanuto, Diodorus Siculus, and others) and even went a step further by exploring in *Marino Faliero, The Two Foscari*, and other poems the different levels of meaning and possibility in any given political episode.[7]

The abundance of such evidence notwithstanding, Byron has seldom been accepted on his own terms, suffering instead accusations that he was seeking "The glorification of a heroic death [to justify] a more dubious life."[8] This critical reluctance to admit the full progressive quality of Byron's thought deserves consideration, for it helps to clarify some practical and theoretical difficulties in interpretation. The temptation to study Byron's psychology rather than his politics has existed since Scott's time and more often than not has led readers to conclude that Byron's aristocratic hauteur prevented him from embracing a truly progressive political position.[9] And his several famous comments to John Cam Hobhouse about leading radicals of the day have confused the issue further. For instance, of William Cobbett and Henry "Orator" Hunt he remarked: "I have always been . . . a well-wisher to and voter for reform in Parliament—but 'such fellows as these who will never go to the Gallows with any credit'—such infamous Scoundrels as Hunt and Cobbett—in short the whole gang (always excepting you [Hobhouse] B. & D.) disgust and make one doubt of the virtue of any principle or politics which can be embraced by similar ragamuffins" (*BLJ*, 7:62–63). But such savage criticism need not be interpreted solely as upper-class contempt for lower-class political enthusiasm (Hunt, in fact, was a gentleman farmer); Byron, after all, just as often dished out severe criticism of "*Gentlemen* reformers" (*BLJ*, 9:194), and indeed his vicious verse satire on Hobhouse's politics almost cost him a lifelong friendship.[10]

Byron was intolerant of Cobbett and Hunt, not because of their lack of social position but because he suspected their motives and more importantly because he disagreed with their political program. Of the major radical spokesmen beginning to emerge in England after about 1807 they were among the most articulate and ambitious, involved fully (as E. P. Thompson puts it) in a "scramble for power" that threatened to defeat the very cause they supported. In addition, although they were "radicals" (for Byron, a new and probably confusing term [see *BLJ*, 7:99]) they were not revolutionaries.[11] Along with Major Cartwright, Sir Francis Burdett, Kinnaird, and others, they believed that social improvement depended entirely on parliamentary reform. Byron, of course, supported reform just as they did, but he had come to believe that this measure alone was incapable of producing substantial and lasting change, for it would merely extend existing political principles without addressing underlying social principles; or, put differently, while the radicals were concerned mainly or wholly with political change, Byron saw the larger need for a full social revolution. Thus he denounced frenzied proclamations that simple change in parliament could rectify severe social ills and attempted in his poetry to demonstrate the level at which truly productive change must take place.

The radicals' reforming zeal, moreover, often combined distrust of any organized militant resistance with commitment to the liberal notion of individual struggle. As Cobbett stated: "I advise my countrymen to have nothing to do with any Political Clubs, and secret Cabals, any Correspondencies; but to trust to individual exertions and open meetings."[12] In Italy Byron not only was busily engaged organizing a secret political resistance group but also in grounding his activities on a careful study of history and society—he refused to rely on simple "trust." Finally, much of Cobbett's social critique, like Car-

lyle's and Ruskin's after him, was idealistic and regressive insofar as
its vision of the future was based upon a rather romantic notion of
the past: "I wish to see the poor men of England what the poor men
of England were when I was born." On this issue Raymond Williams
notes Cobbett's "surprising share of responsibility for that idealization
of the Middle Ages which is so characteristic of nineteenth-century
social criticism."[13] Although Byron himself certainly once had been
absorbed by a vision of an idyllic past, he now was just as certainly
intolerant of such idealization, as *Cain* and *Heaven and Earth* convincingly demonstrate: he denied the possibility of re-creating the green
and pleasant land of some agricultural past that in fact had never really
existed.[14] Byron's position then was not necessarily determined entirely by his private ambitions nor by his elitism; there is a real and
substantive political basis for his criticism of the new radicals that is
at least as important as his personal contempt for them.[15]

Byron's attitude toward the radicals raises the far more thorny issue
of his quarrel with the British liberals, under whose influence he had
first entered politics. It would, of course, be difficult with existing evidence to prove that he remained on the continent after 1816 because he
did not wish to face the strong liberal pressures that inevitably would
be placed on him in England; but his continuing personal friendship
with numerous British liberals, combined with the divergence of his
thought from the developing liberal position, makes such an argument
plausible.[16] He had begun his career in the company of Charles Grey,
Thomas Erskine, and Richard Brinsley Sheridan, whose main goals,
as one historian puts it, were "to defend the liberties of the subject,
freedom of the press and of public meeting against the encroachments
of a panicky Government"; and in his later poetry their influence remains strong.[17] But poems as far back as *The Prisoner of Chillon* and
The Lament of Tasso reveal that he had come to doubt the basic premise
of liberalism, namely its insistence upon absolute individualism as the
starting point of all social inquiry and political conduct. In these poems
Byron depicts characters removed absolutely from any social context,
revealing their inability to rely solely on their individual strength.
Through his treatment of incarceration he arrives at the conclusion that
individualism *must* be defined in social terms if it is to mean anything.

The individualist doctrine was held in common by both radicals
and liberals, who were rapidly aligning themselves against the aristocracy, and its influence was widely felt in every field from economics to

government, from intellectual history to social history. That it would control the British political scene for some years to come was certain, and doubtless Byron sensed this. Jeremy Bentham, Thomas Malthus, David Ricardo, James Mill, John Stuart Mill—these men formulated the theories of the natural law of individualism; and in poetry such writers as Wordsworth, Coleridge, and Keats (even while they energetically resisted specific Benthamite and utilitarian doctrines) converted these theories into artistic truths.[18]

One reason Byron rejected the liberal definition of individualism was his belief that it inevitably generated unresolvable contradictions in the social sphere.[19] He makes this point in his dramas: Sardanapalus's strong individualism contributes to the collapse of a once powerful social order; in *The Deformed Transformed*, Arnold's private pursuit of beauty and perfection leaves a trail of corpses. Outside England Byron's expositions of these contradictions were presented with growing confidence, and as he shed his liberalism he began to ground his thinking upon the need for and possibility of creating a social order that did not work at cross-purposes. Although his analysis is never clearly formulated, his position is implicit in all of his mature poetry; he believed that social amelioration would be possible only when existing values assumed to be natural and universal were understood as being historically and socially determined, serving specific political ends that were not necessarily in the best interest of most people.

To glimpse his position one need only read his Venetian plays, which clearly demonstrate the way a ruling class controls not only the political machinery but also the system of values to which society subscribes, thus assuring the perpetuation of the existing power structure. He had begun to suspect as early as the Eastern Tales that the ostensible universals to which society subscribes were in fact ideologies; but only after leaving England and being forced to reconsider the values by which he judged experience did his poetry—particularly his dramas—begin to convey the depth and many dimensions of ideology.[20] His natural detestation of cant and hypocrisy gradually transformed into a much more profound concept of social order.

That Byron wanted to develop a political poetry capable of providing a more progressive vision than the liberal vision would allow is obvious from his comment to Kinnaird that "I shall not be deterred by any outcry—they hate me—and I detest them—I mean your present Public—but they shall not interrupt the march of my mind—nor prevent me from telling the tyrants who are attempting to trample upon all thought—that their thrones will yet be rocked to their foundation" (*BLJ*, 9:152). Byron, of course, was unsure what a kingless society would be, and he always feared a "Democratical tyranny" (*BLJ*, 7:99) that would simply reverse existing social structures without actually improving them. But his general understanding is plain: he believed that prevailing structures of authority at their most fundamental level were oppressive and inadequate, and that liberal thinking lacked a plan to substantially alter this fact. As he remarked to Thomas Moore: "I think it [society], as now constituted, *fatal* to all original undertakings of every kind" (*BLJ*, 9:119).

The challenge that he faced in writing poetry was to determine exactly the kinds of change that were needed and how these might best be effected. His thinking on these matters was influenced significantly by Vittorio Alfieri, whom he held in high esteem; indeed, in the above remark to Kinnaird he directly echoes the great Italian dramatist, identifying himself with the prestigious tradition of opposition literature in which Alfieri stands. With *Marino Faliero* Byron had begun to experiment with Alfieri's poetic method (for instance, see *BLJ*, 7:182) and although he never was so daring as to dedicate his work to George Washington or to The People—as Alfieri did—he followed Alfieri's example of combining art and politics. In fact, he eventually surpassed Alfieri's rather limited juxtaposition of tyrant and hero—which Byron believed often reduced art to "political dialogues" (*BLJ*, 7:150)—and created a more subtle and sophisticated political poetics based upon the unspoken assumptions encompassing social relations. Significant as it is, this dimension of his art is difficult to understand because his use of literary sources often is confusing and, more importantly, because he continually experimented with poetic ideas and methods rather than resting with a fixed and clearly defined form. He moved easily from historical drama to metaphysical drama, from energetic satire to sentimental narrative (for instance, *The Island*), clouding the common principles he felt to be at the center of each.

Byron's view of drama provides the clearest guide to his poetics. As mentioned above, he believed himself to be writing under a different system from the mainstream drama of the day; he explained in his usual epigrammatic fashion that his aim was "to make a *regular* English drama—no matter whether for the Stage or not—which is not my object—but a *mental theatre*" (*BLJ*, 8:187; see also *BLJ*, 8:185, 210).

I understand this to mean that he wanted to produce drama that was at once highly creative and unrestricted by conventional representationalism and at the same time intellectually and analytically sound.[21] Poetry was to assume an unusually flexible role. Although it was "the expression of *Excited passion" BLJ*, 8:146) rather than a carefully reasoned portrayal of life, it nonetheless could provide a heightened apprehension of fundamental and unifying principles by combining its imaginative quality with a disciplined methodology. In his dramas he plunged beneath surface considerations, such as episode and spectacle, in an attempt to develop a coherent imaginative portrayal of these principles and thereby to extend the definition of historical truth. This poetic premise suggests the important role that he believed his mental theater could play in addressing the personal, social, and political matters of everyday experience.

Byron's thinking about the imagination was probably sharpened and clarified by his reading during this period. He spent the early part of 1821 reading Friedrich Schlegel's *History of Literature*, and though he praised the German literary historian only reluctantly (probably because of political differences), he certainly was sensitive to his powerful and probing intellect. In particular, he would have responded to Schlegel's keen historical awareness. As Arnold Hauser states, Schlegel was one of the first to recognize "that the nature of the human mind, of political institutions, of law, language, religion and art are understandable only on the basis of their history, and that historical life represents the sphere in which these structures become incarnate in the purest and most substantial form."[22] Schlegel's ability to perceive and articulate the essential importance of history determined his approach to literature. One major assumption of his book is that in its highest form the imagination is both literary and historical. Thus, for instance, Thucydides' greatness lay in his genius for "historical drama"; his capacity for uncovering and imaginatively re-creating the inner workings of history made him, in Schlegel's opinion, "the first great writer" to explain fully the decline of Greece.[23] Further, Schlegel believed that the imagination discovers historical truth not simply through creative but also through analytical and intellectual means; or, as he put it, "The clearness of an enlightened judgment must watch over those mighty energies of reason and of fancy [imagination]. True judgment depends in all things upon universality of observation, and discernment of that which is right, in the midst of much more that is wrong."[24]

Byron was also reading British literary histories at this time and seems to have been attracted especially to Thomas Campbell's *Specimens of the British Poets*. If he enjoyed pointing out Campbell's "slips of the pen," he nonetheless thought this "a good work," particularly in its defense of Pope, which he called "glorious" (*BLJ*, 8:21). And here again one appeal of the work would have been Campbell's argument that the poetic imagination is not merely picturesque and descriptive but analytical and moral, penetrating through simple, external nature to "life in all its circumstances." According to Campbell, this meant that the true poet must possess a profound understanding of society. The poet "deepens our social interest in existence. It is surely by the livelihood of the interest which he excites in existence, and not by the class of subjects which he chooses, that we most fairly appreciate the genius of the life of life *[sic]* which is in him." Pope, he says, was "a great moral writer" precisely because his imagination was fed by this powerful social awareness that could plunge beneath class biases to the most basic "manners and affections of his species." [25] Although Campbell's discussion of Pope never develops much beyond polemic, it nevertheless reveals his understanding of a depth and complexity in Pope's imagination (and in the imaginations of all great poets) that many nineteenth-century critics were unable to discern.

Such principles as these informed Byron's regular mental theater, placing demands on the imagination that could not be met by most popular drama, and thus he refused to court the stage. Rather than produce the "rant" and excessive splendor that the Drury Lane crowd applauded, he favored "simplicity" that was *"studiously Greek"* (*BLJ*, 8:186). Only in this way could he capture "the *higher* passions" (*BLJ*, 8:223) that alone made drama more than mere distraction. He defended his position at length against Teresa Guiccioli and friends, emphatically denying the current prevailing assumptions about drama, particularly the popular belief that love was the sacred theme of great tragedy (for instance, see *BLJ*, 8:26). [26] As he told Kinnaird: "I understand what you want—you want me to write a *love*-play—but this were contrary to all my principles—as well as those of Aristotle.—I want to simplify your drama" (*BLJ*, 8:223).

Exactly how Byron's poetic principles were drawn from Aristotle is difficult to comprehend, because Byron integrated Aristotle's poetics with other writings and then adapted them all to his own system. *Werner* and *The Deformed Transformed*, for instance, grew out of a Gothic convention long popular on the British stage, and certainly owe as much to Maturin as to Aristotle. Still, the Aristotelian influence is considerable, even in those works which seem farthest removed from Greek standards. Byron himself emphasized this fact; he states clearly his acceptance of certain fundamentals such as *"Simplicity of plot"* (*BLJ*, 8:218), the unities (though he sometimes veered from these), and the independence of good tragedy from performance and actors.[27] But even more than these he was influenced by Aristotle's understanding of character:

> I must remark from *Aristotle* and *Rymer*, that the *hero* of tragedy and . . . a tragic poem must be *guilty*, to excite *"terror and pity,"* the end of tragic poetry. But hear not *me*, but my betters. "The pity which the poet is to labour for is *for* the criminal—not for those or him he has murdered—as who have been the occasion of the Tragedy. The terror is like-wise in the punishment of the said criminal, who, if he be represented too great an offender, will *not be pitied;* if altogether *innocent* his punishment will be unjust. In the Greek tragedy Innocence is unhappy often, and the Offender escapes." (*BLJ*, 8:115).[28]

This passage reveals unreservedly one important tendency in Byron's poetic method; he cites Aristotle's authority and influence while at the same time conflating Aristotle's views with those of Rymer, Dryden, Johnson, and perhaps even others,[29] to express criticism of the prevailing notion of love and spectacle in drama and to establish the central, unique role of criminality in his own tragedies. Byron's comments suggest much more than a revision of conventional nineteenth-century poetic attitudes; they suggest a serious reinterpretation of the role and scope of drama. As his plays attest, Byron wished not simply to shift dramatic focus from love to crime, in the belief that criminal episodes or heroic guilt were inherently of greater interest than love, but to show how drama could be used to express deeper levels of meaning than a narrowly focused love interest would allow. To this end he attempted to *interpret* crime through the medium of mental theater, here again building upon Aristotle's dictum of describing "what can happen" rather than specifically what did happen. This position stresses judgment and analysis as key imaginative instruments and brings into focus once more Byron's overriding concern with contexts (again an Aristotelian idea) and with unifying principles.

It is Byron's particular understanding of crime that makes all of his dramas (not simply those specifically labeled tragedies) unique and compelling. Byron carefully avoids reducing crime to an easy or pat explanation, but rather explores his subject from various and some-times quite opposite perspectives, frequently concluding that guilt and innocence exist alongside one another in a single character. More im-portantly, he never identifies guilt in his characters with wrong per-sonal choices; their guilt is always presented as somehow socially de-termined or mediated. This method focuses individual relations with culture and society, providing the basis for an imaginative examination of particular social systems within which human life creates meaning. It is at this deep level of analysis, interpretation, and articulation that Byron's mental theater is most alive and penetrating.

Byron's clearest handling of crime appears in such plays as *Cain* and *Sardanapalus*, in which he depicts individuals who knowingly and firmly reject both their specific social roles and the society that has assigned them these roles. In each case private ego is at most only a secondary motive for action; the difficulty of accepting social roles is generated by society itself. Cain, for instance, is required to be "cheer-ful and resign'd" (*Cain*, I.i.51) with his daily punishment—a life of "toil" (*Cain*, I.i.65)—despite the fact that he has committed no crime; he is expected to praise as good a social life that gives him no free-dom and that to him is physically and emotionally burdensome.[30] His inability to ignore such contradictions generates his widening divi-sion from society, creating the frustration that leads him eventually to murder Abel. In tracing the play's action Byron is careful to show that Cain is never malicious, never criminally insane, but rather driven to distraction by "the politics of Paradise" (*BLJ*, 8:216); thus even his murderous action cannot be comprehended in purely psychologi-cal terms but must be viewed within its larger social context.[31] This social focus on murder illuminates Cain's certain innocence, despite his obvious guilt: although he is indeed guilty of fratricide, he is beaten down and driven to distraction by a social order that makes criminal activity virtually inevitable. Endorsement of the existing unjust order would have been neither moral nor conducive to social amelioration, and yet society allows Cain no expression except endorsement; in such a world *any* resistance would be extreme and violent. Cain's action then, although disturbing and repulsive, is inevitable, and it carries within it the strong human need for the freedom to be moral.

Cain clearly displays the extent to which Byron's thought had veered from the liberal position. Here as elsewhere in his later dramatic work (for instance, *Marino Faliero* and *Sardanapalus*) he refuses to set individual and society against each other as though they were equally autonomous entities that somehow must learn to live together. Rather, he maintains, it is social being that determines individual consciousness, so that personal life *is* social life.[32] Cain's frustration and unhappiness are shown to arise from the actual conditions that he confronts, just as his options for action are socially determined. From this perspective, crime is removed from the purely private origin that it so often is assumed to have and traced to a much more complex source within society.

In his final dramas, *Werner* and *The Deformed Transformed*, Byron seems to have developed a more sophisticated perspective on crime based upon the realization that crime can result from social conformity as easily as from dissidence. Of course, he had long entertained this idea, though his earlier responses were often more emotional than analytic; his political remarks in verse dating at least from the first canto of *Childe Harold's Pilgrimage* and his lifelong resistance to conventional religious and moral codes indicate his strong impression of the evils inherent in existing social structures. However, it was not until he became directly involved in revolutionary politics and also began experimenting with drama that he developed a coherent (though admittedly elusive) analysis of this issue. In his final plays he creates protagonists who fully accept prevailing social attitudes and who seek to embody specific social values absolutely. In *The Deformed Transformed*, for instance, the major character, Arnold, is defined entirely in terms of his struggle to overcome alienation from society; he desperately searches for power and beauty, the supreme virtues his culture celebrates, which therefore alone can make him socially and morally whole. But, ironically, his quest generates crime upon crime. Although he understands power and beauty in the highest moral terms, his actual path to realizing them, as he is forced to admit, "Has been o'er carcasses" (I.ii.2); and, worse, his beliefs lead him to a steadily increasing use of force and violence. His honest expressions of compassion and love are continually blackened by actual experience.

Although this play perhaps is artistically inferior to *Cain* and somewhat tentative in its presentation, it nonetheless adds a new dimension to the social analysis provided by the earlier mystery play, because (as

I shall argue at length below) it captures the ever intensifying contradictions at the core of an entire social order. Arnold is guilty *with*
his culture; it is his attempt to overcome alienation, to integrate himself fully into society, that generates evil. That he is implicated repeatedly in crime despite his sincere profession of integrity calls into
question the most deep-seated assumptions that he shares with his
society—assumptions about what is moral, what is natural, what is
social rather than universal. Like Sardanapalus, Arnold fails because
his society fails; inherent in its order are injustice and inequality, both
of which preclude true harmony and durability, as the biting scenes
in St. Peter's Church so convincingly illustrate. These final scenes,
revealing unresolvable contradictions accompanied inevitably by ex-
cruciating violence, emphasize the certain collapse of a social order
that cannot work.

   Byron's concentration in his dramas on the fundamental social dimension of crime (as defined in its broadest possible terms) brought
him to understand that the most powerful threats to any given culture
are *internal;* thus he undertook a detailed examination of the underlying and far-reaching factors within society that might elucidate the
deeper meanings of crime. He studied the encompassing system of
values and structures of authority that bind society and determine
individual assumptions about "right and wrong"; or, put differently,
he became increasingly absorbed by the distinction between *structure*
and *event,* that is, with the relations between the abstract ideas governing culture and society and the actual conduct of people within given
social orders. This focus directed his interest beyond crime itself to
careful consideration of such abstractions as state and law (as in *Marino
Faliero* and *The Two Foscari*) and also to society's more sacred repositories of truth: religion and art. In all of his dramas, after *Manfred,*
he gives special attention to one or all of these, criticizing them not
simply for their surface inadequacies but more importantly for their
claims to an absolute ideal, claims that ignore historical process and
so often confuse basic human needs.

   I now want to consider Byron's dramas individually and at some
length in an effort to elucidate the general ideas just presented.[33]

Manfred

Three years prior to the period considered in the above discussion
Byron had already made his first serious venture into the area of poetic

drama, producing his most popular (though not his most successful) work in that genre. While *Manfred* (1816–17) is more closely aligned— in its tone, style, and "Byronic" posturing—to the Eastern Tales and *Childe Harold's Pilgrimage* than to the dramas written after 1820, it none- theless provides an important early example of some of the principles and themes that were to come to maturation only a few years later. It might be helpful, therefore, to provide here a general sketch of the social content of the drama, considering it as a sort of preliminary effort on Byron's part to find a suitable dramatic form and voice for ex- ploring and articulating the large historical interest that is more clearly defined in the later works.

It is common knowledge that *Manfred* is shaped by specific and in- tensely personal difficulties in Byron's life. As Leslie Marchand aptly states, "All the unhappiness, the sense of guilt, the frustrations, and the dismal broodings which had grown out of his reflection during the summer [of 1816] on his relations with Augusta, his marriage, and the separation found relief in a poetic drama that had been conceived in the high Alps and now burned for expression."[34] Edward Bostet- ter makes essentially the same point: "*Manfred* is the drama in which Byron symbolically works his way through to mental sanity, to the psychological perspective that made *Don Juan* possible. It is a thera- peutic drama into which Byron pours off all of the pent-up, confused, and conflicting attitudes growing out of the debacle" of the immedi- ately preceding years in England.[35] Certainly this personal dimension of the drama cannot be ignored, and indeed perhaps it is the neces- sary starting point for any critical consideration of such a strongly autobiographical poet as Byron.

Still, as the recent excellent editions of the letters, journals, and poetry (as well as the critical work of Jerome McGann) make emphati- cally clear, Byron's thought and imagination were shaped not only by personal matters; there is a vitally important public dimension to all of his work, one which includes a variety of political, social, and historical issues. Despite his obvious sensitivity to his status within society, his deep-seated fear that his personal entanglements would jeopardize that status, and his distasteful egotism and "Byronic" pos- turing when the public eye was on him, he rarely lost sight of the larger contexts and consequences of his particular situation, and indeed often responded to personal pressures by seeing his life in historical terms. This is evident, to take only one example, in a brief comment that he made to Leigh Hunt during the earliest period of his domestic troubles; speaking of his inactivity in Parliament at a time when public affairs were becoming increasingly tumultuous and of his desire for significant political change, Byron remarked:

> [W]hen a proper spirit is manifested "without doors" I will endeav-
> our not to be idle within—do you think such a time is coming?
> methinks there are gleams of it—my forefathers were of the other
> side of the question in Charles's days—& the fruit of it was a title
> & the loss of an enormous property.—If the old struggle comes
> on—I shall lose the one & shall never regain the other—but—no
> matter—there are things even in this world—better than either.
> (*BLJ*, 5:19)

One poetic formulation of the sort of large historical change that is anticipated in this statement appears in *Manfred*, though it is a for-mulation expressive of considerably more anxiety than Byron, in his typically self-confident manner, admits in his letter to Hunt. *Manfred*, indeed, is not only about the breakup of his marriage, his incestu-ous affair with Augusta, and his Promethean defiance in the face of personal and public scandal, but also about complex struggles and con-flicts defining the entire Romantic age. The darkly imagined, mythic situation and characters in the play embody and project, in abstract form, an alienating, anxiety-ridden social situation that is anterior to Manfred's personality, his power, and even his conjuring of spirits. Taken together, the governing structures of authority and systems of belief in the drama, the hierarchy of relations among characters, and Manfred's desperate attempts to find personal meaning in the face of these show the unavoidable claim that a barely acknowledged history and society have on him—despite his own tendency to deny that claim and to see his situation in purely personal terms. Moreover, the con-text within which Manfred's actions and statements are placed reveals a consuming interest in much of Byron's writing: namely the giant disparity between, on the one hand, intellectual awareness of the false grounds of power used to control people and, on the other, individual ability to destroy or even to avoid this power.

One reason criticism has devoted so much attention to the psycho-logical and biographical elements in the drama to the exclusion of the political and social is that it offers such a powerful and lengthy por-trayal of the world of spirits, a world which seems to have little to do with social or public life, and much to do with the life of the individual mind.[36] But this mysterious spiritual world has direct social significance (I want to suggest presently that it has specific class significance as well) for it is presented as a *result* or *effect* of deeply rooted material conditions—inscribed within the text of the drama—which haunt Manfred and with which he is obligated to deal, even if against his wishes. The relation of social life and the black arts is seen directly in the opening scenes of the drama. Here Manfred notes that, like Faust, he has studied philosophy, science, "the springs / Of wonder, and the wisdom of the world" (I.i.13–14), all of which "avail not" (I.i.17); he has also "done men good, / And . . . met with good even among men" (I.i.17–18),[37] but finds no more purpose in this than in the intellectual pursuits that have occupied him. For this reason he has begun to study and to conjure spirits from the forbidden deep, in the hope that these spirits will give him power and hence the peace of mind that he has been unable to find in the public endeavors that he once pursued. This scene focuses the dilemma at the center of the drama: Manfred's problem is not simply that he possesses a unique personality (though he perhaps believes he does) that is strangely, instinctively drawn to forbidden subjects, but rather that the public world within which individuals such as Manfred once flourished has lost its meaning, a fact that (he believes) forces him to look elsewhere than in the world for the meaning of his life. In other words, Manfred's particular situation, as he describes it in these early comments, is not entirely self-defined; it is symptomatic and not constitutive, an effect of what has come before. The drama does not so much explore the specific causes that may lead to the withering of social life—although the characterization of Astarte does provide an important context for understanding those causes—as show the features and consequences of it, specifically presenting what it means to live in a world that allows one to measure and value reality only in terms of private desire.

It is in terms of this extreme alienation from any meaningful social life that Manfred's consorting with spirits must be understood. He proves repeatedly not only that he has the power to call these spirits from the darkness at his whim but also to resist the demands they place on him, however threateningly these demands are presented. But this power, as Manfred himself finally understands, is sheer mystification; it is a power that involves a claim of freedom under the very conditions of its denial. For if the spirits cannot harm Manfred, neither can he direct them to alleviate or change in any way the world of "breathing men" (I.i.8) among whom he, of necessity, must move. Calling the spirits is a futile and pointless exercise, a sort of mental masturbation (to use the phrase that Byron once used to described Keats's poetry) and not a sign of Manfred's real power or independence. While Manfred's commitment to the black arts shows his disillusionment with any kind of human exchange, at the same time it demonstrates compellingly the hopelessness of looking outside the world for solutions to human problems. Manfred realizes the limitations of his world, he imagines greater possibilities than those he sees before him, and he recognizes the potential power of his own mind; and yet—as he learns—these neither constitute true freedom from the world nor enable him to create another world that would make personal fulfillment possible. If the presence of the spirits in the poem illustrates anything, it is that Manfred's home is in the world of people and that whatever hope or despair there is in his life must be measured in terms of this world.

That Manfred's situation is of more than psychological interest, that it reflects more than abstract human nature driven to despair by an eternal conflict between spirit and flesh (as it is sometimes said to do), and that it is in fact socially entangled is seen in two related issues. First, in the early scenes, where he describes the power and knowledge that seem to separate him from other men, Manfred admits that "The Tree of Knowledge is not that of Life" (I.i.12), a statement that acknowledges the priority of life over knowledge and the inability of knowledge alone to change life. This comment locates human possibility not in the mind and not in the imagination—the mind is *not* its own place, despite Manfred's desperate claim to the contrary—but firmly in the world of human experience or life which, as the drama makes increasingly clear, is ineluctably rooted in social and historical processes. That Manfred develops a special knowledge that in turn enables him to consort with spirits and dreams of other worlds is therefore not a sign that there exists an alternative world of untapped possibility someplace outside human history to which that special knowledge will lead him; rather, it is a sign of the extent to which Manfred's world is torn by strife, denying him personal fulfillment within its borders. Even if Manfred himself sees life only in terms of absolutely contradictory alternatives—sheer unfettered knowledge shaped by imagination and desire on the one hand or, on the other, overwhelming hopelessness and despair—his own statements show this position to be grounded in the conflicts of his own material situation. As M. I. Finley has argued (writing in a different context) the utopian impulse—and this finally is how we must see Manfred's indulgence in the black arts—always reflects social and historical reality; it always points to the material conditions from which it arises.[38]

The second consideration—Manfred's obsessive concern with the past—helps to elucidate the historical dimension of the above issue. Questions about the nature and significance of the past run through much of Byron's poetry and are most often treated in purely personal terms and in terms of the Byronic hero's guilt over some past crime or sin, in this case the apparent incestuous affair that Manfred has with Astarte. While the autobiographical and sexual emphasis here cannot be denied, neither can it account satisfactorily for the large structures of authority governing the action of the drama or for Manfred's intense struggles with both conventional and unconventional institutions, powers, and attitudes that pervade the dramatic action. The problem of the past is not simply that Manfred once committed a sin (although he does refer to his love for Astarte as a sin) which he now repents or even feels guilt for—his love for Astarte clearly has never diminished. The problem is rather that the past which he continues to love and desire provides him with no comfort and even drives him to despair. Like his desperate effort to achieve personal power through study of the black arts, his attention to Astarte points toward the inability of the present to inspire his life with meaning and purpose.

Unlike the dark spirits, however, who can be called and dispersed at will, Astarte has a claim on Manfred that he can neither deny nor resist, and this claim anchors the drama's various thematic concerns in historical reality. Astarte is emphatically drawn as part of history, as part of the living past that both haunts and determines the most personal dimensions of Manfred's life, and yet Manfred, despite his knowledge and his exceptional strength of will, can never control or even contain that past. In calling out to the past Manfred asks Astarte to "Forgive me or condemn me" (II.iv.475), neither of which is possible because even as Astarte—as the representative voice of the past—points him toward his personal destiny ("Tomorrow ends thine earthly ills," she tells Manfred [II.iv.521]) she cannot be summoned through a sheer act of individual will to settle the struggles and conflicts of the present. That he hopes otherwise is but a further sign of alienation and desperate need.

I want now to touch glancingly upon the significance of the chamois hunter and the abbot in terms of these various historical crosscurrents, because these characters are the foremost representatives in the drama of conventional belief, and thus they provide additional insight into the context within which Byron develops Manfred's thoughts and actions. While in his letters and poetry Byron often makes bitter comments about institutional religion and engages in vicious attacks on Wordsworth (in many later letters, for instance, Byron refers to the great nature poet as "Turdsworth"[39]), in his handling of the abbot and the chamois hunter (a sort of Wordsworthian devotee of nature) he displays sincerity and even sympathy for their respective beliefs. One reason for this is that both of these characters embody personal integrity in their ability to live peacefully and even productively in the world from which Manfred is alienated. They accomplish this through a philosophy of individual forbearance. As the chamois hunter tells the despairing Manfred: "[W]hatsoe'er thine ill, / It must be borne, and these wild starts are useless" (II.i.40–41). The abbot's position is identical to this, defined by the saving personal belief in reconciliation and in "Our institutions and our strong belief," which alone "Have given me power to smooth the path from sin to higher hope and better thoughts" (III.i.60–62). These positions, as attractive as they are even to Manfred, have not yet felt the awful and far-reaching threats that Manfred feels but cannot identify or explain. The abbot and the chamois hunter live by values that, in the case of the chamois hunter, look outside history and society to nature for fulfillment or, in the case of the abbot, outside history and society to God for fulfillment. Manfred, on the other hand, is so troubled by loneliness, dread, and the threat of irrevocable change—that is, by the debilitating fact of historical pressure—that he is unable to consider these seriously as a path to personal salvation.

I noted at the beginning of this discussion that Manfred's various actions have class significance, and indeed it is the class issue which connects the other episodes and ideas, combining them into a coherent statement about social and historical processes. David Erdman once remarked that "Byron and his heroes often appear acutely conscious of the mortality of their own class," and this is explicitly the case in *Manfred*.[40] The extreme alienation and the conviction of certain defeat and death that Manfred everywhere expresses; his desperate search for some as yet untried transhistorical power to solve personal difficulties; his acute awareness of the inability of conventional actions and systems of belief to provide comfort: all these suggest powerfully the imminent demise not only of Manfred himself but also of the aristocratic class to which he belongs. The past will neither condemn nor forgive this aristocracy, telling only of its certain extinction, and this is why Manfred looks to the spirits of the deep and to the spirit of Astarte for counsel, but never to the chamois hunter or to the abbot, characters who are implicated as fully as Manfred himself (though they do not see this) in the historical and social changes that Manfred feels beginning to take place. As the abbot tells Manfred:

> . . . Rumours strange,
> And of unholy nature, are abroad,
> And busy with thy name; a noble name
> For centuries: may he who bears it now
> Transmit it unimpair'd. (III.i.29–33)

What the abbot cannot know, but what Manfred feels at every turn, is that this noble name most certainly will not be transmitted unimpaired, and Manfred's personal tragedy is that he cannot change this historical fact, despite his superior intellectual and imaginative powers. Looking desperately for an avenue of escape by denying through sheer will the claim that history has on him, he learns finally that there is no solution, no life on the backside of history. This lesson, difficult and painful as it is to learn, is at last accepted and even faced with a sort of Byronic dignity, as Manfred dies in continued defiance of the historical changes that have sacrificed him. At the moment of death he tells the abbot, the supreme representative of traditional thought and belief: "Old man! 'tis not so difficult to die" (IV.iv.411).

The social and historical concerns sketched here do not deny the presence or significance of the psychological and biographical matters in the drama that traditionally have interested readers; but they do, I believe, allow us to glimpse a dimension of Byron's imagination that is central to his best work and that encompasses and gives meaning to the many particular issues that appear on the surface of these works. *Manfred* marks an important step forward for Byron, who until now had been working mainly with Eastern subject matter and with a simple narrative framework to formulate a workable social poetry.

With *Manfred* he discovered the suitability of mental theater for exploring not specific historical events but the structures of authority and belief surrounding those events. In subsequent dramas his handling of these structures becomes more sophisticated and powerful.

Marino Faliero

After completing *Manfred*, Byron's thinking about history, politics, and society—and about the connections between these and literary production—matured remarkably. In his next three dramatic poems (*Marino Faliero, Sardanapalus,* and *The Two Foscari*) he abandoned the mythic scope of *Manfred* in favor of specific, if remote, historical situations, attempting to imagine the operations of social life within those situations and the demands and challenges that society-in-crisis pose for personal life. While the dramas lack the strong personality of a hero such as Manfred, they make up for this lack with an intelligent portrayal of the networks of power, structures of belief, and categories of social life that both enable and constrain individual need, desire, and action.

As Byron himself understood, however, the larger interests of the dramas would be lost to most readers. The flurry of letters that he sent back to England during and after the composition of the plays reveals his impatience with the inability of his (mostly critical) audience to get beyond what were to his mind relatively minor or tangential concerns; he assured friends that these dramas were not what people thought they were and, moreover, predicted that the criticisms aimed at them would dissolve when people understood them better. As he told Murray when the tenor of criticism was unusually high-pitched even in those corners that had always and without question supported him: "I have a notion that if understood they [the plays] will in time find favour (though *not* on stage) with the reader" (*BLJ,* 8:218). They have seldom been understood as Byron hoped they would be, as readers—then and now—have tended to reduce them to narrowly political commentaries, to see them as autobiography, to debate their suitability for the stage, or to consider such exterior issues as the accuracy of a given historical detail. Their portrayal of the deep structures of social life remains largely unconsidered. But, as a considered critical investigation shows, it is precisely the portrayal of these structures that distinguishes the history plays from *Manfred,* and suggests the deepening intelligence and broadening scope of Byron's historical vision.

The various difficulties and accomplishments associated with the history plays can be seen most readily in *Marino Faliero* (1820). While critics of this drama have written well about its historical accuracy, its prophetic political commentary, and its political opportunism—as well as its imagery and symbolism and its psychological interest—they have said little about the larger social frames of references within which these concerns are developed.[41] One reason for this is that the play's surface political interests are so powerfully and specifically presented that more abstract issues are hard to see. It is difficult, for instance, to read such an obviously sympathetic exposition of treasonous conspiracy without suspecting Byron of simpleminded "radicalism." Yet he insisted that the tragedy was *"Not a political* play" (*BLJ*, 7:184). While, as some readers have suggested, this comment may be disingenuous, calculated to palliate the politically conservative Murray to whom he was writing, to dismiss it too readily is to risk misunderstanding Byron's meaning, which was not to deny out of hand the play's politics (he tells Murray plainly in the same letter that "you and yours won't like the *politics* which are perilous to you in these times") but rather to direct attention to the deeper social motives that created the political turmoil being dramatized.

Both in his letters and within the play itself he voices this as his main interest. As early as 1817, when he first contemplated the Faliero conspiracy as a subject for a play, he wrote to Murray: "Look into 'Moore's (Dr. Moore's) view of Italy' for me—in one of the volumes you will find an account of the *Doge Valiere* (it ought to be Faliero) and his conspiracy—or the motives of it—. . . . I want it—& can not find so good an account of that business here. . . . I have searched all the libraries—but the policy of the old Aristocracy made their writers silent on his motives which were a private grievance against one of the Patricians" (*BLJ*, 5:174). Toward the end of the play too, Byron has Faliero ask: "Were it not better to record the facts, / so that the contemplator might approve, / Or at least learn *whence* the crimes arose?" (V.i.508–10).[42] The motives of the conspiracy, Byron believed, transcended readily apparent political considerations and traced back to larger questions of the dynamics of Venetian society itself. To understand the conspiracy, therefore, it was necessary to re-create Venice as

it must have been in Faliero's time: the atmosphere that found aristocrat and plebian joining forces to defeat a common enemy; the passions
of individuals who lived in that society; and the obstacles and choices
that could have arisen in the minds of the discontented citizenry. This
social perspective, more than a narrowly conceived political interest,
begins to suggest some of the deeper concerns of the drama.

Just as he wanted *Marino Faliero* to be more than a political drama,
Byron also wanted it to be more than a revenge drama portraying
psychological unrest, and thus he chose not to found the play's action
on jealousy. Michael Steno's irreverent conduct, he explained, provides only a "first motive"[43]—not a complete explanation of the conspiracy. The central issue, as critics since Samuel Chew's day correctly
have remarked, is "the conflict . . . between the patricians and the
people";[44] the "private wrongs" recorded in the play "spring from
public vices, from the general corruption generated by the foul aristocracy."[45] We need now to understand what this means in terms of
the social world that Byron is re-creating.

To say that the aristocracy is corrupt is not necessarily to indict
their private conduct or to suggest that they publicly and physically
abuse the Venetian citizenry. Their corruption, as the drama shows,
lies largely in their consuming self-interest. They are morally blamable
because they manipulate the prevailing networks of power to benefit
only their own class, without regard to the larger body of individuals
who compose society. As rulers they disseminate and uphold values
which ostensibly represent the best interests of everyone, but which in
reality do not recognize the needs or the integrity of private citizens.

One of the key ways Byron defines this corruption and pinpoints
the built-in injustices of Venetian society is by emphasizing the disparity between the nobility of the aristocracy's language and the actual
self-interest of their actions. They disguise their selfish motives and
subdue the Venetian citizens with a hollow rhetoric that serves as an
outward show of sincerity, dignity, and humility. For instance, while
on the one hand the patricians insult the doge's private integrity as well
as his public office by imposing only a token punishment on Steno, at
the same time their verbal position is one of esteem and concern for
Faliero: "The high tribunal of the Forty sends / Health and respect to
the Doge Faliero" (I.ii.45–46).

This kind of disparity is seen again in the episode with the patrician Lioni and the plebian Bertram. Motivated by true friendship and

concern for human life, Bertram tries to save Lioni from imminent assassination. Lioni, however, uses Bertram's sincerity to extort information concerning the conspiracy. Speaking in noble language that professes the encompassing value and importance of the state ("who are traitors save unto the State?" "Say, rather thy friend's saviour and the State's" [IV.i.299, 317]), he persuades Bertram to compromise his personal integrity to save the patricians. The irony of this is underscored by the fact that Lioni's noble language consistently is contrasted to his fast regard not for the state but specifically for aristocracy. His interest in Bertram never extends beyond what "Beseem[s] one of thy station" (IV.i.137); he is willing to assist Bertram only if Bertram "hast not / spilt noble blood" (IV.i.144–45). Also, once the conspiracy has been prevented, the patricians justify their brutal treatment of the prisoners in noble language. After being tortured on the rack and before finally being executed, Israel Bertruccio and Philip Calendaro are told by the Chief of the Ten that they have committed treason "Against a just and free state, known to all / The earth as being the Christian bulwark 'gainst / The Saracen" (V.i.10–12); further, they are told that they can save their soul only by confessing the injustice of their actions against the state: "[W]e would hear from your own lips complete / Avowal of your treason . . . . / . . . [T]he truth / Alone can profit you on earth or Heaven" (V.i.29–32).

What critics mean—and what Byron likely meant—when they speak of the play's criticism of a corrupt aristocracy is that the ruling class value system does not serve the Venetian citizenry at large. The dominant values of the society, reflected in the language of the patricians, consist largely of an abstract rhetoric of honor that practically and materially benefits only a few people. Those who do not benefit (for example, Faliero and the plebians) eventually come to see themselves as slaves rather than citizens (I.ii.106–8, 461–62). The corruption, then, that generates the revolutionary conspiracy does not rest solely in the Steno decision or in the physical abuse of Israel Bertruccio: it lies in the system of values that not only produces such atrocities but also sanctifies them.

Byron develops his characters' sensitivity to unjust Venetian values in terms of their growing awareness of social class. It is common for critics to comment on Faliero's "aristocratic contempt for the mob," his desire to "win real power," or his adherence "to a princely code of honor."[46] But Byron's treatment of Faliero involves more than this; it involves the sentiments and conflicting passions of an individual who finds himself standing outside the social sphere that he and his forbears have been bred into. Attention is not focused mainly on Faliero's drive for power or on his princely conduct but, as Andrew Rutherford puts it, on "the tensions in Marino's mind when he made common cause with the plebians against his own class."[47] The play examines Faliero's awareness that his class position allows only a narrow social perspective, incapable of alleviating the pervasive social injustices plaguing Venice, and follows him as he develops a fuller understanding of society's needs.

Byron's emphasis on class consciousness is seen again in his handling of the conspiring plebians, who—like Faliero—must wrestle with the problem of class relationships. The conspirators are keenly sensitive to their position in the social hierarchy. When Israel Bertruccio informs Calendaro that a new member will shortly join their ranks, Calendaro responds: "Is he one of our order?" (II.ii.161). And later when Faliero is introduced to the conspirators, reaction to him is unanimous: "To arms!—we are betrayed—it is the Doge! / Down with them both! our traitorous captain, and / The tyrant he hath sold us to" (III.ii.90–92). Their initial response is as expressive of class prejudice as Faliero's. They, too, are presented the challenge of admitting that integrity and moral passion—and political allies—can be found outside their own class.

Byron's depiction of class consciousness suggests the range of social perspectives that is possible in any given culture. But more importantly it illustrates the necessity of becoming aware of class roles in order to overcome the barriers they impose. Both Faliero and the plebians must realize that their specific class interests do not reflect the views of all society and cannot answer to the needs of the Venetian citizenry at large. They must learn to set particular class differences aside and explore their common social needs as human beings; only in this way can they begin to generate social solidarity capable of defeating the injustices inflicted on them by the patricians. Moreover, only by developing a social rather than simply a class perspective can they hope to mount a revolutionary campaign that will do more than merely reverse existing class structures.

The play explores not only the necessity of recognizing and overcoming ideological assumptions and class barriers to bring about social change, but also the difficulty of rationalizing the physical violence that must accompany any effort to change the social structure. Violence against one's own state is perhaps the most sensitive issue in the play, and indeed the problem which finally destroys revolutionary hope. Even before Faliero meets with the conspirators he tells Israel Bertruccio that he cannot unfeelingly "take men's lives by stealth" (III.i.108). And again, after the doge has held commune with the plebians and agreed to lead them in the conspiracy, he asks: "And is it then decided! must they die?" (III.ii.449). Though he realizes that " 'Tis mine to sound the knell, and strike the blow" (III.ii.491), still he "quiver[s] to behold what I / Must be, and think what I have been" (III.ii.498–99).

In two main ways Faliero justifies the violence that he knows must accompany the revolution. First, he convinces himself that he has no choice; he is, as it were, entirely a creature of circumstance who must perform the deeds that fate has destined for him: "[T]he task / Is forced upon me, I have sought it not" (III.i.9–10). He resorts to this justification more than once, giving the impression, as Jerome McGann puts it, that he "act[s] freely against . . . [his] own will and feelings."[48] In trying to explain his actions, Faliero remarks that "there is *Hell* within me and around, / And like the Demon who believes and trembles / Must I abhor and do" (III.ii.519–21).

Another more practical and realistic way in which he comes to terms with political violence is by refusing to see the patricians as individual human beings. He identifies them with the abstract mechanisms of the ruling social order: "law," "policy," "duty," and "state" (III.ii.351–54). Instead of looking on them as former friends, he tries to see them only as "Senators" who inveterately have viewed him as "the Doge" (III.ii.377–78):

> To me, then, these men have no *private* life,
> Nor claim to ties they have cut off from others;
> As Senators for arbitrary acts
> Amenable, I look on them—as such
> Let them be dealt upon. (III.ii.382–86)

It is in this way that he must finally account for revolutionary violence. He must identify the individuals of the ruling class entirely with the corrupt political machine that is to be destroyed; only then can his sympathy for human life be contained and prevented from interfering with the demands of revolution.

Byron does not treat the horrors of violence as uniquely a problem for leaders: all persons engaged in revolutionary activities must come to terms with violence. He illustrates this point in the character of Bertram, a plebian involved in the conspiracy. Bertram focuses the moral question that Faliero had raised: how does one rationalize the violence that seems to be a necessary part of the drive to establish a right and just social order (III.ii.64–69)? Unlike the doge, however, he cannot separate the political machine from those who run it: "[E]ven amongst these wicked men / There might be some, whose age and qualities / Might mark them out for pity" (III.ii.24–26). Though he is as eager for the revolution as Faliero or his fellow plebians, he ultimately destroys the possibility of revolution by his inability to resolve the moral question of political violence; and his decision not to betray his patrician friend Lioni transforms him into an unwilling informer: "Then perish Venice rather than my friend! / I will disclose— ensnare—betray—destroy —/ Oh, what a villain I become for thee" (IV.i.314–16).

If Marino Faliero gives the question of political violence its noble, tragic dimension, Bertram gives it a broader social significance. His concern with the morality of violence assures that we do not read the play as a narrow or incomplete picture of a moral dilemma unique to aristocracy. As with the other prominent social issues treated in the play, Byron implicates all classes of individuals, making them equally responsible for the condition of society and for meeting the practical demands of social life.

Despite certain expository weaknesses, *Marino Faliero* effectively presents some possible private and public motives for engaging in political struggle and forcefully illustrates some of the moral questions that necessarily arise during this struggle. Byron probably found the play difficult to write (he contemplated it for more than three years) because he could not satisfactorily understand and present the social issues he thought to be important to the political episode he was describing. But once his understanding of these issues matured, he produced a play that represents a vital part of his developing historical and social vision.

Sardanapalus

Though *Sardanapalus* (1821) was, like *Marino Faliero*, a play about princes, queens, and popular disturbance, Byron trusted that it would "not be mistaken for a *political* play—which was so far from my intention that I thought of nothing but Asiatic history" (*BLJ*, 8:152). Like *Marino Faliero, Sardanapalus* re-creates a historical situation in order to explore various dynamics of social reality. The play, however, does not simply duplicate the earlier drama. Although it treats some of the same themes that had marked the Venetian tragedy (violence, ideology), *Sardanapalus* displays in greater detail both the circumstances that could make an individual feel out of step with the values of his culture and the difficulties of overcoming alienation when the circumstances that caused it have not changed. Moreover, it attempts to distribute the blame for individual and social corruption more evenly than *Marino Faliero* had done. In the earlier play the doge had been shown to be clearly in the right and the patricians in the wrong; but in *Sardanapalus* the prince is shown to be as mistaken in his view of himself and his world as Nineveh in the values it tries to uphold.

Marino Faliero begins at the moment of Faliero's decision to join the plebian conspirators, and thus does not dramatize preexisting social conditions that could explain how the doge came to be so far removed from the values of his class as to commit treason. *Sardanapalus* attempts to correct this deficiency by providing a background sufficient to explain its hero's alienation. In Acts I and II Sardanapalus is not drawn abstractly as a "luxury-loving and easy-going monarch," nor is he simply "a debauchee who wants only to renounce his power."[49] Rather, his character reflects disgust for a society marked historically by violence. When Salemenes tries to inspire Sardanapalus by recalling the exploits of Semiramis, an illustrious ancestor, Sardanapalus asks: "And how many [corpses] / Left she behind in India to the vultures?" (I.ii.131–32).[50] And when Myrrha, attempting to instill in him a sense of civic responsibility, encourages him to read the histories of his culture, he replies: "They are so blotted o'er with blood, I cannot" (I.ii.548). The Nineveh of the present, too, demands blood. When Sardanapalus is faced with the prospect of a rebelling populace he exclaims: "The ungrateful and ungracious slaves! they murmur / Because I have not shed their blood" (I.ii.226–27). In short, Sardanapalus is not blindly hedonistic but is driven (he feels) to hedonism in a protest against the blood-drenched values of the society he is born to rule; his conduct expresses discontent with and condemnation of violence as a way of life.

This is not to say, however, that his hedonism—though explainable in social terms—is admirable, or even preferable to the values to which it is a response. The drama shows that, as a way of life, it is as unaccept-able as Nineveh's history of violence. Though he wants to make "The weight of human misery less" (I.ii.264), and thinks he can accomplish this best by leaving people to themselves (I.ii.268–78), Sardanapalus actually helps to create misery by leaving people defenseless; he fails to acknowledge any need whatsoever for the physical protection of life. When Salemenes warns him of imminent danger, Sardanapalus feels no compulsion to defend himself: "What dost dread?" "What must we dread?" (I.ii.280, 285). Myrrha's efforts, too, to make Sardanapalus understand that "Kingdoms and lives are not to be so lost" (I.ii.488) are met with the same simplistic and passive response: "Why, child, I loathe all war, and warriors; / I live in peace and pleasure: what can man / Do more?" (I.ii.529–31). Myrrha realizes that his attitude is potentially destructive both for himself and for society (I.ii.526–28) for it rests, finally, on the assumption that life is not worth defend-ing. Sardanapalus admits as much, claiming that life "is not worth so much" that he should always be "guarding against all [that] may make it less" (I.ii.392–93). The weakness of his hedonistic philosophy is that it denies that Sardanapalus should accept responsibility for his own life; by implication this form of hedonism makes it impossible to accept responsibility for any life.

The initial actions of the play dramatize the struggle between equally unsatisfactory social philosophies. The Nineveh that Sardana-palus inhabits—and that his forbears inhabited—places an undue em-phasis on violent aggression; Sardanapalus's attitude refuses to admit the value of any kind of physical defense of human life. The central purpose of the play appears to be to show how these divergent outlooks are brought into line with one another. The conspiracy of Arbaces and Beleses reveals to Sardanapalus the insufficiency of his hedonis-tic creed and forces him to bear arms in defense of himself and his society. And, since he "fights as he revels" (III.i.213)—that is, enthu-siastically—he seems able at last to take up the duties required by the state. The final scene of the play, too, seems to mark the degree to which he has changed, for he commits suicide to escape the ignominy of being captured by the revolutionaries and to prevent them from defiling his heritage.

The full social significance of this interior conflict is revealed in the dream that Sardanapalus recounts to Myrrha, for it illustrates the de-gree of Sardanapalus's continued alienation. In his dream Sardanapalus sees himself in the company of his ancestors, all of them ghastly and repulsive because of the violent atrocities they have committed in the name of the state. One holds "A goblet, bubbling o'er with blood" (IV.i. 111); others, "crowned wretches" (IV.i. 114), stare steadfastly at Sardanapalus, producing, he says, "a horrid kind / Of sympathy between us" (IV.i. 124–25). These descriptions reveal Sardanapalus's instinctive fear of becoming such a villain as he considers his ancestors to have been, and his reluctance to commit himself fully to their program of violence. Further, his description of the dream to Salemenes suggests his sense of personal superiority over his glorious ancestors and his wish to remain apart from them: "[A]ll the predecessors of our line / Rose up, methought, to drag me down to them" (IV.i. 174–75). In short, the dream shows that Sardanapalus has not changed suddenly from a hedonistic and irresponsible monarch to a decisive and noble leader but rather, in assuming a military role, has acted against his principles, which remain unchanged. It shows, moreover, that despite his display of military virtuosity, his pacifist sympathies remain strong. Finally, the incongruity between his thoughts and actions shows that the conflict between individual and society presented at the beginning of the play is no closer to resolution.[51]

Indeed, the conflict is never resolved. Sardanapalus's hatred of war and his refusal to see any sort of violence as necessary to human freedom continue unchanged until the final collapse of Nineveh is imminent. Near the end of Act IV, when his commitment to defending his country is ostensibly total, he tells Myrrha:

> To me war is no glory—conquest no
> Renown. To be forced thus to uphold my right
> Sits heavier on my heart than all the wrongs
> These men would bow me down with. (IV.i. 505–8)

He indicates here that he still sees no middle ground between the views he held at the outset of the play and the needs of his country. His longing continues for "An era of sweet peace" (IV.i. 512). Though forced by circumstance to don armor and weapons, his escapist desire to make "my realm a paradise" (IV.i. 517) persists. The "thirteen hundred years of Empire" (I.i. 7–8), the war, and the lure of conquest: all the details and episodes that represent Nineveh's glory burden him.

This inability to resolve the conflict between his thoughts and actions is Sardanapalus's tragic flaw. He goes through the motions of leading his followers in combat, but he clings tenaciously to his belief that it is senseless and degrading to do so. By operating on two radically different levels, he creates a situation that will be fatal for himself and for his country.

Only after Salemenes' death and after the throne is doomed does Sardanapalus fully understand the error of his isolationist and individualist views—and even then he views himself as a victim rather than an accomplice in his downfall (V.i.205–9). Whereas earlier in the play he had despised his ancestry for its bloodthirstiness, he now vows full commitment to defending "our long royalty of race" (V.i.155). In the end his suicide illustrates and confirms his understanding that one cannot commit oneself only partially to social life; one must accept that individual or private life is entirely defined by social reality, and therefore that the desire for personal fulfillment must be pursued within the realm of social life, rather than apart from it. The suicide is intended not only to prevent the defilement of the throne by rebels but also to show Sardanapalus's full acceptance, at last, of social life and social responsibility. His action is neither melodramatic nor escapist but tragic, for it is a sign of understanding that comes too late to save his kingdom or his life.

Byron does not lay the blame for Nineveh's destruction entirely at Sardanapalus's door. Sardanapalus is the tragic hero, to be sure, the one who must suffer for his personal sins; but the drama makes clear that his sins arise from the kind of world that he has inherited. The main plot (the story of Sardanapalus changing from hedonist to military leader) is vital for this reason: it completes the interior drama by keeping in our minds the bloodshed and inhumanity that mark Nineveh's history and that Nineveh requires Sardanapalus to accept. Sardanapalus's initial impulse toward hedonism and his later inability to commit himself fully to the defense of his country when it needs him have their roots at least partly in social contradiction—not wholly in character deficiency. Looking at the play from this perspective, we see that the conspiracy of Arbaces and Beleses is not only Sardanapalus's fault but also Nineveh's fault, and consequently both are doomed to destruction. For just as Sardanapalus is unable to resolve the conflict between his thoughts and actions, Nineveh is unable to meet fully the needs of its citizens, unable to resolve the conflict between social glory and vicious conquest. The funeral pyre that ends the play marks not only the tragic suicide of Sardanapalus but also that of Nineveh.

The Two Foscari

The Two Foscari (1821) takes the social concern that Byron had developed in *Marino Faliero* and *Sardanapalus* yet a step further. Building carefully on issues of political violence and ideology presented in the previous works, the drama suggests that the various personal and political conflicts depicted in the plot action arise because both the doge and the state, as Jerome McGann puts it, have allowed "a gulf" to separate "the standards of public and private life."[52] I want to clarify and develop this observation to show that the problem Byron tries to expose by writing about the two Foscari rests ultimately in the prejudices of Venetian ideology.

That the play describes a corrupt political machine is generally recognized.[53] But why or how it is corrupt has not been adequately explained, mainly because commentary tends to concentrate on details and actions presented in the plot, rather than on the social structure within which those details and actions are contained. If the ruling class portrayed in the drama oppresses people—as it most certainly does—then there must be a specific social location for that oppression beyond the obvious physical abuse of individuals. That location, as in *Marino Faliero*, involves the values and beliefs that underlie state actions against individuals. To glimpse these values and beliefs, it is necessary to look beyond plot to what various characters take for granted as being true about their social world and at what they consider to be morally just; only then can we begin to uncover the sources of corruption in the political machine and understand how that machine can protect and excuse such mad individuals as, for example, James Loredano.

First, everyone in the play except Marina takes for granted that the Venetian state is an abstract and mysterious power beyond individual comprehension. As one senator comments to Memmo: "[M]en know as little / Of the state's real acts as of the grave's / Unfathomed mysteries" (I.i.184–86).[54] This attitude is reflected as well in the doge's several comments to Marina that she cannot understand the workings of the state (II.i.84, 115, 125–26). This belief is accompanied by a corollary assumption: that the state is beyond reproach and thus commands absolute submission (usually represented in the drama as "commitment"). Cursed by Jacopo for presiding over his torture, an officer explains: "The sentence was not of my signing, but / I dared not disobey the Council" (I.i.153–54). Loredano, as a representative of state authority, implies the righteousness of state power when he asks: "[W]ho shall oppose the law?" (IV.i.258). These are the major ingredients of Venetian ideology; individuals measure justice, morality, and humanity against them, accepting without question that they represent "truth" and "reality." It is within the context of these generally accepted values that such individuals as Loredano wield political power.

This picture of Venice closely resembles that presented in *Marino Faliero*, except that here it is more clearly shown that such values as these do not simply fall out of the sky or exist abstractly above and beyond humanity. Rather, the drama insists that they are created by people like the doge and Loredano who sincerely or otherwise commit themselves so completely to a vision of society that they are blinded to the needs and feelings of the individual people within society. The doge's character is a vivid example of how the Venetian power structure has become corrupt. Through most of the play (until his son dies) the doge denies his own and others' needs when those needs conflict with the policies of state. He is, he says, "the State's servant" (II.i.38), with "other duties than a father's" (II.i.184). When Marina expresses her anger at the vile injustices of the state, the doge admonishes her: "That is not a Venetian thought" (II.i.276). Completely submissive to the state apparatus and its dictates, he gives "deference due even to the lightest word / That falls from those who rule in Venice" (II.i.298–99).

This philosophy, which insists upon the absolute subordination of individuals to the state, though superficially noble, is dangerous and potentially destructive. For what it means in practical terms is that neither the doge nor anyone else is materially and morally responsible for what the state does. By serving as willing "slaves" (II.i.357) of Venice and by "administer[ing] / My country faithfully" (II.i.369–70) the Venetian ruling order is able to absolve itself of the moral burden of dealing with and administering to *people*. This logic, to be sure, allows the state to expand and strengthen itself—"Under such laws, Venice / Has risen to what she is" (II.i.400–401)—but only by setting up laws and policies that excuse the doge and his fellow rulers from blame for acts of human atrocity. The doge actively embraces and helps to strengthen this system of personal irresponsibility by defining himself as "more citizen than either" doge or father (II.i.415). This cold reasoning allows him to accept Loredano's vindictive conduct as proper to state business, and to see his own son as a "traitor" (II.i.385) and a "disgrace" (II.i.175). The elder Foscari reminds one of Blake's Urizen:

he acts from what he considers to be noble and serious desires to create and preserve "order," but his actions in reality are nonproductive and contribute to the sum of human misery.

Byron's handling of the doge's character shows that the play is not simply about personal allegiance either to Venice or to Jacopo but about skewed thinking, that is, thinking which is unable to acknowledge that values rest as much in people as in ideas. The conflict of allegiances exists because the doge has created it, along with others who think like him. By attaching the doge to the matrix of Venetian ideology and having him represent Venetian values, Byron assures that the play is not primarily about private choices but about ways of perceiving individuals and society. The Venice that the drama portrays does not allow one to imagine that the doge could have resolved the conflict by showing more sympathy for Jacopo, for we are faced throughout the play with a dominant structure of values that makes no allowances for its citizens. It is not the doge alone but the doge and the Venetian network of power that would need to change in order to resolve the conflict at the center of the dramatic action.

Marina provides the key to the social perspective of the play, for she consistently disentangles the confused logic and mistaken social notions of the other major characters (the doge, Loredano, and Jacopo). Only she, for instance, recognizes the difference between people and the state and understands the proper relation between them. Despite the doge's objection that she "speaks wildly" (II.i.318) because of her "clamorous grief" (II.i.132), in fact, Marina provides a corrective to the dominant attitude toward society and social responsibility and offers the only balanced perspective in the play. She alone is fearless (II.i.312) before the state and its ministers; she alone sees through the oppressive ways of the patricians.

Her clear-sightedness is best illustrated in her ability to take the un-questioned assumptions of the other characters and apply them to real people and situations so that they become visible in practical terms. For instance, when Memmo speaks of the ruling council's "duty" (I.i.261) as a natural part of state matters, Marina points out to him, " 'Tis *their* duty / To trample on all human feelings, all / Ties which bind man to man" (I.i.261–63). Her exchanges with Loredano also show her ability to define Venetian ideology in practical terms. When the patrician visits Jacopo's dungeon cell Marina "let[s] him know / That he is known" (III.i.267–68); that is, she shows that she does not confuse his "office" with his personal malice but understands that he is using one to practice the other. Refusing to defer to his political position, she launches a verbal attack that exposes both the real evil of his person and of the Venetian power structure that he represents (III.i.252–433).

The full extent of Marina's understanding emerges in her conversation with the doge. With acuity and force she batters the "maxims" (II.i.300) that the doge and Venice live by, demonstrating how these maxims have turned both individuals and the state into arch villains. She maintains that the gross injustices visited on her husband have their source not only in Venice but also in the doge. Again, the clarity of her thinking rests in her refusal to subject herself blindly to Venetian values and expectations. When the doge attempts to explain that she cannot understand the workings of the state (II.i.115), she retorts: "I do—I do—and so should you, methinks— / That these are demons" (II.i.116–17). The doge's remark had been the common one that those who do not occupy a ruling position cannot understand the ways of political power. This translates, of course, into an endorsement of mass ignorance: it is the role of the citizenry (that is, everyone not in a position of public authority) to be ruled, not to understand or question the forces that rule them. Marina dashes the logic of this argument by looking directly at people and their actions rather than at the great mystery of the state and its power. She teaches the obstinate doge how the political system works, showing him that underneath the exteriors of noble Venetian precepts are to be found dishonor and malice: "Venice is dishonoured; / . . .'Tis ye who are all traitors, Tyrant!—ye!" (II.i.164–67). Her viewpoint is explained best in her comment to the doge that her thoughts are "human" rather than Venetian (II.i.277). By refusing to accept a priori that Venetian structures of authority are right and good, and by looking directly at the material relationships between the people of Venice, she exposes the faults of the individuals and power that rule the state.

The truth of Marina's assertion that Venetian ideology works against the best interests of its citizens and, indeed, victimizes them, is evident in the character of Jacopo who, from a purely dramatic point of view, is perhaps the least satisfying character in the play.[55] He seems to possess an unnatural affection for a country bent on torturing him, and, moreover, he is characterized by a melodramatic emotionalism that compromises his believability. Still he is proof of the evils embedded in the Venetian value system. His attachment to Venice shows his need for society; as he explains to Marina: "[M]y soul is social" (III.i.109). More specifically, it shows the vital significance of place in shaping his views of his personal identity and of the world. Venice contains the materials of his experience and it contains his heritage, and thus it provides the only context for whatever meaning his life possesses. That Venice tortures him without regard to his innocence or guilt[56] substantiates Marina's claim that the state is "traitor" to its citizens.

The Two Foscari advances the social interests of *Marino Faliero* and *Sardanapalus* by focusing more clearly on the relationship between individuals and the dominant ideology of their society. The social problems described in more or less general terms in the earlier dramas are shown here to lie ultimately in rules, policies, and creeds that do not properly acknowledge the passions and needs of individuals. As the old doge realizes too late, the fault with Venice is that

> There's no people, you well know it,
> Else you dare not deal thus by them or me.
> There is a *populace,* perhaps, whose looks
> May shame you; but they dare not groan nor curse you,
> Save with their hearts and eyes. (V.i.257–61)

Taken together, the history plays show Byron's attempt to cut through the obvious and largely superficial explanations of why social injustices exist and to uncover some of the more primary—and difficult—causes. *Marino Faliero*, written first, is the least satisfying of these plays because it turns on the easy assumption that an oppressive political machine is solely responsible for the stifling social situation described in the plot action, and that the overthrow of this machine is all that is needed to create a better society. Only when the revolution fails does it become apparent that social problems are not so easily explained or resolved. *Sardanapalus* marks a step forward by illustrating that political machinery provides only a partial explanation of social injustice; individuals who serve in the power structure must be held equally accountable. Finally, *The Two Foscari* attempts to show in greater detail the precise relations between individual and state in order to suggest that social problems arise often from the division of life into private and public duties, which often are mutually exclusive. This gradually sharpening perspective of social reality overrides the purely political or psychological elements in the plays and suggests that Byron's interest was not simply in political structures, political actions, or in individual characterizations, but rather in how the relations between and among them make society what it is.

Another way of explaining the plays' social content is by looking at the way Byron restricts and focuses his thematic concerns from one play to the next in order to eliminate secondary considerations and bring primary social questions into view. *Marino Faliero's* three major themes—class allegiance, ideology, and political violence—too numerous and too difficult to be treated effectively in a single historical drama, are presented indiscriminately as being equally important. *Sardanapalus* attempts to alleviate this problem by minimizing the plot significance of class and concentrating on ideology and violence. *The Two Foscari* then focuses on the social content even further by omitting violence (except as a minor issue) and examining ideology in detail. This perhaps is a crude reduction of the plays' thematic interests, but it nonetheless suggests their developing perception that one important way to understand society is to understand the structures of value and belief that govern it.

Perhaps the single greatest strength of the history plays is that they refuse to offer quick and ready explanations of complicated social issues. Their method is tentative, interrogative; they admit the reality of social injustices, but they refuse to admit that simple-minded notions of political revolution can by themselves lead to action capable of alleviating these injustices, just as they refuse to admit that uncritical commitment to existing social codes can make society better. Their fundamental argument is that any positive action to improve society must be accompanied by an understanding of a wide network of social forces and energies. This understanding can best be achieved by looking at the assumptions and beliefs that motivate certain kinds of social action. In exploring these assumptions and beliefs the history plays help to uncover problems with conventional social thinking, point to reasons for social unrest, and provide a groundwork for social involvement.

Heaven and Earth

The social perspective presented in the history plays is developed further in Byron's two "mystery" plays, *Cain* (1821) and *Heaven and Earth* (1823), which focus sharply on underlying structures of social authority and value, and specifically on why and how social systems of belief often create strife and unrest. Like *Heaven and Earth, Cain* is not so much about theology as about what religion means in terms of political and social reality. The play depicts a society built on a religious foundation, allowing Byron to stress the way religion can dictate society's conduct and outlook on life; every major character except Cain submits unquestioningly to the sacred order that people must toil, pray, sacrifice, and generally ignore the possibility of independent human activity and dignity. Cain's unhappiness and restless opposition to prevailing beliefs offer a vantage point from which to examine the justice of a religious code that demands self-denial and to measure religious values against the material situation in which they find expression.

Each act of the play treats an aspect of the social implications of religion. Act I presents "the accepted social order,"[57] that is, the combination of fundamental religious and political ingredients that make Cain's society what it is. Cain at this point is not yet consciously rebellious because he is as yet unsure about the source of his distress; but he is alienated, torn by his inchoate sense that something is wrong with what is described as God's order, and driven to question the values that require his submission. The cosmic journey of Act II provides him with a perspective that is larger than the narrowly ideological one of his own society, enabling him to assess the way religion and society work together to control people's thinking and behavior. The voyage shows Cain both the insignificance of the world when measured against the vastness of the universe, and—by revealing previous, greater races than the human race—undercuts the assumption of humanity's central role in God's scheme. Act III then returns Cain to the world, where his frustration with the oppressive and evidently unjust "politics of Paradise" (*BLJ*, 8:216) leads him to murder Abel. At every point the drama makes the religious story bear on conventional assumptions about individuals and society; it takes a hard and honest look at the practical significance of a subject most people of Byron's day preferred to regard as sacrosanct and to leave unconsidered; and he suggests that social unrest often traces back to the system of values that motivates human action. In short, the play indicates the social context in which Byron had come to consider religion, and provides a firm foundation for the questions he raises later in *Heaven and Earth*.[58]

Heaven and Earth pursues many of the interests established in *Cain*. The play describes both a ruling order and individual dissatisfaction with that order; it offers a perspective on social life that is not dictated by the prevailing structures of social authority themselves; and it presents an openly defiant reaction against the way society is set up. But *Heaven and Earth* is more complex than *Cain* because it confuses even further the issues of good and evil. Rather than having Lucifer lure humanity into defiance of God's proclamations, Byron here has God's own unfallen angels perform the deed; instead of having a traditional villain such as Cain question the laws of God and society, Byron has one of the Elect—Japhet—do so; and rather than having the defiant rebels punished by the Deluge, Byron allows them to escape with God's legions—who become rebels to save them. These points emphasize the drama's refusal to label values abstractly as sacred or profane, and more importantly they suggest that a value system is logically subordinate to social circumstance: no predetermined structure of values exists above and beyond society.

As the patriarch of antediluvian society, Noah represents the controlling orthodox attitude in the play; he embodies a set of idealistic principles against which the other characters measure their individual worth, needs, and desires. Noah believes that society is built upon laws and morals handed down by God; they are not created by people. In fact, he believes that people have no real control over the world in which they live nor, indeed, any *right* to govern themselves. A person gains social power, he believes, only when he is preordained (as Noah himself has been) by God to voice the creator's wishes.

This outlook generates at least two disturbing practical consequences. First, it promotes a rigidly authoritarian power structure that uses religion to justify political and social tyranny. By attributing his power to God, Noah relieves himself of the human responsibility attendant upon his position as a leader of people. As God's mouthpiece he controls every facet of social conduct, not only sexual and domestic habits but even geographical mobility. If individuals deviate from accepted social norms Noah recalls them not by a threat of physical punishment but by the stronger threat of God's vengeance. To illustrate: Noah claims that his son, Japhet, has no business wandering the Caucasus because "It is an evil spot" (II.91), nor any right to seek Anah's love because she is "of a fated race" (II.94); Japhet's errant conduct in both cases is considered to be an affront to God, and punishable by "doom" (III.466).[59] The sanctions are vague but effectively intimidating, and they systematically overawe the sensual through their reference to the sacred.

A second, more disturbing consequence of Noah's Calvinist understanding of social power is that it deadens human sympathy for individual people and endorses a vicious drive for self-preservation at the expense of others. Noah shows no compassion for the daughters of Cain; he is willing, even eager, to see them destroyed by the flood. And he warns Japhet to dismiss them also. Noah states that if Japhet hopes to survive the impending flood he must "forget / That [the daughters of Cain] exist" (III.495–96). The selfishness inherent in Noah's power is displayed even more bluntly when it becomes evident that he is willing not only to let the daughters of Cain die but also to let his own son die for loving Anah, despite his commands that Japhet abandon her:

> Then die
> With them!
> How darest thou look on that prophetic sky,
> And seek to save what all things now condemn,
> In overwhelming unison
> With just Jehovah's wrath! (III.756–61)

Noah's power rests not only on his ability to convince society that he is administering God's wishes but also on his ability to keep individuals fixed in their assigned social positions. The importance of social stratification to Noah's rule is presented most clearly in the Caucasus scene, which brings together the range of characters representing antediluvian society: Japhet, the tempted son who must be recalled to the moral norms of society so that eventually he can inherit his father's power; Anah and Aholibamah, the temptresses who defy Noah's power, both by luring Japhet away from his father and by consorting with beings beyond Noah's control; the angels, overt representatives of religion and explicit justification for Noah's power; and later Noah himself, the exemplar of proper conduct within the prevailing social order. Noah's frantic response to these characters collected together, exchanging ideas openly without any apparent regard for their appointed social positions, suggests the important role hierarchy plays in maintaining the social order over which he rules. He angrily reminds the others of their proper stations, threatening them with God's vengeance if they continue to violate the decreed order. He describes Anah and Aholibamah as "children of the wicked" (III.465) who deserve no human sympathy; he insists that the angels belong in heaven, not in the daily routines of society: "Has not God made a barrier between Earth / And Heaven, and limited each, kind to kind?" (III.475–76). He reminds Japhet that he is better than his associates, and that if he is to be assured of future social and sacred favors he must forego such unseemly company (III.494–98).

Plainly, Noah's heated, politically motivated commands—which go so far as to call God's angels themselves into question for intruding uninvited into the world—illuminate the requisites of the power he wields: the regimentation of individuals, the snuffing of any possible opposition before it can solidify, and a single authoritarian ruling voice. Moreover, his comments reveal once more the way religion can be used to strengthen political authority: Noah justifies the division of society not in terms of his personal aspirations to rule the world but rather in terms of *God*'s orders. These points not only show the close connection between Noah's religion and politics but also suggest the inhumanity and injustice at the heart of his religious beliefs.

One of the ways Byron makes the play's social theme more complex than in *Cain* is by having Japhet—traditionally associated with unquestioning conformity to God's commands—express many of the same social and religious doubts that Cain had expressed in the earlier mystery play. Japhet is alienated from the blind movements of society, he is expressly unhappy, and he questions many of society's accepted values. Although his immediate cause for distress is Anah's lack of interest in him, he is disturbed also because his personal and emotional needs cannot be satisfied within the scope of Noah's power. He is told bluntly (III.464–66) that Anah is off-limits to him because she is wicked and thus unacceptable to both Noah and to God. Compared with the ringing finality of this pronouncement, it actually matters little whether Anah loves him.

Further, Japhet is bothered not only by his private difficulties with Noah and God but also by the impending flood, which he doubts can be justified, even by God. If his initial prayer to God to preserve Anah (II.74–75) suggests his desire for a single exception to God's will rather than his discontent with the decree that everyone shall die, his later sympathy for all people doomed to die and his questioning of the logic and virtue of God's plans show a more general concern for humanity and a profound dissatisfaction with God's law:

> My kinsmen,
> Alas! what am I better than ye are,
> That I must live beyond ye?
> . . .
> Can we in Desolation's peace have rest?
> Oh God! be thou a God, and spare
> Yet while 'tis time. (III. 16–18, 703–5)

Japhet's position here recalls the defiant Cain boldly defending what he instinctively knows to be humanly right; he tells Noah that he would have his lot with humanity: "Let me die with *this,* and *them*" (III.498).

Unlike Cain, however, Japhet's gnawing sense of injustice in the world is outweighed by the heavy hand of religious and social authority, and thus he never openly breaks with society. He is a potential son of Cain in his unrest and doubt that willful harm—even if it is decreed by God—to humanity can be good, but he does not have the courage to side with Anah (though he loves her) in opposition to Noah and God. Traditional attitudes eventually control his thinking and weaken his independence until finally he succumbs to his father's obviously unsatisfactory explanation that God's tightening hold on the human race is necessary because "The Earth's grown wicked" (II.65), and he denies his own power to alleviate injustice (III. 51). He expresses his rejection of the freedom that had attracted him and, by implication, his acceptance, finally, of Noah's authority when he learns that Anah is consorting with angels:

> [U]nions like to these,
> Between a mortal and an immortal, cannot
> Be happy or be hallowed. We are sent
> Upon the earth to toil and die; and they
> Are made to minister on high unto
> The Highest. (III.369–74)

This passage echoes Noah's law that humanity's role is to "die when he [God] ordains, / A righteous death" (III.687–88), and indicates Japhet's inability to stand against the controlling codes of social and religious conduct. Pressed to choose between open defiance and reluctant submission, Japhet cannot sustain the Cain-like posture, which at various moments he seems to embrace, because underneath his outward discontent he is afraid not to believe Noah's maxim that to "Be a man"

(III.694) means to submit to the dictates of God and society. Still, though he submits, he does point up in his final question the chilling irony of this great system of cosmic and social order that divides individuals from their fellow beings: "Why, when all perish, why must I remain?" (III.929).[60]

Anah and Aholibamah reveal more explicitly the problems embedded in antediluvian society by openly testing and challenging the combined religious and political forces that control their world. Although they display opposite personalities—Anah is introspective, sensitive, and submissive, while her sister is proud, defiant, and caustic—still they both embody the orthodox idea of human evil and both are equally condemned by Noah and God. Aholibamah claims that her spirit, "though forbidden yet to shine" (I.104), demands freer movement than orthodox attitudes and authority permit; in fact, her confidence in her independent strength not only manifests itself in contempt for Noah's power but even prompts her to exhort angels to "Descend and share my lot" (I.96). The gentle Anah expresses with less assurance and vigor essentially the same radical sentiments as her sister. While lamenting that in the world's present condition "Delight [is] / An Eden kept afar from sight" (I.72–73), she also implies at the same time in her patient longing for the angel Azaziel that she intends to find what pleasures she can, despite Noah and God. Her timidity and her natural trepidation notwithstanding (see, for instance, I.139), Anah shares her sister's dogged opposition to Noah's authority and to the existing social order.

Their nonconformity is revealed clearly in their relationship with the angels. This relationship not only exemplifies their decided refusal to accept without question Noah's commands: it furnishes them with a larger perspective of reality than Noah wants to allow individuals, and thus challenges the absolutism of his political power. Moreover, it implies their denial of God's cosmic scheme. Anah and Aholibamah believe in a reality beyond the authoritarian rule that now controls the world; they believe in a human spirit that (they feel) has been smothered unjustly by existing laws and structures of value. Their union with angels manifests these beliefs and actualizes their hatred of the unnecessary and unjust restrictions which govern antediluvian society.

The social relevance of their affair with the angels crystallizes in Aholibamah's exchange with Japhet, who, though frustrated with

Noah and God, finds himself making a clumsy effort to defend the way the world is against what Aholibamah says it can be. The awkwardness of his position highlights the inconsistencies rooted in orthodoxy. For example, he defends his father's willing participation in the impending destruction of humanity as both "well-doing" and "Righteous" (III. 381–82). This statement alone perhaps would not show Japhet in such a bad light, but he follows it with a desperate pronouncement of his love for the clearly wicked Anah, which pathetically demonstrates his dissatisfaction with Noah's "well-doing" and "righteous" ways by betraying his sincere longing for things expressly forbidden by Noah. Worse, like Byron's heroes in the Eastern Tales, he rationalizes his love for Anah by deluding himself as to her real standing in the world: "My Anah! / Thou who dost rather make me dream that Abel / Had left a daughter" (III.402–4). Aholibamah recognizes the inconsistencies in Japhet's comments and condemns his spoutings as unhealthy and destructive hypocrisy: "Get thee hence, son of Noah; thou makest strife" (III.411). She knows that his attitude—less polished but essentially the same as his father's—allows religious fear to fasten unjust authoritarianism and hierarchy on the human race. The clearest material example of the fear that governs his thinking is the ark, which Aholibamah holds up to him as "The bugbear . . . built to scare the world" (III.443) into doing what Noah says. Japhet's bumbling exchange with Aholibamah points up the social injustice at the heart of Noah's political and religious system and, more significantly, explains the importance of the angel-mortal union as a means of combating Noah's authoritarian politics.

Taken together, the various characterizations suggest the drama's twofold interest. First, it shows the way society's religious foundation dictates humanity's outlook on life. The dominant social order of the play echoes that which Byron had presented in *Cain*: it is a paternalistic, restrictive, and authoritarian order that Noah commands as God's regent; it focuses on submission as the central human virtue and thus at least seems to work against the better interests of people. In short, Noah's pact with heaven creates tyranny. This is shown in the flood, which in the context of the play does not so much represent God's cleansing of the earth as the extreme practical consequence of Noah's social philosophy. As the flood gains momentum, doomed humanity repeats Aholibamah's bitter claim that "heaven and earth unite / For the annihilation of all life" (III.770–71; see also III.795–96, 840–43).

The flood is the culminating illustration of the oppressive and destructive tendency of Noah's powers; it is the practical manifestation of how religion can be used to justify even mass murder.

Second, the portrayal of Anah and Aholibamah and their union with the angels provides a positive, even utopian, alternative to the injustice and tragedy associated with Noah and Japhet. In joining the angels, Anah and Aholibamah rise above the system of values and structures of authority that control the world and, further, approach a position that enables them to evaluate life from a perspective other than Noah's. Anah and Aholibamah, in this regard, represent the search for a freer reality principle, one which would allow them to achieve their full human potential in life. Their escape from the flood with angels who desert God's tyranny suggests both the nobility of their resistance and the continuing physical and spiritual opposition to the clearly unjust system administered by God and Noah.

Heaven and Earth examines the source of many social attitudes and assumptions treated in Byron's earlier writings, showing the profound impact of religion on society, and thereby supplying an explanation of how systems of value can be used to manipulate people. Social control, even authoritarian social control, is not necessarily maintained by physical power but very often by ideological means that derive their strength from religion. Byron emphasizes the role religion can play in causing social injustice by clouding the distinctions between characters traditionally assumed to be good or evil, illustrating more clearly than he had in *Cain* that the worth of one's values must be determined by material circumstances. That what Noah calls God's values are not automatically good is made evident both through Japhet's frustration and through the angels' evasion of God's command. The play concludes that "The politics of Paradise," and the politics of society in general, become dangerously oppressive when they are built upon so-called religious ideas that in reality deny people the freedom to pursue their full potential in the world.

Werner

Although *Werner* has been considered by some critics to be "about as complete a failure as anything in literature,"[61] the drama in fact is a fascinating portrayal of the way and the extent to which ideology controls social life. One reason it has received such negative critical response, even when it initially appeared, is that it resists the biographical and psychological methods of analysis most often brought to bear on Byron's work.[62] Absent from the play are the powerful Byronic hero, the captivating lyricism, the swift movement, the psychological depth, and the sharp irony that characterize his more popular poems. In their place are an unlikable, spineless main figure, a rather prosaic and sometimes cluttered verse, and a conspicuously unspectacular setting. Although they mark a radical departure from many of Byron's previous works, these features need not be interpreted as regressions or as a sign that Byron was "now the burlesque of what he was," as one contemporary reviewer stated.[63]

If the play fails to meet conventional aesthetic standards of excellence, it nonetheless provides a highly imaginative and compelling account of the social and political interests that had come to absorb Byron completely. The play studiously avoids the Byronic trademark—with its emphasis on the virtues of absolute individualism—concentrating instead on a social order undergoing radical change and, specifically, on the demise of a once powerful ruling class. This emphasis insists that Werner's story is not his alone; it is not a psychologically compelling tale of a unique individual.[64] Rather, like Arnold (in *The Deformed Transformed*) or Cain's story it is invested with and given significance by the values and assumptions of Werner's society. To understand his crime and his failure, despite his aspirations to honesty and integrity, it is necessary to understand the full network of social relations within which he is obligated to function.[65]

Werner is the only one of Byron's plays that begins with a stage note indicating the time as well as the place of action. This note is important, for it calls attention to a revision of Byron's source—Sophia Lee's *German Tale*—that significantly changes the meaning of the action.[66] Whereas the original tale is set in the midst of the Thirty Years' War, Byron shifts the time scheme to the close of the war and then reinterprets his internal materials accordingly. (For example, the celebration of the signing of the Peace of Prague—1635—in Act V becomes a projection of Siegendorf's domestic life and a celebration of his ostensibly splendid and just rule.[67]) This seemingly minor time change provides Byron with essential artistic flexibility because it allows him to focus the play's action at a moment of great historical crisis—the Thirty Years' War—and to examine various fundamental social structures in the light of this crisis, while at the same time avoiding the difficulties and inevitable distortions that the immediate pressures of the war would present to social analysis.

The Thirty Years' War represents much more than background. It provides both the context and the pulse of the play, the social and historical episode that the characters are most immediately caught in, and thus it gives meaning to the specific events being dramatized. The historical significance of the war has been variously interpreted, and generalizations about such a signal episode are always dangerous. But it is possible, I believe, to offer a set of general statements that, if not pushed too far, can help to elucidate the play's rich historical vision.

It is well known that the Thirty Years' War was one of the bloodiest and most vicious wars in modern Western history; new military tactics produced unprecedented slaughter and this was accompanied by new heights of lawlessness in international relations. Indeed, it was largely from the sweeping chaos created by this war that Hobbes and Locke drew inspiration for their theories of the state of nature.[68] The war took its character from conflicting historical forces that had been developing for hundreds of years. As Georges Pages remarks, "The Thirty Years' War saw the last effort of the Roman Catholic Church and the house of Hapsburg to re-establish unity by the triumph of Catholicism over the Protestant heresies and the renewal of the emperor's universal power."[69] At the same time, resistance to the church and to the house of Habsburg represented Germany's desperate attempt to move from the Middle Ages into the modern world, where most of Europe already stood. To quote Pages: "Politically it [the war] was characterized by the formation of the first modern states; from the religious point of view it witnessed the destruction at the hands of Protestantism of the united Christendom which the Catholic Church had established in the Middle Ages."[70] Although Pages stresses the religious dimension of the war, he makes clear at the same time that this was not mainly a religious war. The causes and consequences on all sides were sweeping, transcending any single issue, attesting that this in fact was a violent struggle to determine the direction that European history was to take.

The war provided an excellent context for Byron's purposes, not only because it was a major watershed in Western history, marking a turn away from feudal structures of authority, but also because its termination crystallized history at a delicate and precarious moment in which numerous crucial social determinants stood exposed. The long, bloody war ended in temporary victory by the old order, briefly freezing the course of history. Arnold Hauser describes the situation precisely: "[I]n Germany . . . the land-owning nobility itself became an official caste and the middle class was pushed back in an even more ruthless fashion than anywhere else into the ranks of the subordinate civil service." And this, of course, "brought the final collapse of German commerce and destroyed the German cities economically as well as politically." [71] Not until Bismarck would Germany finally be united.

At the same time, however, this termination in favor of the aristocracy foreshadowed subsequent and even more extreme turmoil, because the forces that had gained a strong foothold in European culture at large could not be permanently subdued, as history eventually proved. From his vantage point in the nineteenth century, with the fact of the American and French revolutions at hand (the latter Shelley had described to him years before as "the master theme of the epoch in which we live" [*LPBS*, 1:504]), Byron could see the inevitable struggles that still lay ahead; and he was deeply aware that these struggles, including the pervasive European conflicts in his own century, were born from the past. The Thirty Years' War presented him with a clear picture of the major issues that had shaped and continued to shape the course of history, and in *Werner* he used the war to capture and to re-create as precisely as possible the many dimensions of these issues. It is in the context of the Thirty Years' War then that the play's otherwise disparate social, political, economic, and ideological interests are brought to a head in the form of historical fact.

The direction of Byron's social analysis in *Werner* is immediately evident in his treatment of social class, which is here more detailed, intelligent, and imaginative than in his other dramas. He not only offers a fully realized portrait of class structure under feudalism from the serving classes to the nobility, but he also captures the levels of meaning contained in class relations. Further, through his extensive treatment of Werner's poverty, he illuminates the powerful alienation that victimizes lower classes, not so much because they possess very little material wealth as because they are always governed by a set of social and cultural values not their own, values that in fact work against their material and moral betterment.

One of the main assumptions upon which the drama's critique of social class rests is that a ruling order perpetuates its power not only by assuring that subordinate classes remain static but also by maintaining exact order within its own ranks. This fundamental principle is exemplified in Werner's personal history. He is disinherited precisely because he ignores the restraints inherent in his social position. His marriage to Josephine, like Hesperus's marriage to Floribel in *The Brides' Tragedy*, crosses class lines and thus brings upon him the full wrath of his peers, demonstrating explicitly how the ruling class readily and powerfully will exercise its authority, even among its own, to protect class interests. The blow of disinheritance which falls upon him schools him in an important fact of feudal social reality, namely that, even at the top, individuals are always expendable. The tyranny of class stratification described here contributes to the tragic dimension of the play, and Byron's several points of focus on class structure represent developments and clarifications of this tyranny.

The play's emphasis on class is manifested in numerous literal details. In the first three acts of the play, for instance, Byron develops the strong tension between Werner's lower-class disguise (with the many difficulties of conversation, attitude, and conduct that this creates) and his longing for open acceptance into the aristocracy, into which he was born. Werner's deep-seated assumptions of his due social privilege—"I was born to wealth, and rank, and power" (I.i.77)[72]—are set consistently against the harsh fact of his poverty and even more revealingly against the fact of the lower class with which he has been forced to align himself. His discomfort among those he considers to be naturally inferior and his inability to identify himself with them or even to sympathize with them underscore the pervasive power that class stratification exercises in social life. Werner never overcomes his suspicion of Idenstein, and for no other reason than that Idenstein is a servant, which, Werner assumes, means that he should always be deferential and servile, laboring to produce leisure for others. That Idenstein should display ordinary human characteristics, that he should deign to engage Werner in conversation, for instance, insults and shocks Werner, who believes that decency of character depends entirely on rank.

The rigidity of this class structure is not exemplified from one side only. The reason Idenstein approaches Werner at all on topics of everyday life—for instance, about "the way of business" (I.i.192)—is that he assumes Werner to be a social equal, not a superior. Idenstein quickly and enthusiastically fulfills the obligations of his class immediately upon the arrival of Stralenheim, who is obviously from the ruling class;

indeed, Idenstein cannot do enough to serve this complete stranger (I.i.455–59) who, because of his social rank, commands authority and respect even in someone else's domain.

The class issue is manifested in the larger structure of the play as well. The shift of setting in Act IV to the castle of Siegendorf removes the action from the domain of the poor to that of the wealthy. This change in setting allows the drama to present a dual perspective on society. In the early acts, despite Werner's expressed alienation, society is presented mainly through the eyes of its lower orders. Idenstein and his colleagues are shown going about their daily work and in their simplest statements and actions and in their unpremeditated responses to persons of various ranks they provide a compelling social analysis. Even Werner helps to clarify the lower-class view of rank; in an obvious selfish effort to justify his own criminal conduct, he asks his son, Ulric: "Young, / Rash, new to life, and reared in Luxury's lap, / Is it for you to measure Passion's force, / Or Misery's temptation?" (II.ii.101–4). Further, he repeatedly seeks to explain his actions as the consequence of straitened circumstances (see, for instance, II.ii.147–49), betraying, albeit unintentionally, the specific difficulties with which the poor are forced to contend.

Act IV describes society from a radically different perspective. Here the assumptions of the wealthy and powerful prevail; society is shown to be functioning properly, that is, responding unquestioningly to those who rule it. As Siegendorf explains to Ida:

[T]he Heaven
Which gave us back our own, in the same moment
It spread its peace o'er all, hath double claims
On us for thanksgiving: first, for our country;
And next, that we are here to share its blessings. (IV.i.251–55)

As far as Werner is concerned, his personal return to aristocracy vindicates the social system, proving its rightness and its durability. These divergent class perspectives not only provide a means of measuring the underlying causes and ramifications of the tragedy that culminate in Act V: in addition, they demonstrate the importance Byron now attached to a social analysis that would sweep fully across society.

These simple yet compelling insights offered in the plot indicate the drama's sensitivity to the power and unquestioned divisions governing class society. Its emphasis on the central importance of class is given ballast by numerous seemingly minor touches, all of which illuminate the degree to which the social world depicted in the drama stands divided. For instance, names are given special attention. Werner is highly reluctant to identify himself to Idenstein, and when at last he does so Idenstein uses his name to place him socially (I.i. 173–98), even to the extent of calling him "cousin." General vocabulary is similarly focused. When Stralenheim enters the palace in Act I, Werner displays extreme difficulty speaking the language of the class to which he ostensibly belongs. In response to a question from Stralenheim, Werner states: "When I know it [the question] such / I will requite—that is, *reply*—in unison" (I.i. 532–33). Such details are carefully handled throughout, and collectively they display the way language is used as a class weapon. Names, vocabulary, and rhetorical expertise are never in the play simply as a means of conveying objective information: they reflect profound class biases that hold existing social hierarchies in place.

Central to the play's emphasis on class is the question of natural rights and natural order. Werner's disinheritance focuses this question initially by placing him in a position that challenges his most fundamental assumptions about his personal and public role. His various responses to his situation consistently confuse social life and natural life, displaying not only the ahistorical character of his thought but more importantly emphasizing the assumptions that sustain class stratification. His alienation exists not simply because he lacks wealth but also because, in his view, his poverty violates natural order. Indeed, it is the deeper distress of being cast out by his class upon "this desolate frontier" (I.i. 50) that he cannot comprehend: "Something beyond our outward sufferings (though / These were enough to gnaw into our soul) / Hath stung me oft, and, more than ever, *now*" (I.i. 46–48). For Werner, the loss of social position is the loss of "my rights" (I.i. 86). His attitude, at least from his standpoint, is not selfish but in fact highly moral, for it is grounded upon his honest desire to be in a position to provide for his family and, ultimately, to serve the society to which he belongs (for instance, see I.i. 149–65).

Werner, in fact, never understands the social dimension of his situation. Even in the end, when his position is destroyed by his son's confession of murder and open embrace of an independent, criminal life, he confuses social reality with natural order; if Ulric before was suspected of being unnatural, he is now perceived as completely transmogrified (V.ii.57). And, likewise, Werner expresses his own demise entirely in terms of natural order: "No, no; I have no children: never more / Call me by that worst name of parent" (V.ii.54–55). The assumption here is that events are determined by forces that, despite their social consequences, are not of social origin.

The extent to which Werner is governed by this ideology of natural right and natural order is illuminated by his crime against Stralenheim. That his theft of Stralenheim's gold represents more than a momentary lapse of character, more than a psychological quirk, is immediately evident from the context in which Byron places the crime. Werner is consistently described as an aristocrat who lacks the material means upon which aristocracy is predicated. Thus if he appears personally weak and unattractive it is because he has endured twelve poverty-ridden years that necessarily have injured his once powerful independence of mind (recall, for example, his earlier defiance of authority in marrying Josephine). Without wealth his attitudes, his values, and his entire being are hollow. The particular character of his distress is manifested at the moment of the theft, when he compares his present weakened situation with that of the confident, aristocratic, and wealthy Stralenheim:

> I'm alone—
> He with a numerous train: I weak—
> In gold, in numbers, rank, authority.
> I nameless, or involving in my name
> Destruction, till I reach my own domain;
> He full-blown with his titles, which impose
> Still further on these obscure petty burghers
> Than they could do elsewhere. (I.i.625–32)

From this perspective (although Werner does not fully understand this), the theft is a social act, like Fazio's in Milman's play, representing Werner's desperate and impulsive attempt to overcome alienation, to realign himself with his own class (and thus with his own character), and once more to become a fully social individual.[73] As he tells Josephine, the gold "Will rescue us from this detested dungeon" (I.i.738) and "will make us way" (I.i.742), presumably to aristocracy, freedom, and power.

The public response to the theft elaborates the ideological and class pressures controlling the world depicted in the play. When Idenstein remarks that the crime is a blot on the city's honor (II.i.7), he expresses a generally assumed, albeit unconscious, social fact, namely that honor is a concept with distinctive class dimensions. Indeed, his concern arises not simply because there has been a crime but specifically because "A Baron [has been] pillaged in a Prince's palace" (I.i.2). According to this statement, honor clearly is equated with the preservation of aristocracy; a dishonorable act is any act that injures the ruling class. In this view, of course, honor ultimately works against the lower orders by ossifying their subordinate social position. This attitude stands at the center of the prevailing social system and the drama describes its consequences explicitly. When the crime is learned, everyone from Stralenheim to Idenstein automatically assumes the thief *to be poor*. Stralenheim's assertion that to be poor is to be suspect (II.i.290) is carried to its most vicious extreme by Idenstein, who proposes to "send out villains to strip beggars, and / Search empty pockets; also, to arrest / All gipsies and ill-clothed and sallow people" (II.i.69–71). Such a response, of course, indicates the pervasiveness and extreme power of controlling ideas; but, more than this, it focuses the way these values perpetuate ruling class domination. Society assumes that any social disruption (such as the theft) is always attributable to the lower classes; this causes the lower classes perpetually to blame one another (stated bluntly it causes the oppressed to turn on one another) which in turn "proves" their "natural" inferiority and at the same time demonstrates the sanctity and ultimate rightness of aristocratic authority. Or, put differently, the play maintains that class stratification generates an encompassing system of values that in turn perpetuates (or even continues to create) further class stratification. To conduct an honest investigation from the start, to acknowledge the equal possibility of the theft having been committed by an aristocrat, is out of the question; not only would this insult the assumed integrity of the aristocratic class but also it would admit that aristocracy is potentially less than honorable, hence weakening its "natural right" to rule. In short, the controlling system of values protects its rulers by exempting them automatically from suspicion of all wrongdoing.

Byron exposes the faulty assumptions behind the beliefs in natural right and natural order by presenting the various and often contradictory ways circumstance is perceived. This focus anticipates an issue later developed in Marxist thought, namely that individuals cannot be satisfactorily understood in terms of their own perceptions of themselves: they must be understood in terms of the discrepancies between their perceptions and actual material life.[74] While expressing their fundamental and identical belief in a fixed order based on the natural rights of aristocracy, Werner and Stralenheim rely on circumstance to justify their private and mutually exclusive aims; both men assume that their respective values and social situation are or can be made consistent with one another. In his effort to escape poverty and regain his former social position, Werner ardently states that "there are crimes / Made venial by the occasion" (II.ii. 147–48), and one such crime of course is his own against Stralenheim. At the same time, the ambitious Stralenheim asserts that "circumstances . . . have made / This man [Werner] obnoxious—perhaps fatal to me" (II.ii.343–45). In a larger sense, too, Werner believes that circumstance (his birth) gives him the indisputable right of aristocracy (I.i.86), while Stralenheim believes just as strongly that because of circumstance (that is, because Werner is "A disinherited prodigal" [II.ii.388]), Werner has absolutely no rights.

The contradictions here are plain and they suggest that neither character actually understands circumstance, despite his repeated appeals to it, because each interprets as natural and absolute what is in fact ideological and subject to social pressures. Obviously, both men cannot be correct; carried to their extreme, these attitudes cancel one another, which is precisely what happens as Stralenheim is murdered and Werner is destroyed. Notwithstanding the strong mutual claims to universal, indisputable definitions, and the repeated efforts to substantiate these claims by reference to circumstance, neither Werner nor Stralenheim can free himself from social and class reality; their inability demonstrates exactly the fallacy in assuming that an encompassing, ahistorical structure of ideas and relations governs social life.

The extent to which the social world of the play is limited and shaped by ideology is developed in Byron's handling of religion. Like *Cain* and *Heaven and Earth, Werner* refuses to exempt religion from the exchanges of social life, and in fact clearly depicts the particular class role that religion often plays in sustaining a structure of social authority. The melodramatic, sad, comical exchange between Werner and the prior captures the way religion and class often complement one another to maintain and perpetuate the ruling order. Once he regains his aristocratic position, with its accompanying power and wealth, Werner is, not surprisingly, guilt-ridden because of his earlier crime against Stralenheim; he thus donates the dishonest gold to the church in order to expiate his sin. Werner's sincerity here is complete; he does indeed wish to atone for an act that he perceives as immoral. In fact, he is desperate to know the full integrity of his character. But his honesty is very narrowly defined; he is so entirely governed by his desire to preserve his aristocracy that he never really considers making a full confession, even to the prior. To do so, of course, might jeopardize his social position, tarnish his public image, or both. This is not simple hypocrisy on his part (at least in the usual sense), for he cannot perceive the inconsistencies in his position; rather, it is a sign of his need to be personally and socially whole. That the prior readily accepts his donation and his explanations exemplifies the way religion endorses and sanctifies aristocracy's choices:

> *Werner:* I bestow this sum
> For pious purposes.
> *Prior:* A proper deed
> In the behalf of our departed friends.
> *Werner:* But he who's gone was not my friend, but foe,
> The deadliest and the stanchest.
> *Prior:* Better still!
> To employ our means to obtain Heaven for the souls
> Of our dead enemies is worthy those
> Who can forgive them living.
> *Werner:* But I did not
> Forgive this man. I loathed him to the last,
> As he did me. I do not love him now,
> But—
> *Prior:* Best of all! for this is pure religion!
> You fain would rescue him you hate from hell—
> An evangelical compassion. (IV.i.483–95)

This exchange describes the religious justification for Werner's social conduct. The very real issues of social life—the theft, the murder— are insistently relegated by religion to an abstract level that ostensibly transcends class reality, thus freeing Werner from his immediate responsibilities as a social being. In this view, religion serves a very real if subconscious purpose; it subsumes the contradictions in the social order, thus making possible the perpetuation of that order. Once Werner is convinced that "I am *not* guilty" (IV.i.522), he can comfortably resume his position of wealth and exercise his ruling power with a clear conscience. This fact is emphasized in the scene immediately following, which describes a grand celebration in Count Siegendorf's elaborately decorated castle. Marx explains this social perspective on religion perfectly:

> [M]an is no abstract being encamped outside the world. Man is *the world of man,* the state, society. This state, this society, produce religion, an *inverted world-consciousness,* because they are an *inverted world.* Religion is the general theory of that world, its encyclopaedic compendium, its logic in a popular form, . . . its moral sanction, its solemn complement, its universal source of consolation and justification.[75]

The play's most penetrating and original insight into the structures of social order lies in its portrayal of personal life. Here Byron demonstrates the full social character of his imagination, denying conventional abstract assumptions in order to develop an encompassing, socially consistent concept of the family. Restored to aristocracy, Werner responds to strong social pressures—evident in his past life as well as in his continuing doubts about Stralenheim's murder—by drawing his family closely about him. In fact, his family becomes vitally important to him as virtually an open symbol of his personal worth, providing a sanctuary, a source of meaning that he believes, or at least hopes, is independent and self-contained. With its emphasis on personal emotions and on love, his family constitutes for him a domain that is not dominated by everyday public life. It is this understanding and need that prompt his desperate remark to his son, Ulric, that "thou lovest me not! / All hearts but one may beat in kindness for me— / But if my son's is cold!" (IV.i.323–25), as well as his stern warning to Ulric to embrace a conventional domestic life (IV.i.332ff.). But as with his understanding of religion, Werner's domestic choices and attitudes, though perhaps honest, in fact respond to and perpetuate the ruling class as well as his particular position within that class. Not only does he insist on family presence at the Prague festival for the sake of public show, explaining in response to Ulric's proposed absence that " 'twould be mark'd in any house, / But most in *ours,* that ONE should be found wanting / At such a time and place" (IV.i.249–51); but more significantly, he has adopted the orphaned Ida, daughter of the murdered Stralenheim, thus consolidating his power by incorporating a potential enemy into his own camp. As Ulric honestly summarizes the situation: "[T]his union with / The last bud of the rival branch at once / Unites the future and destroys the past" (IV.i.131–33). If Werner's family serves private needs, these needs clearly are connected to social realities and express very real and powerful social values. The full social dimension of his personal life is shown explicitly at the end of the play when the strong pressures with which he has been struggling explode within the family itself, destroying both his domestic and his public life.[76]

One way Byron connects these various social threads is through his characterization of Gabor. Unlike other characters in the play, Gabor is socially unattached, a foreigner, and this fact serves at least two important purposes. First, the vulnerability that issues from his ambiguous social position allows Byron to emphasize the fundamental unity of existing social attitudes. Despite the fact, for instance, that his only real act in the play is to rescue a drowning man, he is suspected by the laboring and ruling classes alike both of theft and of murder. As an unknown he is a convenient victim of social manipulation; his guilt in these crimes would leave the social order innocent and intact, and more significantly would "prove" society's righteousness by cleansing it (with no harm to itself) of an evil that has surfaced. It is thus perfectly understandable that Idenstein and Fritz as well as Stralenheim (and later Siegendorf) would immediately suspect him of the theft that Werner committed.

Further, Gabor's distance from the play's prevailing social order makes him a perceptive critic who sees through complacent assumptions to the serious contradictions threatening the stability of the world he has entered. It is Gabor who announces that the poor are always the first to be suspected of guilt (III.i.23–24) and who explains as well the full social significance of this response to crime. As he tells Ulric: "[Y]ou spared me for / Your own especial purpose, to sustain / An ignominy not my own" (V.i.214–16); and later he makes the same point to Siegendorf: "I conceived myself / Betray'd by you and *him* [Ulric] . . . into this / Pretended den of refuge, to become / The victim of your guilt" (V.i.342–46). The issue at hand here is not a purely private matter emerging from the accusations against an innocent individual; as the play makes clear, guilt is socially assigned to protect ruling-class interests. Gabor, for instance, makes this point explicit numerous times in the play. He explains to Josephine when he first talks with her that "I know well these nobles, and / Their thousand modes of trampling on the poor" (I.i.655–56); and when Stralenheim questions him about the theft he retorts: "[Y]ou / Are practising your power on me—because / You have it; but beware! you know not whom / You strive to tread on" (II.i.261–64).

While other characters conduct themselves according to principles that appear to be universal and beyond criticism, Gabor remains relatively independent from those principles. His relative freedom (as a foreigner) from the structures of authority controlling the world inhabited by all of the other characters enables him to expose the actual social basis of human values and, moreover, to explain how these values in reality can be used to support specific class interests. His perceptions illuminate the social context encompassing the play's disparate issues and amplify the deep-seated contradictions that ultimately destroy the existing social order.

The collapse of the prevailing structures of social authority involves at the same time the slow creation of a new system of values. Both the direction of and the particular motivating impulses behind this system are most fully embodied in Ulric. Of course, Ulric is a product of the social world into which he is born, as is evidenced in his aristocratic hauteur, his assumptions of privilege, and his readiness to command authority; and his character is necessarily shaped by the various social and personal contexts of his life. But he is also an imaginative individual, attempting to overcome these contexts and to carve a new life free of the contradictions that demand ever greater compromises from his father. Werner's life magnifies the very real inadequacies of the prevailing system, bringing fully into Ulric's view the "inherent weakness, half-humanity, / Selfish remorse, and temporising pity, / that sacrifices your whole race" (V.ii.36–38). Thus while Werner, Stralenheim, and most of the others accept the natural and universal validity of ideas binding their society, only to find themselves victimized in trying to justify their beliefs by means of religion, family, circumstance, and so on, Ulric attempts to live unhypocritically, without relying on an abstract system to justify his life. He abandons entirely the ethic to which his father blindly subscribes in favor of a more individual, private, even bourgeois ethic, one that places the value and right of "ownership" and privilege on one's ability to attain them— hence his life of murder and plunder. He always takes the most expedient course of action to attain his goals, without respect to conventional assumptions about right and wrong. Along with his large group of marauders, he illustrates, as it were, the inchoate existence of a new class; born into a crumbling aristocracy, he frees himself from its confining value system and way of life and begins constructing his own renegade social context.

This, of course, is not to say that Ulric is morally right in the life he has chosen. Indeed, the extreme physical violence he unquestioningly and unflinchingly performs foreshadows future atrocities to match or surpass those of the culture he rejects.[77] Rather my point is that he, like Cain, faces a given set of circumstances and assumptions that determine his choices. His conduct simply exemplifies the developing process of social change being charted in the play: just as Werner had defied the right of society to govern personal life (note, for instance, his marriage to Josephine), Ulric defies the right of society to govern public life. His final confession and then departure with his fellow banditti ("men—who are worthy of the name" [V.ii.48]) mark the triumph of the strongly individual ethic he represents, illuminating the dominant characteristic of a new social order beginning to emerge.

The diverse social issues and perspectives developed in the play bring into focus the complex role and significance of inheritance. The conventional psychological explanation generally brought to bear on this issue (that the son inherits the sins of the father) is inadequate, because it reduces a contextual matter to purely private terms that are badly inconsistent with the public character of inheritance as it is presented in the drama. The various social issues around which the plot revolves, I believe, combine into a unified and highly critical reevaluation of inheritance. The main concern here is neither psychological nor legal (that is, the concern is not with the question of who is entitled to succeed Werner's father as count), but social. In ascending to the position of count, Werner does not simply achieve a private aim; he inherits and accepts a full system of beliefs with its attendant social reality. Karl Mannheim (writing in a different context) clarifies this larger social view of inheritance:

> Strictly speaking it is incorrect to say that the single individual thinks. Rather it is more correct to insist that he participates in thinking further what other men have thought before him. He finds himself in an inherited situation with patterns of thought which are appropriate to this situation and attempts to elaborate further the inherited modes of response or to substitute others for

them in order to deal more adequately with the new challenges which have arisen out of these shifts and changes in his situation.[78]

This point is exemplified in Werner's adoption of Ida, in his search for the (presumed) guilty Gabor, and in his public show of power and wealth—all public actions that reflect his embracement of a received situation and which are meant to secure his personal integrity, as well as the integrity of the ruling class, within that situation.

Such an explanation of inheritance within the broad historical context of social life illuminates more immediate concerns of the play. That Werner is implicated in crime after crime (both material and moral) and that finally these destroy entirely his private and public life are signs of the severe evils that necessarily emerge when social principles go unexamined. In this view, inheritance becomes a symbol of the entire social order that the play describes; although it is never explicitly defined or fully understood by Werner, inheritance (or the *idea* of inheritance) is perceived as natural and universally valid, just as the existing social and class relations are perceived as natural and universally valid. The conclusion of the play powerfully illustrates the narrowness of these assumptions and stresses the true social and historical conditions that have governed the action from the beginning. When Ulric blatantly refuses to become "the vain heir / Of your [Werner's] domains" (V.ii.44–45) and leaves his father for the last time, the stunned Werner announces that "The race of Siegendorf is past" (V.ii.66). Even if his remark is understandable because of the pressures on him at the moment, it is incorrect (Ulric is not dead), and this fact is important. Given his class position and its absolutely encompassing set of beliefs, Werner cannot understand that in fact what is past is a way of life, a social system in which individuals passively and uncritically inherit their wealth (or poverty), their status, and their values, and that it is being replaced by a new system in which merit is determined by individual action. His confusion of natural and social phenomena at this extreme moment illuminates the complete control that his society exerts over him and, in larger terms, it represents the final blow to a system destroying itself by its own internal limitations, injustices, and contradictions.

Without attempting to press the issue too far, I should note that Werner's story parallels exactly the course of the Thirty Years' War, so that the play may be viewed as a particular manifestation of a larger historical crisis. Although the war ended in momentary triumph by the old order, it sounded at the same time the certain eventual demise of aristocratic hegemony; likewise, Werner's inheritance marks a temporary restoration of social order and also crystallizes the various inconsistencies that eventually must destroy this order. Or, put differently, just as Werner is defeated in his efforts to reestablish his personal life as it once was, his social class is defeated in its efforts to halt the course of history.

These, of course, are vast simplifications, but nonetheless they may be used as a gloss on the drama's method of presenting history. It sets the action at the time of the Thirty Years' War to focus the importance of specific events, to give them historical depth and dimension. This particular appropriation and presentation of historical and social life have never been fully appreciated because, as the foregoing discussion stresses, the drama avoids conventional positivistic biases. *Werner* is not concerned with charting a linear, cause–effect course for historical events; rather, it dramatizes social structure, emphasizing the contradictions, the faulty assumptions, the dominant philosophy and character types, the economic forces at the center of a specific social system.

The lengthy analysis that I have here provided of *Werner* should indicate my belief that this is Byron's most sophisticated and historically compelling drama. Behind this portrayal of deep and severe social contradictions are Byron's extensive reading in history, literature, and politics; his personal experiences in family and public life; the turmoil and apocalyptic fervor of the American and French revolutions; the unprecedented extravagance, oppression, and poverty of Regency England; the Peterloo Massacre; the revolutionary writings and political activities of Shelley; the Napoléonic campaigns; the Austrian domination of Italy; the Carbonari resistance; and more.[79] In *Werner*, as in all of his works after about 1820, Byron attempts an imaginative synthesis, not of the details of these forces but rather of their ideological currents; implicit in this attempt is the assumption that social change can become truly progressive and productive only when the structures of authority and belief encompassing events and attitudes are clearly understood.

The Deformed Transformed

That *The Deformed Transformed* (1822) has rarely been viewed as a work
with anything serious to say about politics and society is at least partly
Byron's fault. He wrote the drama with even less patience and precision than usual, allowing his ego and impulse toward autobiography
to obscure other interests. Consequently, readers unanimously have
brought an exclusive psychological perspective to the play, arguing
that in it can be found autobiographical references to Byron's physical
deformity, his turbulent relationship with his mother, and his long-
standing fascination with the idea of a doppelgänger.[80] These psychological imperatives notwithstanding, *The Deformed Transformed* is most
fully understood in terms of its radical critique of social order. The
play presents an array of ostensibly isolated topics from alienation
to violence, from religion to art, affirming their vital connectedness
in society. Moreover, it articulates the complex relation between abstract or transhistorical ideals and the material conditions of everyday
personal and social life, thus demystifying the powerful ideological
processes that both reflect and shape human perceptions of the world.

These matters are presented through the experiences of what must
be Byron's oddest character creation, an ugly and physically deformed social outcast named Arnold. Like the stereotypical romantic
hero, Arnold displays a "natural" attraction to the noblest qualities in
life: "beauty" (I.i.191), "peace" (I.ii.21), "honor" (II.iii.80), "mercy"
(II.iii.93–94), and "forgiveness" (II.iii.111); and he sincerely wishes to
be loved (I.i.29–31, 421–22).[81] But these noble and abstract ideals emphatically elude him, never becoming part of his ordinary everyday
experience. His mother looks on him as an "incubus" (I.i.2), a "night-
mare" (I.i.2), an "abortion" (I.i.3), and a "monstrous sport of Nature"
(I.i.15); and when he reflects upon his situation he reluctantly agrees
that he is despicable (I.i.46), fit only for slave labor despite his desperate
and sincere longing for something better.

Arnold's unfortunate predicament, of course, traces immediately to
his physical deformity but, as the drama gradually shows, this is only
the literal manifestation of a deeply ingrained and unquestioned set of
social beliefs. The public scorn generated by his ugliness rests upon
the prevailing assumption in his world that he is too ugly and weak to
deserve better than what he has, that his situation is his fault alone. Or,
put bluntly, he is despised because he is unable to be anything other

than what he is; he cannot attain full integration into the mainstream of life because of his own limitations. These assumptions make human life fundamentally individual, untouched by historical and social determinations, and they deny that real human value derives in any way from the texture of material social existence. Further, it makes circumstance a fixed, static, unyielding arena that does little more than test one's private strength and serves as a measure of one's success or failure. In short, the assumptions behind the public condemnation of Arnold set up an absolute dichotomy between private character and overriding "real" values, without admitting the active, mediating role of history and society. In this view, to be loved and appreciated, to experience freedom and meaning, Arnold would need first the strength to overcome the severe limitations that presently make him seem worthless; and then he would need somehow to embody the ideals held up to him as sacred.

The consequences of this ethic, which he has inherited and fully embodied, are exemplified in his eventual transformation into the physically beautiful Achilles. His transformation (he thinks) marks his first step toward social acceptance and love, and therefore toward personal fulfillment; it gives him a near perfect human form and bestows on him unsurpassed physical skills as well, enabling him to overcome those individual deficiencies that previously had limited him and made him the scorn of other people. That he understands his heroic acquisitions in moral rather than selfish terms is evidenced in his initial exclamation as Achilles: "I love, and I shall be beloved! Oh, life! / At last I feel thee! Glorious spirit" (I.i.421–22). Yet, once he has actually achieved his idealized vision of himself, his desire for love modulates rapidly into a wish to go "Where the World / Is thickest" (I.i.494–95), or as his accomplice, the Stranger, realistically states it, where "the whole race are just now / Tugging as usual at each other's hearts" (I.i.500–501). And once he finds his way into the thick world, moreover, he begins to display gross selfishness and inhumanity. As a soldier in action, for instance, not only does he insist on preceding his commander, Bourbon, into battle but he also fights with savage disdain of bodily injury and even skirmishes bitterly with his own soldiers when they beat him to the spoils of war. He proceeds relentlessly until he becomes the single greatest living man, blatantly superior to his fellow soldiers and in complete possession not only of fallen Rome but also of Olimpia, Rome's most beautiful and distinguished survivor.

Although he confesses at one point that his path to glory "Has been o'er carcasses" (I.ii.2), he never realizes that there has been a radical change in his thinking. Worse, he never realizes that his actions, from the moment of his transformation into Achilles, produce the exact reverse of what he most desires. His inability to evaluate experience accurately and to discriminate such significant shifts of thought illuminates the true object of his desire. His consuming effort to free himself from all restraints and thereby to confirm his real virtue translates into his strong need to embody an image of himself that always stands just outside experience as he knows it; *he envies what he might be,* and this of course always precludes satisfaction with what he is (even if he is Achilles and the conqueror of Rome). In the final, incomplete section of the drama the Stranger makes this point explicit:

> *The Stranger:* You are jealous.
> *Arnold:* And of whom?
> *The Stranger:* It may be of yourself, for Jealousy
> Is as a shadow of the Sun. The Orb
> Is mighty—as you mortals deem—and to
> Your little Universe seems universal;
> But, great as He appears, and is to you,
> The smallest cloud—the slightest vapour of
> Your humid earth enables you to look
> Upon a Sky which you revile as dull;
> Though your eyes dare not gaze on it when cloudless.
> Nothing can blind a mortal like to light.
> Now Love in you is as the Sun—a thing
> Beyond you—and your Jealousy's of Earth—
> A cloud of your own raising. (III.i.69–82)

This view of Arnold's character explains why he sees his persistent campaign to make himself "the superior of the rest" (I.i.317) as both moral and consistent with his original desires, and why at the same time he becomes increasingly frustrated with every achievement. His ongoing search for his elusive and ever changing Self steadily destroys his public or social awareness, and necessitates the continual redefinition of values in progressively narrow terms. Like Mary Shelley's Frankenstein, his motives and goals are honest but sadly misguided by an isolating subjectivism, and thus doom him to confusion and despair.

The dangers of self-idealization, associated here with the character of Arnold, are presented as well in some of Byron's earlier poems, and it may be helpful to consider them briefly in this context. "Ode from the French," written shortly after the Battle of Waterloo, depicts Napoléon's rise to greatness and his subsequent demise, emphasizing that the powerful general's downfall was due at least partly to his diminishing understanding that accompanied his successful military exploits. Though beginning with a sincere desire to secure France's liberty, and building a broad power base from popular support, Napoléon gradually became consumed by his lust for ever greater control over those he was fighting to defend; and once "goaded by Ambition's sting, / The Hero sunk into the King" ("Ode from the French" [32–33]).[82] This transformation from noble hero into despised conqueror involved a steadily narrowing vision to the point of private desire only, and the poem would have Napoléon realize this: "I [Napoléon] have warred with a World which vanquished me only / When the meteor of conquest allured me too far" ("Napoléon's Farewell" [5–6]). He is depicted similarly in *Childe Harold* 3. To achieve his increasingly private vision of greatness he was compelled to ignore public concerns; he became obsessed with his own accomplishments, losing touch with the masses of people who were the ultimate source of his greatness. And finally, when he became "A God unto thyself" (*Childe Harold* 3, xxxvii), he became vulnerable.[83]

The Deformed Transformed expands the subjectivist and self-idealizing perspective associated in these poems with Napoléon by depicting in greater detail its social implications. These implications are pursued primarily through the mysterious and often misunderstood character of the Stranger. With bitterness and cynicism unrivaled even by the narrator of *Don Juan*, the Stranger assails those idealizations which pass for truth and which deny the social dimension of the most cherished human values. He makes the drama more than a psychological curiosity, more than a study in the disparity between individual ideals and actions, by insisting that every facet of human life is vitally connected with every other; that every act, on some level, has both public motive and consequence; and that the pervasive violence around him traces directly to ignorance of these facts.

The Stranger's role as spokesperson for the realities of everyday social life is established from the beginning. His initial appearance as a black man emerging from a smoke screen immediately causes Arnold

to suspect him of being a diabolical figure (I.i.85). Conventional oc-
cultish descriptions associate him both with soul-selling (I.i.144) and
with the standard devilish blood-compact (I.i.154). But this entire
scene is farcical, a devil-man encounter only because Arnold insists
on making it one. It is Arnold, after all, who labels the Stranger a
devil—a term, incidentally, applied earlier in the drama to Arnold
himself (I.i.40ff.)—and it is Arnold who introduces the issue of soul-
selling, as well as the blood-compact. The Stranger does nothing more
than play along good-humoredly with Arnold's wild surmisings and
accusations, occasionally providing revealing glimpses into Arnold's
shallowness. (For example, while Arnold never realizes it, the Stranger
lambastes conventional notions of devil-man agreements by accepting
blood from an accidental rather than self-inflicted wound.) He is not so
easily made into the devil that Arnold perceives him to be; and if he is a
tempter, he is so in the same way Lucifer is a tempter in *Cain*: "I tempt
none, / Save with the truth" (*Cain*, I.i.196–97). He functions mainly as
a satirical practical consciousness, remaining throughout essentially a
truth-representing force who sees through the assumptions, motives,
and goals that bind Arnold's character and society at large, and who
offers a sometimes bitter, sometimes humorous commentary on the
limited views that perpetuate social strife and injustice.[84]

The Stranger criticizes Arnold's purely private ethic and establishes his own opposing perspective by transforming himself into
Arnold's old, deformed shape. By confidently embracing the body
which Arnold disdainfully rejects as "horrible" (I.i.482), the Stranger
condemns Arnold's belief that his difficulties are entirely physical,
but more importantly he asserts the unavoidable truth of historical
context. Although Arnold prefers to forget his past, even to deny it,
the Stranger insists upon its continuing influence. According to the
Stranger, Arnold's deformity is biological fact and thus cannot be refused or ignored, despite Arnold's total commitment to beauty and
truth. In this view, the Stranger's transformation is much more than
cynicism in action: it is positive criticism that places a supposed individual matter in its proper historical perspective. It is a corrective, a
bitterly realistic statement of what Arnold must understand if he hopes
to survive. As the play bears out, only at his own peril can Arnold
ignore the Stranger's wisdom.

Central to the Stranger's philosophy—and in contrast to Arnold's
thinking—is the assumption that social relations are the basic principle

of human life, and that failure to understand their truth and absolute priority produces humanity's alienation. This view develops with increasing poignancy as the Stranger witnesses the impact of Arnold's self-absorption. The Stranger maintains that Arnold is discontented, even after his transformation, because he "know[s] no better than the dull / And dubious notice of your eyes and ears" (II.ii.14–15). And what is true for Arnold is true in general; humanity "thinks chaotically" (I.ii.318) about social relations. Society, the Stranger emphatically states, is all-embracing, created by people, and connected by human thought and actions on every level; the many elements of social life—language, religion, art, law, and morals—are a single, unified *human* product. Any system of values (such as the idealist one to which Arnold subscribes) that divides the social properties of human existence from one another and from basic individual concerns must ultimately collapse:

> [People] have built
> More Babels, without new dispersion, than
> The stammering young ones of the flood's dull ooze,
> Who fail'd and fled each other. Why? why, marry,
> *Because no man could understand his neighbors.* (I.i.676–80; italics mine)

The drama sharpens this focus and establishes Arnold's thinking as part of a set of social relations by moving the action to Rome, which manifests socially those issues heretofore manifested personally in Arnold's character. The city shows how extreme individualism and idealist thinking can both control life and breed pestilence through an entire culture. Built upon the most extreme selfishness—"Rome's earliest cement / Was brother's blood" (I.ii.83–84)—the city symbolizes in both its art and religion Western culture's most esteemed values. This biting irony is captured in the Stranger's running commentary, which describes in gory detail the vile contradictions embedded in Roman culture. The Stranger does not merely lament the sack of the ancient city at the hands of Charles of Bourbon, but rather explains it as an inevitable result of a system of values that has actually sanctified violence and caused strife through the course of Western history.[85]

In its description of Rome the drama concentrates on art and religion to express the Roman experience. But it stresses that these are not simply passive reflections of Rome's character. While they do indeed powerfully articulate a set of values, they also operate as rigid controls, holding those values in place by reacting back on every facet of human experience.

This point becomes clear in the play's brief but telling depiction of Benvenuto Cellini, one of the most representative of Italian Renaissance sculptors. In fewer than fifteen lines the drama introduces and dismisses Cellini, as though the artist were an afterthought or a minor concern. But the brief treatment accomplishes several very significant tasks. First, it allows Byron to mention an otherwise unacknowledged major source for the play; his description of the sack of Rome is taken directly from Cellini's autobiography.[86] But, more significantly, the presence and role of Cellini provide a compelling analysis of art in its social context. By having the sculptor simply appear and disappear without forewarning or comment, Byron creates the impression that there is no need to question the artist's actions. Cellini's noble, even ethereal sculpture speaks for itself, attesting to his belief in the values and ideals of Roman culture; in common with his fellow Romans, he would naturally defend this culture against siege.

But as a source for the play, the autobiography provides a behind-the-scenes look at Cellini and a gloss on the real significance of his art. Cellini's defense of Rome was not exactly what we commonly regard as natural, patriotic, and noble. His involvement was vigorous, to be sure, but not because he was inspired by high purpose and patriotic passion; according to his own account he was motivated by his love for bloodshed and physical violence. Three passages from the autobiography illustrate his character:

> [D]irecting my arquebuse where I saw the thickest and most serried troop of fighting men, I aimed exactly at one whom I remarked to be higher than the rest. . . . When we had fired two rounds apiece, I crept cautiously up to the wall, and observing among the enemy a most extraordinary confusion, I discovered afterwards that one of our shots had killed the Constable of Bourbon; and from what I subsequently learned, he was the man whom I had first noticed above the heads of the rest.
>
> I fired, and hit my man exactly in the middle. He had trussed his sword in front, for swagger, after a way those Spaniards have; and my ball when it struck him, broke upon the blade, and one could

see the fellow cut in two fair halves. The Pope, who was expecting nothing of this kind, derived great pleasure and amazement from the sight.

I was perhaps more inclined by nature to the profession of arms than to the one [sculpture] I had adopted, and *I took such pleasure in its duties that I discharged them better than those of my own art.* [italics mine][87]

Cellini's art stands in direct contrast to this savage mockery of human life. His best work—the *Nymph of Fontainebleau*, the *Apollo and Hyacinth*, even the violent *Perseus*—is ornate, intricate, and sensitive, and enthusiastically celebrates the beauty of the nude human figure. Defective as much of the sculpture is, it offers an impassioned vision of unchanging beauty and truth (the very ideals that Arnold early in the play had admired) that is characteristic of so much Italian Renaissance art.[88] In relying on the autobiography, however, Byron's play is not simply depicting the grave disparity between Cellini's personal character and art in order to call attention to a psychological curiosity; rather, it focuses on the ideological function of art. Cellini's sculpture in all its grandeur embodies the highest values to which Roman culture aspired. The universal laws of beauty upon which it insists mystify actual experience—including the violence to which Cellini is partner—and thus mask the ugly machinations of the culture from which it grew. In this way it actually shapes and controls individual expectations, preventing a true knowledge of society.

The drama's depiction of Cellini, however, does not dismiss all art out of hand as deceptive or useless; nor does it suggest that biography is the determining property of the value of art. Rather, it deplores the common tendency of ignoring the contextual nature of art, suggesting that to do so is to reduce artistic expression to a largely ideological function of endorsing existing power structures (if only tacitly by throwing obstacles in the way of social and political awareness). Viewed as the sacred preserver of transhistorical, timeless ideals, art relegates to virtual insignificance complex social relations, thus radically limiting people's social knowledge and social power. The drama implies that if it is to realize its full human potential, art must be understood as a social product within a full network of social relations. By presenting Cellini as a momentary, almost intrusive element in the action, the play punctuates our persistent ignorance of this social dimension, and implies that outside its social and historical context Cellini's art is mere abstraction, an illusion that ever further alienates people from their real social world.

Religion serves essentially the same ideological function as art. It is a structurally coherent system that both mirrors a society's noblest principles and at the same time creates social attitudes consistent with the prevailing structures of a specific social authority. The drama captures this vital connection between religious belief and social reality, and traces the pervasive trouble and discord that plague Western culture to a set of values protected by Christian religion. This radical position is evidenced in the Stranger's sporadic jibes at Christianity (for instance, II.i.137ff., 161–62), but Byron makes the point vivid by moving the play's climactic and goriest scene into the interior of St. Peter's Church. This scene magnifies the gross contradictions that Roman society allows to go unquestioned and that somehow are upheld and even sanctified by prevailing attitudes.

The Stranger has carefully guided Arnold to the very center of Western culture, and now exposes him to "the two great professions" (II.iii.30)—of priest and soldier—which are its most powerful representatives. It becomes evident in St. Peter's Church that Arnold's character cannot be understood in purely psychological terms; he is shown to be merely one participant in a sick culture. Ignorance, violence, and noble rhetoric are pervasive and presented indiscriminately, constituting an uncamouflaged savage critique of the motivating values that have stood behind Arnold's character from the beginning. The cries for "eternal glory" (II.iii.22) and the pleas "In the holy name of Christ" (II.iii.6) justify murder and plunder; the altar becomes both a place of death and a vantage point for killing (see, for instance, the various stage directions in this scene); and even the crucifix is used as a murder weapon (II.iii.63ff.). This scene represents the play's most extreme and inclusive statement about the power and pervasiveness of ideology. The events in St. Peter's Church bring to a head the Stranger's contention that alienation and social strife trace directly to the comprehensive system of values that determine human actions and hopes. From the very start of the play he has maintained that idealist thinking governed by assumptions of transhistorical truth is destructive, and that deeds are the only true measure of human virtue (I.i.151–52). And here his point is made convincingly, as the desperate struggle for love, honor, glory, and beauty—for a permanently ennobling ideal—totally deadens Arnold and the warring soldiers to genuine human compassion (see, for instance, the exchange between Arnold and Olimpia, II.iii.105ff.), and makes them contributors to public chaos and madness.

The play's final fragmentary section restates in simpler terms the issues that have been presented heretofore, namely that Arnold's unhappiness results from his obsessive search for "the Philosopher's stone" (III.i.57), that his desire in fact is for self-idealization (III.i.69–82), and that social relations alone are redemptive and truly meaningful (III.i.99–101). But the play does not develop these concerns beyond what is suggested in the first two acts, perhaps because Byron feared that the introduction of Olimpia threatened to reduce the larger social interests to a simple love relationship. Still, even in its fragmentary state *The Deformed Transformed* stands as a radical and compelling analysis of the powerful function of ideology. It bitterly records the fundamental contradictions at the core of Western culture that are concealed by the specific structures of social authority and belief. These contradictions—as the depictions of Arnold and of Rome graphically illustrate—produce alienation and perpetuate a social system that demands human sacrifice.

CHAPTER

৵ৡ৵

10

"The Act Seals All"

Conclusion

Before offering a final set of general remarks about the place of drama in the historical study of Romanticism, I want to comment briefly on Keats's *Otho the Great* (1819), an important drama omitted from examination in the above chapters only because I have written in the past at some length about its historical and social dimensions.[1] In recalling here certain details of the main argument of my earlier discussion, I hope to suggest the relevance of *Otho* to any historical study of English Romantic drama and, more specifically, to recall once more the concentration of much Romantic drama on the deteriorating social authority of aristocracy.

Among the many rich historical interests in *Otho*—ranging from religion to patriarchy, from love to madness—is its primary and intelligent consideration of the material and ideological dimensions of feudal state authority. Specifically, it elaborates the contradictions between that authority's representation of its own interests and values and the actual political apparatus in place to preserve itself. These issues unfold on at least two levels in the plot action. First, the story begins with a description of the just-ended military confrontation between Hungary and Otho's Germany in the tenth century and describes the apparent benevolence of the victorious Otho toward Gersa, a captured Hungarian soldier. Second, the military conflict finds a corollary trauma in the relationship between Otho and his prodigal son, Ludolph, who (according to one of Keats's possible historical sources) led an unsuccessful revolt against his father,[2] but who, at the time of the action described in the drama, fights secretly on behalf of Germany against Hungary. This loyal activity wins for Ludolph the affection of his father, who embraces his son warmly upon welcoming him back into the good graces of state and family.

Both of these plot-level episodes focus on an important dimension of state authority, namely its exercise of both physical and ideological force to maintain and extend its command of German society. As the drama compellingly demonstrates, when the contradictions of social life intensify to the point of threatening the prevailing structures of authority—as they necessarily do in the tightly controlled world ruled by Otho—military force is called in as a proper, order-restoring response. The preferred force of social control, however, is ideological in nature (as exemplified most clearly in Otho's ostensible benevolence toward Gersa and Ludolph), not only because ideological authority is socially more palatable but also because it publicly demonstrates the ability of the state to incorporate dissidence into itself and therefore gives the appearance of integrity and liberality. Thus it is that Otho, while relying on military force when he must, throughout attempts to control society by showing that the specific political interests of the state he governs are consistent with the personal interests of individuals.

One remarkable feature of the drama is that it recognizes and exposes the impossibility of Otho's position, revealing the contradictions inherent in the German state's own representation of itself and of the better interests of society. As both Keats's historical sources and the text of his drama emphatically show, the benevolent authority of which Otho is so fond is ineluctably tied to the violent abuse of people, though he makes every effort to hide this fact. He pardons Gersa, for example, not simply because he has a generous heart but because he knows that Gersa had not been a conspirator against him; as he puts it, with the pardon of Gersa "a marble column do I build / To prop my empire's dome" (I.ii.160–61).[3] The same is true with his warm and fatherly handling of Ludolph, which is motivated, at least partly, by his knowledge that Ludolph had fought secretly on behalf of Germany in the recent Hungarian uprising. Only after verbally toying with his son, using the most violent terms—"No, obstinate boy, you shall be kept cag'd up, / Serv'd with harsh food, with scum for Sunday-drink"

(II.i.88–89)—that is, only after emphasizing in the grossest terms the boundlessness of his authority, does Otho pardon Ludolph and embrace him once more as a member of the family and citizen of the state. Clearly, the real power of Otho's regime, despite the ruler's many expressions of humane regard for others, is grounded ultimately in tight physical control over both the political and everyday structures of social life; his leadership is compassionate only in self-description and only after all opposition has been entirely crushed.

The contradiction between ideological representation and material reality is tracked through the course of the plot action, and is shown to increase in intensity until it explodes the stability that Otho has insistently (and convincingly) associated with his position as emperor. In tracking this growing contradiction the drama discloses a full range of anxiety-ridden feudal relations, including religion, family life, law, marriage, and so on. While its portrayal of these relations is silent about class conflict or about the threat to an old aristocracy by an emergent, hostile, and external social force, the drama effectively displays—in its presentation of these feudal relations among the larger contradictions of feudal society—the internal erosion of feudalism; in its final portrayal of Ludolph's madness, indeed, we recognize that personal and historical moment when neither material nor ideological authority is sufficient any longer to preserve social stability.

The abiding concerns of the preceding chapters have been to show that Romantic drama is haunted by class anxiety and social instability and to elaborate the various social relations that become visible through a materialist critique of that anxiety. From *The Borderers*, where an aristocratic worldview is shown to be under fire from the modern intellect of Rivers, to *The Deformed Transformed*, where the old structures of authority in Western culture are tracked to their source in Rome and exposed in all their dehumanizing atrocity, the dramas are shaped by the fact of historical change from aristocratic to bourgeois forms of social life. Even when they do not place class conflict at the level of plot or theme (as, for instance, in *Halidon Hill, Otho the Great*, or *Heaven and Earth*), they vividly describe both vicious, threatening turmoil and paralyzing convictions of imminent doom in their social worlds, thus encouraging historically minded readers to investigate the deeper structures of social life that may account for the intimations of mortality besieging the characters who inhabit those worlds. I have tried to show that the result of such dramatic description is a body of work that is rich in social and historical significance.

At the same time, the very details that make the dramas ripe for historical investigation make them problematic for literary critics who like their literature formally stable and stylistically consistent. Historically prepared to describe the activities and values of an aristocratic world in the early nineteenth century, while facing the hard realities of a triumphant bourgeoisie, drama was incapable of presenting a sharply defined worldview or of sustaining a strong and stable dramatic voice. From a purely formal point of view, Romantic drama was fatally injured by its inability to negotiate these competing sets of historical pressure—it suffered defeat along with the worldview that had given it life during the Renaissance. As Raymond Williams remarks, the result is that "the period from 1750 to 1850 is the most barren in our dramatic history, if it is work of any lasting value we are looking for."[4] As if to assure that the drama of the period will continue to be seen as lacking durable value, most scholars and critics of Romanticism have complacently ignored it, written only disparagingly about it, or studied it only for its expressions of conventional Romantic themes and attitudes.

But Williams's comment, while certainly accurate in a narrowly critical sense—many of these dramas, such as *Halidon Hill*, are simply difficult to like—too readily accepts the standard portrayal of Romantic drama as a form unable to bear close investigation. As the above chapters demonstrate, the specific historical situation that Williams rightly adduces to explain the unhappy fate of Romantic drama in literary history is not simply an external authority that assigns death to certain literary forms while energizing and valorizing others. That historical situation is necessarily inscribed in those literary forms most vulnerable to its pressure. That is, although Romantic drama had a vested interest in social structures of value and belief that were on the verge of extinction by the early nineteenth century, it is not a simple literary record of a dead or dying world. Rather, it is a complicated, historically dense record of the struggle between competing structures and relations of social life. Class, religion, family, personal life, state, law, economics, labor, gender, and more: these social relations were all transformed during the transition from aristocratic to bourgeois structures of authority and belief, and one record of that transformation is Romantic drama. Further, the anxieties, violence, and fear accompanying the structural change of social life haunt Romantic drama, which compellingly (if at times awkwardly) reveals the astonishing scope of that change during the Romantic period. For this reason, rather than dismissing it, historical criticism and scholarship should recover Romantic drama from the margins of literary history and subject it to systematic historical explanation. Such an effort—to which the present study is meant to contribute—would bring into the light of literary history the social historical imperatives that not only govern Romantic drama, but also all other literary forms of the period.

NOTES

1 Toward a Theory of Romantic Drama

1. A younger generation of scholars and critics has, in one way or another, absorbed these ideological biases in their own work. Jerome J. McGann discusses these biases in *The Romantic Ideology: A Critical Investigation*, especially 19, 21–24, 59–63.

2. For a discussion of these matters in terms of categories put forward by Michel Foucault, see Clifford Siskin, *The Historicity of Romantic Discourse*.

3. McGann's *Romantic Ideology* is now the standard work on this topic.

4. I am here offering a thumbnail sketch of now common ideas. For a thorough discussion of these and related matters, see, for instance, Marjorie Levinson, Marilyn Butler, Jerome McGann, and Paul Hamilton, *Rethinking Historicism: Critical Readings in Romantic History*; Marjorie Levinson, *Keats's Life of Allegory*; and Fredric Jameson's important theoretical work, *The Political Unconscious: Narrative as a Socially Symbolic Act*.

5. See Joseph W. Donohue, Jr., *Dramatic Character in the English Romantic Age*; Terry Otten, *The Deserted Stage: The Search for Dramatic Form in Nineteenth-Century England*; and Erika Gottlieb, *Lost Angels of a Ruined Paradise: Themes of Cosmic Strife in Romantic Tragedy*.

6. I want to be clear here that I am not offering a negative assessment of the outstanding work of Cox, Burwick, and Richardson, but rather attempting to situate their arguments within recent critical debates over Romanticism. It should be mentioned as well that Cox's recent work shows that he is acutely aware of the sorts of issues I am raising and that he engages directly certain

materialist questions that bear on the study of Romantic drama. See especially his fine essay, "Ideology and Genre in the British Antirevolutionary Drama of the 1790s," 579–610.

7. Lamb's famous comment, directed specifically to the work of Shakespeare, reads as follows: "It may seem a paradox, but I cannot help being of opinion that the plays of Shakespeare are less calculated for performance on a stage, than those of almost any other dramatist whatever. Their distinguishing excellence is a reason that they should be so. There is so much in them, which comes not under the province of acting, with which eye, and tone, and gesture, have nothing to do. . . . But the practice of stage representation reduces everything to a controversy of elocution." See Charles Lamb, "On the Tragedies of Shakespeare," in *The Complete Works and Letters of Charles Lamb*, 291–92.

8. For excellent considerations of these questions, see John D. Kinnaird, *William Hazlitt: Critic of Power*, 167–71; and Marilyn Gaull, *English Romanticism: The Human Context*, 81–108.

9. The relations between drama and theater in the Romantic period have been discussed in detail by Terence A. Hoagwood, "Prolegomenon for a Theory of Romantic Drama," 49–64; and by Greg Kucich, " 'A Haunted Ruin': Romantic Drama, Renaissance Tradition, and the Critical Establishment," 64–76. Both essays appear in a special issue of *The Wordsworth Circle* on Romantic drama. Also on this subject, see Gaull, *English Romanticism*, 81–108.

10. Christopher Caudwell, *Illusion and Reality: A Study of the Sources of Poetry*, 108.

11. G. V. Plekhanov, *Art and Social Life*, 14.

12. John Fekete, *The Critical Twilight*, 6.

13. Raymond Williams, *The Long Revolution: An Analysis of the Democratic, Industrial, and Cultural Changes Transforming Our Society*, 264.

14. Ibid., 263.

15. For an excellent discussion of these matters, see Hoagwood, "Prolegomenon"; Kucich, " 'A Haunted Ruin' "; and Gaull, *English Romanticism*. For an excellent and useful discussion of Coleridge's attempts to reform the stage, see Julie Carlson, "Command Performances: Burke, Coleridge, and Schiller's Dramatic Reflections on the Revolution in France," 117–34.

16. Kenneth Neill Cameron, *Shelley: The Golden Years*, 396.

17. I take the term political unconscious from Jameson, *The Political Unconscious*.

18. Raymond Williams, *The Sociology of Culture*, 164.

19. Lucien Goldmann, *Towards a Sociology of the Novel*, 13.

20. Ibid., 14.

21. For a discussion of the social dimensions of *Cain*, see Terence A. Hoagwood's forthcoming book *Byron's Dialectic: Skepticism and the Critique of Culture*.

See also Edward E. Bostetter, *The Romantic Ventriloquists: Wordsworth, Coleridge, Keats, Shelley, Byron*, 282–91. For a discussion of the social dimensions of *The Cenci*, see Michael H. Scrivener, *Radical Shelley: The Philosophical Anarchism and Utopian Thought of Percy Bysshe Shelley*, 187–96.

22. The phrase appears both in *The Borderers* (III. v. 1496) and in *The Prelude*, and in both places it carries explicit political associations. In *The Borderers*, Rivers says to Mortimer:

> You have taught mankind to seek the measure of justice
> By diving for it into their own bosoms.
> To day you have thrown off a tyranny
> That lives but by the torpid acquiescence
> Of our emasculated souls, the tyranny
> Of moralists and saints and lawgivers.
> You have obeyed the only law that wisdom
> Can ever recognize: the immediate law
> Flashed from the light of circumstances
> Upon an independent Intellect. (III. v. 1486–96)

In *The Prelude* Wordsworth describes his early enthusiasm for the French Revolutionary period in strikingly similar terms:

> What delight!
> How glorious! in self-knowledge and self-rule
> To look through all the frailties of the world,
> And, with a resolute mastery shaking off
> Infirmities of Nature, time, and place,
> Build social upon personal Liberty,
> Which, to the blind restraints of general Laws
> Superior, magisterially adopts
> One guide, the light of circumstances, flashed
> Upon an independent intellect. (XI. 235–44)

The reference to *The Prelude* is taken from William Wordsworth, *The Fourteen-Book "Prelude."* All references to *The Borderers* are taken from William Wordsworth, *The Borderers*, ed. Robert Osborn. Act, scene, and line numbers are cited parenthetically in the text.

23. Wordsworth's early attitude toward political violence is explicitly evident in the following quotation from his letter to the bishop of Llandaff: "Alas! the obstinacy & perversion of men is such that she [Liberty] is too often obliged to borrow the very arms of despotism to overthrow him, and in order to reign in peace must establish herself by violence." This passage appears in William Wordsworth, *The Prose Works of William Wordsworth*, ed. W. J. B. Owen and Jane Worthington Smyser, 1:33.

24. See Reeve Parker, " 'Oh Could You Hear His Voice!': Wordsworth, Coleridge, and Ventriloquism," 125–43; and Theresa Kelley, *Wordsworth's Revisionary Aesthetics*, 72–90. Both of these studies explore the ways in which action and identity are formed by language. My concern is quite different, focusing instead upon how language, under certain circumstances, comes to be seen as having authority over the determining power of social relations.

For an excellent historical analysis of *The Borderers*—one that is considerably more thorough than what I can offer here—see Alan Liu, *Wordsworth, The Sense of History*, 225–310 passim.

25. Fekete, *Critical Twilight*, 20.

26. All quotations from the second edition of the *Lyrical Ballads* are taken from Wordsworth, *Prose Works of William Wordsworth*, vol. 1. Page numbers are cited parenthetically in the text.

27. Fekete, *Critical Twilight*, 4.

28. For a helpful, brief discussion of the importance of *The Borderers* in terms of Wordsworth's developing conservative vision, see James K. Chandler, *Wordsworth's Second Nature: A Study of the Poetry and Politics*, 227–29.

2 Samuel Taylor Coleridge's Osorio

1. Coleridge's sensitivity to the political nature of his poetry can be seen in a comment he made to William Lisle Bowles concerning the *Ode*: "My Ode you will read with a kindly forbearance as to it's [sic] political sentiments.— The base of our politics is, I doubt not, the same. We both feel strongly for whomever our imaginations present to us in the attitude of suffering.—I confess, that mine is too often a *stormy* pity." Samuel Taylor Coleridge, *Collected Letters of Samuel Taylor Coleridge*, ed. Earl Leslie Griggs, 1:318. All subsequent references to Coleridge's letters are cited in the text as *LC*.

2. See John Colmer, *Coleridge: Critic of Society*, 49–52.

3. For excellent discussions of the connections between *Osorio* and Coleridge's politics in the 1790s, see Carl Woodring, *Politics in the Poetry of Coleridge*, 204–5; and Paul Magnuson, *Coleridge and Wordsworth: A Lyrical Dialogue*, 52–66.

4. See Coleridge's letter to Sheridan in February 1797: "I received a letter last Saturday from a friend of the Revd W. L. Bowles, importing that *You* wished me 'to write a tragedy on some popular subject.' I need not say, that I was gratified and somewhat elated by the proposal; and whatever hours I can win from the avocations, by which I earn my immediate subsistence, shall be sacred to the *attempt*" (*LC*, 1:304).

5. Magnuson is particularly good on drawing out this theme of the drama. See Magnuson, *Coleridge and Wordsworth*, 60–62.

6. On the critical tendency to duplicate Romantic values and attitudes, see Jerome J. McGann, *The Romantic Ideology: A Critical Investigation*.

7. Robert Weimann, *Structure and Society in Literary History: Studies in the History and Theory of Historical Criticism*, 6.

8. This quotation is taken from the stage note at the beginning of the play. This and all quotations from *Osorio* are taken from Samuel Taylor Coleridge, *The Complete Poetical Works of Samuel Taylor Coleridge*, ed. Ernest Hartley Coleridge, vol. 2. Act, scene, and line numbers are presented parenthetically in the text.

9. Coleridge's most immediate source for *Osorio* is Robert Watson, *The History of the Reign of Philip the Second, King of Spain*, 1:341–66. While it is not my intention to offer a source study of *Osorio*, I should mention that in this work many of the names Coleridge uses in his drama appear in Watson's history, including Velez, though Coleridge has altered their roles for the sake of dramatic need and action.

The violence enacted against the Moors, and about which Coleridge remains silent, is described vividly by Watson as follows:

Philip had disapproved of the lenity with which the Morescoes had
been treated by the marquis of Mondejar, and, while he listened only
to the voice of superstition or resentment, forgot what every wise
King will regard as the most sacred maxim of his policy, that the
strength and glory of a prince depend on the number and prosperity of
his subjects.

But this bigoted monarch set no bounds to his abhorrence of those
who deviated, or whom he suspected of deviating, from the Catholic
faith. Agreeably to his instructions, great numbers of the Morescoes,
living peaceably in the plains of Granada, were, upon suspicion of
their corresponding with the insurgents, put to death. All the inhabitants of some villages and districts, men, women, and children, were
extirpated. All the prisoners of both sexes were either executed or
deprived of their liberty. And of those Morescoes who had refused
to join in the rebellion, all but a few, without whom certain manu-
factures could not be carried on, were torn from their native homes,
and transported into the interior provinces; where they were exposed
to the injuries and insults of a haughty people, and many of them
by their poverty reduced to a state of dependence on the Castilians,
which differed little from the condition of such of their countrymen as
had been sold for slaves. (1:364–65)

10. Byron's Gulnare (see *The Corsair*, 1814) displays many of the same characteristics as Alhadra—courage, willingness to act, bold conviction—and, as
with Alhadra, is one of the most interesting female figures in Romantic literature. For a discussion of the social significance of Gulnare's character see

Daniel P. Watkins, *Social Relations in Byron's Eastern Tales*, 83–85; and Susan Wolfson, "Couplets, Self, and *The Corsair*," 491–513.

11. Note, for instance, her remark in Act III, as she feels herself drawn to the disguised Albert:

> This dead confused pain! [*A pause—she gazes at* Albert.]
> Mysterious man!
> Methinks, I cannot fear thee—for thine eye
> Doth swim with pity—I will lean on thee. (III. 145–47)

Her regard for Albert is here accompanied by willing dependence upon him.

12. For a very different view of Alhadra's final speech, see John Beer, *Coleridge's Poetic Intelligence*. Beer views the drama's ending as a call for bloodshed and therefore as cynical:

> After the long clash of Moorish and Catholic forces in the play, she [Alhadra] . . . delivers the final speech, announcing that if she had a band of suitable men she would destroy all the strongholds of the cruel,
>
> > Till desolation seem'd a beautiful thing,
> > And all that were and had the spirit of life
> > Sang a new song to him who had gone forth
> > Conquering and still to conquer!
>
> Such an ending explicitly affirms the "spirit of life" only to assert that before the spirit can assert itself properly in such a place, bloodshed must be endured. The logic of drama, with its need for a strong ending, has enforced a final dominant note that is sardonic and even borders on the cynical. (110–11)

3 Joanna Baillie's DeMonfort

1. Stuart Curran, "The I Altered," 185–86.

2. For an example of the typical critical attitude toward Baillie's work, see Om Prakash Mathur's remark that "She tends to forget the man in her passion, and so even within the limited range of passions she attempted to portray, the main characters seem to be in line with case-histories reported in medical bulletins rather than human beings with whom we come in contact every day." *The Closet Drama of the Romantic Revival*, 315; or W. L. Renwick's dismissive comment about Baillie that "No real dramatist would deliberately sit down to write a whole series of *Plays on the Passions*." *English Literature 1789–1815*, 232. For a more favorable assessment, see Bertrand Evans, *Gothic Drama from Walpole to Shelley*, 200–215.

3. Curran, "The I Altered," 203.

4. It is true, of course, that at the level of plot Rezenvelt is located securely within the ranks of the aristocracy: he is a marquis who, according to Jane DeMonfort's comment toward the end of the play, will likely be buried "with his noble ancestors" (V.iv). But his social position, which gives his character credibility within the plot action, must be distinguished from the ethic, or structure of values, that defines his relation to other characters and to his world; that ethic is uniquely bourgeois insofar as it is shaped and energized by self-interest, consumerism, and competition.

5. All quotations are from Joanna Baillie, *DeMonfort*, in *British Theatre: Eighteenth-Century English Drama*, ed. Natascha Wurzbach, vol. 20. Act and scene numbers are cited parenthetically in the text.

6. It is worth remarking that the portrayal of gender relations in this scene reflects a common concern among some feminists in the 1790s with a masculine tendency to treat women merely as ornaments and objects, lacking the ability to think or act as men do. Mary Wollstonecraft's *A Vindication of the Rights of Women* specifically discusses the means by which socially powerless women attempt to attach themselves to masculine power. See Mary Wollstonecraft, *The Works of Mary Wollstonecraft*, ed. Janet Todd and Marilyn Butler, vol. 5.

7. In these respects, the relationship between Jane and DeMonfort not only recalls some of the details of Coleridge's *Osorio*, but also looks forward to the semi-incestuous relationships depicted in Byron's poetry, for example the Selim-Zuelika affair in *The Bride of Abydos*, or the Hugo-Parisina affair in *Parisina*. For a discussion of the social dimension of incest in these works, see Daniel P. Watkins, *Social Relations in Byron's Eastern Tales*, 51–52, 134–35.

8. Other writers of the Romantic period made more explicit statements about the effect of large-scale societal structures on individual life. Note, for instance, Wordsworth's letter to the bishop of Llandaff defending the French Revolution; Mary Wollstonecraft, *Vindication of the Rights of Men*, in *Works of Mary Wollstonecraft*, vol. 5; and William Godwin, *An Inquiry Concerning Political Justice and Its Influence on Morals and Happiness*, ed. F. E. L. Priestley.

9. I am, of course, here using the vocabulary of contemporary feminism. See, among other works, Simone de Beauvoir's *The Second Sex*, especially xix–xxv, 160–63.

10. Evans, *Gothic Drama from Walpole to Shelley*, 200.

4 Charles Lamb's John Woodvil

1. Om Prakash Mathur, *The Closet Drama of the Romantic Revival*, 328. Mathur goes on to remark that "the very soul of the drama is . . . diseased" (328). See also A. H. Thorndike, *Tragedy* (London, 1908), who calls the drama

silly (343); and W. L. Renwick, *English Literature 1789–1815*, who sees it as an unequivocal failure (233).

2. One singular exception is Joseph Nicholes's important essay, "Politics by Indirection: Charles Lamb's Seventeenth-Century Renegade, John Woodvil," 49–55. Among the recent good work on Lamb over the past twenty years or so, see especially Winifred F. Courtney, *Young Charles Lamb, 1775–1802*; Gerald Monsman, *Confessions of a Prosaic Dreamer: Charles Lamb's Art of Autobiography*; George L. Barnett, *Charles Lamb*; Wayne McKenna, *Charles Lamb and the Theater*; and John I. Ades, "Charles Lamb, Shakespeare, and Early Nineteenth-Century Theater," 514–26.

3. The general point I am making here is related, in ways that will become clear shortly, to Raymond Williams's larger argument about the declining and emergent elements of culture. See Raymond Williams, *Marxism and Literature*, 120–27.

4. Lamb, of course, is a major critic of Shakespearean and Renaissance drama, and he and his sister, Mary, brought out several important editions of Renaissance drama, as well as rewriting many of Shakespeare's plays to make them accessible to children. See, for instance, their children's volume *Tales from Shakespeare*, or Charles Lamb's essay "On the Tragedies of Shakespeare," in *The Complete Works and Letters of Charles Lamb*.

5. Mathur, *The Closet Drama of the Romantic Revival*, 329. For an outstanding discussion of the historical relations between Renaissance and Romantic drama, see Greg Kucich, " 'A Haunted Ruin': Romantic Drama, Renaissance Tradition, and the Critical Establishment."

6. W. L. Renwick, *English Literature 1789–1815*, 233. This particular relation is explored intelligently in Nicholes's "Politics by Indirection."

7. I am thinking here of Lewis's *Castle Spectre*, which treats such pressing political issues as racism and slavery within a context of a melodramatic and action-driven plot, and Shelley's *Prometheus Unbound*, which idealizes and displaces onto mythic structures actual historical struggle and political conflict.

8. All quotations from *John Woodvil* are taken from the Modern Library edition of Charles Lamb, *The Complete Works and Letters of Charles Lamb*, 426–57. Act and scene numbers are cited parenthetically in the text.

9. This is admittedly a rather confusing scene that may be read as a prelude to a plan to reveal Sir Walter's whereabouts. Certainly this is the way old Sandford reads their comments as he overhears their conversation. Even so, the overall intent of the scene appears to me to reflect the servants' admiration for Sir Walter; Sandford's accusations, which immediately follow their speculations on Sir Walter's hiding place, reflect the old steward's intense fear that his last hope of social stability, and hence personal integrity, is being threatened.

10. One example of the sort of character that has come to define John Wood-

vil's world is Harry Freeman, whose politics are defined entirely in terms of alcohol. The exchange between Freeman, Woodvil, and Lovel illustrates this world perfectly:

> *Freeman* (who is drunk): Honest Jack Woodvil,
>   I will get drunk with you to-morrow.
> *Woodvil:* And why to-morrow, honest Mr. Freeman?
> *Freeman:* I scent a traitor in that question. A beastly question.
>   Is it not His Majesty's birthday? the day of all days
>   in the year, on which King Charles the Second
>   was graciously pleased to be born.
>   *(Sings.)* "Great pity 'tis such days as
>   those should come but once a year."
> *Lovel:* Drunk in a morning; foh! how he stinks!
> *Freeman:* And why not drunk in a morning? canst tell, bully?
> *Woodvil:* Because, being the sweet and tender infancy of the day,
>   methinks, it should ill endure such early blightings.
> *Freeman:* I grant you, 'tis in some sort the youth and tender
>   nonage of the day. Youth is bashful, and I give it
>   a cup to encourage it. (II.i)

11. Raymond Williams, *Problems in Materialism and Culture*, 80.

12. See Christopher Caudwell, *Illusion and Reality: A Study of the Sources of Poetry*, 108; and John Fekete, *The Critical Twilight*, 6.

13. This language may be too strong to describe Margaret accurately in the early portions of the play, but I am thinking of the stage note in Act I that describes her "as in a fright, pursued by a Gentleman," and of John Woodvil's belittling remarks about her after she has left him: "Gone! gone! my girl? so hasty, Margaret! / . . . / . . . Foolish wench" (II.i).

5 Henry Hart Milman's Fazio

1. See Henry Hart Milman, *The History of the Jews from the Earliest Period Down to Modern Times*, 1:9–10; and Henry Hart Milman, *History of Latin Christianity, Including That of the Popes to the Pontificate of Nicholas V*, 1:v–vi.

2. Perhaps the most famous example of the historicist thought during this period is David Friedrich Strauss's *Das Leben Jesu (The Life of Jesus)*.

3. Quotations from *Fazio* are taken from Henry Hart Milman, *The Poetical Works of the Rev. H. H. Milman*, vol. 3. Act and scene numbers are cited parenthetically in the text.

4. I am here drawing upon Marx's discussion of commodity fetishism: "Value, therefore, does not stalk about with a label describing what it is. It is value, rather, that converts every product into a social hieroglyphic. Later

on, we try to decipher the hieroglyphic, to get behind the secret of our own social products; for to stamp an object of utility as a value, is just as much a social product as language." See Karl Marx, *Capital: A Critique of Political Economy*, 1:79.

5. The comments on patriarchy that follow are influenced, most immediately, by Veronica Beechey, *Unequal Work*, 95–116. But see also Zilla R. Eisenstein, *The Radical Future of Liberal Feminism*, 14–26.

6. Hidden in these contradictions is an even greater irony that would be a proper subject for future consideration, namely that the duke, an aristocrat from a clearly feudal tradition, oftentimes in the drama sounds very much like the defender of bourgeois values.

6 Charles Robert Maturin's Bertram

1. Ian Jack, *English Literature 1815–1832*, 181.

2. Bertrand Evans, *Gothic Drama from Walpole to Shelley*, 192–99. Note his remark, for instance, that "mere failure to relate *Bertram* to that large share of the eighteenth century represented by the Gothic tradition would perhaps not in itself be a grave matter. But this failure illustrates a general misconception which is important. To misjudge the relation of *Bertram* to the Gothic tradition is to misjudge the relation of the Byronic in general to that tradition" (199).

3. Joseph W. Donohue, Jr., *Dramatic Character in the English Romantic Age*, 88–89.

4. Dale Kramer, *Charles Robert Maturin*, 69.

5. See Willem Scholten, *Charles Robert Maturin: The Terror-Novelist*, 30–42, which offers a summary of the play's plot, a consideration of Maturin's borrowing from Schiller, Scott, and others, and a discussion of preproduction revisions of the drama that were urged upon Maturin; Robert E. Lougy's brief comments on Maturin's revisions and upon the extreme popularity of the drama, *Charles Robert Maturin*, 44–49; and Jeffrey Cox's more recent and fine discussion of *Bertram* in his book, *In the Shadows of Romance: Romantic Tragic Drama in Germany, England, and France*, 119–26.

6. Samuel Taylor Coleridge, *Biographia Literaria, or Biographical Sketches of My Literary Life and Opinions*, ed. James Engell and W. Jackson Bate, 211. Subsequent references appear parenthetically in the text.

7. To cite only two examples, note the Hesperus-Olivia marriage in Thomas Lovell Beddoes's *The Brides' Tragedy* and the Elvira–Conde de las Cisternas marriage in Matthew Lewis's *The Monk*. For a discussion of class issues in these works, see the chapter on *The Brides' Tragedy* below; and Daniel P. Watkins, "Social Hierarchy in Matthew Lewis's *The Monk*," 115–24.

8. Quotations are from Charles Robert Maturin, *Bertram*, in *British Theatre:*

Eighteenth-Century English Drama, ed. Natascha Wurzbach, vol. 19. Act and scene numbers are cited parenthetically in the text.

9. To say this, of course, is not to deny the importance of individuals but to insist upon their absolute importance within the context of social life.

10. It should be noted that one main difference between Maturin's handling of cross-class marriage in the Gothic imagination of 1816 and Matthew Lewis's handling of it in *The Monk* in 1795 is that Lewis condemns it, resolving social tensions by re-creating an aristocratic and stable world which excludes all other classes from the realm of real social authority. Maturin, on the other hand, does not seek any sort of resolution, allowing his play to end on a note of utter violence and social and religious confusion—which, of course, explains Coleridge's particular condemnation of Maturin's work. For a discussion of this matter in Lewis, see Watkins, "Social Hierarchy in Matthew Lewis's *The Monk*."

11. Maturin's handling of this issue of class authority anticipates Byron's treatment of it in *Werner* (see chapter 9), where Byron's aristocratic hero possesses little individual identity and autonomy.

12. To cite only one example of Bertram's defiant attitude toward religion, note the prior's attempt to convince him to seek mercy after Saint Aldobrand has been murdered:

Bertram: Why art thou [the prior] here?—There was an hovering angel
Just lighting on my heart—and thou hast scared it—
Prior: Yea, rather with my prayers I'll woo it back,
In very pity of thy soul I come
To weep upon that heart I cannot soften—
(A long pause.)
Oh! thou art on the verge of awful death—
Think of the moment, when the veiling scarf
That binds thine eyes, shall shut out earth for ever—
When in thy dizzy ear, hurtless the groan
Of those who see the smiting hand upreared,
Thou canst but feel—that moment comes apace—
(Bertram smiles.)
But terrors move in thee a horrid joy,
And thou art hardened by habitual danger
Beyond the sense of aught but pride in death.
(Bertram turns away.)

13. My general thinking about the significance of punishment in the drama has been influenced by Michel Foucault's *Discipline and Punish: The Birth of the Prison*, though certainly my interpretive comments do not trace to Foucault.

These have been influenced rather by (among others) Eli Zaretsky's argument about the historical formation of subjectivity and Antonio Gramsci's comments on the social functions of law. See Eli Zaretsky, *Capitalism, the Family, and Personal Life*; and Antonio Gramsci, *Selections from the Prison Notebooks*, especially 195–96, 246–53.

14. Zaretsky, *Capitalism, the Family, and Personal Life*, 40.

15. For an excellent discussion of the interpretive and reception history of the *Rime*, see Jerome J. McGann, "The Meaning of the Ancient Mariner," 35–67.

16. Coleridge, *Biographia Literaria*, 286.

7 *Thomas Lovell Beddoes's* The Brides' Tragedy

1. For studies pursuing one or both lines of argument, see Northrop Frye, *A Study of English Romanticism*, 51–55; James R. Thompson, *Thomas Lovell Beddoes*, 24–41; Lytton Strachey, "The Last Elizabethan," in *Books and Characters: French and English*, 235–65; and Harold Bloom, *The Visionary Company: A Reading of English Romantic Poetry*, 428–34. While these conventional explanations may help to clarify certain isolated psychological or literary historical matters, at the same time they run the risk of distorting literary history in their attempt to find a suitable vocabulary for discussing the drama. To identify *Bride* primarily in terms of Jacobean tragedy, for instance, is to forget that the central feature of most Jacobean tragedies is the destructive power of lust; in *Bride* this is not the case. Hesperus's murder of Floribel is encouraged not at all by lust but rather by jealousy in conjunction with the incarceration of Hesperus's father and by the larger domestic and social situations flowing from these. Moreover, the argument that Beddoes's obsession with death in the drama represents the end of Romanticism is confusing when we consider that earlier Romantic works—for instance, *The Monk* or even the *Rime of the Ancient Mariner*, both written in the 1790s—are as extreme in their portrayal of these matters as *Bride*, and that works written in the later nineteenth century—for instance, James Thomson's "City of Dreadful Night" (1874) and Thomas Hardy's *Jude the Obscure* (1898)—are equally given to physical violence and existential despair. If the work signals the demise of Romanticism, it is for reasons other than those most often cited.

Two studies that, in my view, provide more helpful considerations of *Bride* are Horace Gregory, "The Gothic Imagination and the Survival of Thomas Lovell Beddoes," 81–95; and especially Eleanor Wilner's excellent historical assessment of Beddoes in *Gathering the Winds: Visionary Imagination and Radical Transformation of Self and Society*, 73–106.

2. For an excellent discussion of this dark side of the Romantic imagina-

tion, from a psychological perspective, see Edward E. Bostetter, *The Romantic Ventriloquists: Wordsworth, Coleridge, Keats, Shelley, Byron.*

3. Quotations from *Bride* are taken from Thomas Lovell Beddoes, *The Works of Thomas Lovell Beddoes*, ed. H. W. Donner. Act, scene, and line numbers are cited parenthetically in the text.

4. Eli Zaretsky, *Capitalism, the Family, and Personal Life*, 70.

5. Ibid., 71.

6. Ibid., 40.

7. It should be noted that Hesperus's jealousy when he catches Floribel kissing Orlando's page is created as much by the patriarchal pressure from his father to wed Olivia as by his selfish and bourgeois desire to possess Floribel absolutely apart from the world.

8. This disempowerment, while enduring from an aristocratic to bourgeois social formation, gets redefined in ways that Olivia cannot here see. As suggested in the above descriptions of Hesperus, the isolation of the woman from female companionship involves at the same time her conversion into an ideal of pure value divorced from the world, a conversion which secures the individual subjectivity and power of men.

9. Zilla R. Eisenstein, *The Radical Future of Liberal Feminism*, 25. My general arguments here regarding the distinctions between bourgeois and bourgeois patriarchy draw very heavily on Eisenstein, especially 14–49.

8 Sir Walter Scott's Halidon Hill

1. In addition to composing four dramas, Scott also translated several dramas from German, including August Wilhelm Iffland's *Die Mundel*, Jakob Maier's *Füst von Stromberg*, Steinberg's adaptation of Joseph Franz Marius von Babo's *Otto von Wittelsbach*, and Friedrich von Schiller's *Fiesko*. See Duncan M. Mennie, "Sir Walter Scott's Unpublished Translations of German Plays," 234–39. See also Om Prakash Mathur's brief discussion of the translations in *The Closet Drama of the Romantic Revival*, 280–82.

2. An account of the composition of the drama can be found in J. G. Lockhart, *Memoirs of the Life of Sir Walter Scott, Bart.*, 2:267–68.

3. Note, for instance, the dramas of Byron (*Sardanapalus, The Two Foscari,* and *Marino Faliero*) that portray the debilitating impact on cultures of internal conflict. Keats approaches a similar view in *Otho the Great*, and Shelley in *The Cenci*.

4. On this latter point, note Swinton's stern reminder to the complaining Reynald: "Peace, Reynald! Where the general plants the soldier, / There is his place of honour, and there only / His valour can win worship. Thou'rt of those, / Who would have war's deep art bear the wild semblance / Of

some disorder'd hunting" (I.i). Quotations from *Halidon Hill* are taken from Sir Walter Scott, *Scott: Poetical Works*, ed. J. Logie Robertson. Act and scene numbers are cited parenthetically in the text.

5. For a very brief discussion of the economic dimension of the Crusades, see Carl L. Becker, *Modern History: The Rise of a Democratic, Scientific, and Industrialized Civilization*, 28–30. See also Aziz Suryal Atiya, *Crusades, Commerce, and Culture*; and Edward W. Said, *Orientalism*, passim.

6. He did not leave England seeking fortune but was in fact cast out by his countrymen. Note Chandos's remark to Percy, in response to a comment by Baliol lamenting the violent military defeat of his former countrymen: "His conquerors, he means, who cast him out / From his usurped kingdom" (II.i).

7. For a sketch of some of these matters, see David Erdman's excellent essays on Byron: "Byron and Revolt in England," 234–48; "Byron and 'the New Force of the People,'" 47–64; "'Fare Thee Well'—Byron's Last Days in England," 203–27; "Lord Byron and the Genteel Reformers," 1065–94; and "Lord Byron as Rinaldo," 189–231. See also A. D. Harvey's excellent social history of early nineteenth-century England, *Britain in the Early Nineteenth Century*.

8. The reference here is to Hob Hattely, who remarks to Swinton: "It is my purpose, / Having lived a thief, to die a brave man's death; / And never had I a more glorious chance for it" (II.iii).

9 The Dramas of Lord Byron

1. The best work on Byron's relation to Shakespeare is G. Wilson Knight, *Byron and Shakespeare*.

2. Susan Wolfson has begun to examine in detail the function of gender in Byron's work, including the drama. See, for instance, her fine essay, "'A Problem Few Dare Imitate': *Sardanapalus* and 'Effeminate Character.'"

3. All quotations from Byron's letters and journals are taken from Lord Byron, *Byron's Letters and Journals*, ed. Leslie A. Marchand, and appear in the text as *BLJ*.

4. Note, for instance, Shelley's comment to Mary Shelley that Byron had adopted "a system of criticism fit only for the production of mediocrity," Percy Bysshe Shelley, *The Letters of Percy Bysshe Shelley*, ed. Frederick L. Jones, 2:317. All quotations from Shelley's letters are from this edition and are cited parenthetically in the text as *LPBS*.

5. For a detailed study of Byron's developing political attitude, see David V. Erdman's painstakingly researched essay, "Lord Byron and the Genteel Reformers"; see also his excellent essays on Byron, "'Fare Thee Well'—Byron's Last Days in England," and "Lord Byron," 161–227.

6. See Leslie A. Marchand, *Byron: A Portrait*, 341; see also *BLJ*, 8:45–46.

7. See Aristotle's *Politics*, Book 2, in his *Works*, ed. W. D. Ross, 10:1260–74. Byron may have had Aristotle's ideas directly before him in the works of Samuel Johnson. See especially *The Rambler*, no. 154, in which Johnson states: "The Direction of *Aristotle* to those that study Politicks, is, first to examine and understand what has been written by the Antients upon government, then to cast their Eyes round upon the world, and consider by what Causes the Prosperity of Communities is visibly influenced, and why some are worse and others better administered" (*The Rambler*, ed. Donald D. Eddy, 2:917).

8. Christopher Caudwell, *Illusion and Reality: A Study of the Sources of Poetry*, 105.

9. Note, for instance, Scott's assessment of Byron:

Our sentiments agreed a good deal, except upon the subjects of religion and politics, upon neither of which I was inclined to believe that Lord Byron entertained very fixed opinions. On politics he used sometimes to express a high strain of what is now called Liberalism; but it appeared to me that the pleasure it afforded him as a vehicle of displaying his wit and satire against individuals in office was at the bottom of this habit of thinking. At heart, I would have termed Byron a patrician of principle. (John Nichol, *Byron*, 80–81)

Hazlitt's assessment, though more severe, also interprets Byron's politics in terms of personality. For Hazlitt, Byron's expressed political position was insincere, no more than another example of his wish "to shine by contrast": "His [Byron's] ruling motive is not the love of the people, but of distinction; not of truth, but of singularity." In short, for Hazlitt Byron was "a pampered egotist." William Hazlitt, *Complete Works of William Hazlitt*, ed. P. P. Howe, 9:70–77.

10. This funny but very serious poem appears in Lord Byron, *Lord Byron: The Complete Poetical Works*, ed. Jerome J. McGann, vol. 4. That it expresses much more than simply contempt for Hobhouse's association with "the mob" has been convincingly argued by David V. Erdman in "Byron and 'the New Force of the People,'" 57ff. For the difficulties the poem caused Byron see *BLJ*, 7:99, 104.

11. I am relying here mainly on E. P. Thompson, *The Making of the English Working Class*, 451–71. Note also R. W. Harris's comment that "After 1807 Cobbett, Sir Francis Burdett, Major Cartwright, Orator Hunt and Francis Place were the leading Radicals, and none of them was a revolutionary. Their way out of the perplexing difficulties of the time lay through parliamentary reform." *Romanticism and the Social Order, 1780–1830*, 77.

12. Quoted in Harris, *Romanticism and the Social Order*, 77. It should be remarked that such comments as this notwithstanding, Cobbett did in fact support labor unions, especially later in his career as he became increasingly

radicalized, though he resisted all *violent* political activism. For Cobbett's views on unions, see Raymond Williams, *Culture and Society, 1780–1950,* 16–18.

13. Williams, *Culture and Society,* 19. Cobbett's statement (quoted in ibid., 13) dates from 1807. For Cobbett's changing attitude, see Thompson, *Making of the English Working Class,* 459.

14. For a discussion of *Cain* in the light of its pressing and immediate political concerns, see Edward E. Bostetter, *The Romantic Ventriloquists: Wordsworth, Coleridge, Keats, Shelley, Byron,* 282–91. See also Terence A. Hoagwood, *Byron's Dialectic: Skepticism and the Critique of Culture.*

15. It should be noted that while Byron was usually critical of the radicals, he nonetheless selectively used their writings and ideas in his own work. Note, for instance, his reading of Cobbett's *Political Register* during the composition of *The Age of Bronze* (1823). It should be noted as well that in the 1818 Westminster elections Cobbett supported Cartwright over Byron's friend Hobhouse; it is possible that this event helped to shape Byron's prejudices.

16. On this topic, see Edward Dudley Hume Johnson, "A Political Interpretation of Byron's *Marino Faliero,*" 417–25; and Leslie A. Marchand, *Byron's Poetry: A Critical Introduction,* 101.

17. The quotation is from the introduction to Alan Bullock and Maurice Shock, eds., *The Liberal Tradition from Fox to Keynes,* xxi. The enduring influence of certain liberals on Byron is seen, for instance, in the fact that the epigraph to Byron's *The Two Foscari* is taken from Sheridan's *The Critic.*

18. That artists and intellectuals often endorse on a deep level the very ideas that they reject on another level has been noted frequently. See, for instance, G. V. Plekhanov, *Art and Social Life,* passim; or Antonio Gramsci, *Selections from the Prison Notebooks,* 333.

19. Indeed, it is precisely this problem that historically has troubled liberal thought. For example, liberals have attempted repeatedly to resolve their assumption of an antithesis between individual and society, as well as their conflicting support for both full democracy and a powerful ruling class. Even John Stuart Mill's famous clarification of liberalism as a defense of intellectual and moral freedom rather than of political freedom has not been satisfactory, as the subsequent writings of T. H. Green and Leonard Hobhouse (among others) have shown. On this issue see Bullock and Shock, eds., *The Liberal Tradition from Fox to Keynes,* xxxiv–lv. For an excellent general study of the crisis of liberalism in our own century see George Dangerfield, *The Strange Death of Liberal England, 1910–14.*

20. For a discussion of the Eastern Tales from a historical materialist perspective, see Daniel P. Watkins, *Social Relations in Byron's Eastern Tales.*

21. Jerome J. McGann has noted this particular characteristic of Byron's imagination. See Jerome J. McGann, *"Don Juan" in Context,* ix.

22. Arnold Hauser, *The Social History of Art: Rococo, Classicism, Romanticism*, 3:170.

23. Friedrich Schlegel, *Lectures on the History of Literature Ancient and Modern*, 33.

24. Ibid., 422.

25. Thomas Campbell, *Cyclopoedia of English Poetry*, 59–60.

26. His attitude toward the love theme is made explicit in *The Deformed Transformed*, which breaks off precisely at that moment when love intrudes and threatens to become a dominant issue.

27. On Byron's adherence to the dramatic unities see Samuel C. Chew, *The Dramas of Lord Byron*.

28. It is curious, and indicative of his method of selection, that Byron here is quoting from Dryden (as represented in Samuel Johnson's *Lives of the Poets*), who relies very heavily on the love theme in his own tragedies.

29. In *BLJ*, 8:218, for instance, Byron states that his dramas are more in line with Alfieri's system than with the English.

30. Quotations from *Cain* are taken from Truman Guy Steffan, ed., *Lord Byron's "Cain": Twelve Essays and a Text with Variants and Annotations*.

31. For an interesting discussion of crime that may have influenced Byron, see Aristotle's *Politics*, Book 2.

32. I am here, of course, echoing Karl Marx in his preface to *A Contribution to the Critique of Political Economy*, 21.

33. I omit *Cain* from this discussion because between them Bostetter and Hoagwood have already covered much of the ground that I consider to be most important to understanding that play's social dimensions. See Bostetter, *Romantic Ventriloquists*; and Hoagwood, *Byron's Dialectic*.

34. Marchand, *Byron: A Portrait*, 252–53.

35. Bostetter, *Romantic Ventriloquists*, 278.

36. For a sustained and persuasive analysis of the relations between the world of spirits and psychological and biographical considerations, see Stuart Sperry, "Byron and the Meaning of 'Manfred,'" 189–202.

37. All quotations from *Manfred* are taken from Byron, *Complete Poetical Works*, vol. 4. Act, scene, and line numbers are cited parenthetically in the text.

38. M. I. Finley, "Utopianism Ancient and Modern," 3–20.

39. See, for example, Byron's letter to John Murray, August 12, 1820, which refers to the "male Tadpole of Poet Turdsworth" (*BLJ*, 7:158).

40. Erdman, "Byron and 'The New Force of the People,'" 54.

41. See, for instance, Boleslaw Taborski, *Byron and the Theatre*, 108ff.; Marchand, *Byron's Poetry: A Critical Introduction*, 98–101; Peter J. Manning, *Byron and His Fictions*, 107–22; Jerome J. McGann, *Fiery Dust: Byron's Poetic Development*, 205–16; Edward Dudley Hume Johnson, "A Political Interpretation of Byron's

Marino Faliero," 417–25; Thomas L. Ashton, "*Marino Faliero*: Byron's 'Poetry of Politics,' " 1–13; and Carl Woodring, *Politics in English Romantic Poetry*, 181–86. More recent studies have begun to provide helpful discussion of the play's social dimensions. See especially A. B. England, "Byron's *Marino Faliero* and the Force of Individual Agency," 95–122.

42. All quotations from *Marino Faliero* are taken from Byron, *Complete Poetical Works*, vol. 4. Act, scene, and line numbers are cited in the text.

43. Quoted in Byron's preface to the play. See Byron, *Complete Poetical Works*, 4:301.

44. Chew, *Dramas of Lord Byron*, 92.

45. B. G. Tandon, *The Imagery of Lord Byron's Plays*, 68.

46. M. K. Joseph, *Byron the Poet*, 113; Paul West, *Byron and the Spoiler's Art*, 102; and Woodring, *Politics in English Romantic Poetry*, 181.

47. Andrew Rutherford, *Byron: A Critical Study*, 186. The dramatic action, indeed, is largely mental. Note Byron's letter to Murray in August 1821: "I want to make a *regular* English drama—no matter whether for the Stage or not—which is not my object—but a mental theatre" (*BLJ*, 8:186–87).

48. McGann, *Fiery Dust*, 207.

49. Francis M. Doherty, *Byron*, 97; and Manning, *Byron and His Fictions*, 135.

50. Quotations from *Sardanapalus* are taken from Byron, *Works of Lord Byron: Poetry*, vol. 5. Act, scene, and line numbers are cited in the text.

51. For a helpful discussion of these and other matters as they relate to the issue of gender, see Wolfson, " 'A Problem Few Dare Imitate': *Sardanapalus* and 'Effeminate Character,' " 867–902.

52. McGann, *Fiery Dust*, 218.

53. See, for instance, Chew, *Dramas of Lord Byron*, 100; Marchand, *Byron's Poetry*, 102; or John W. Ehrstine, *The Metaphysics of Byron: A Reading of the Plays*, 69.

54. Quotations from *The Two Foscari* are taken from Byron, *Works of Lord Byron: Poetry*, vol. 5. Act, scene, and line numbers are cited parenthetically in the text.

55. See McGann's comments in *Fiery Dust*, 220.

56. See the exchange between Loredano and Barbarigo (I.i.9–18), or Marina's comments to the doge (II.i.156–67, 181–83).

57. Bostetter, *Romantic Ventriloquists*, 287.

58. Bostetter sums up *Cain's* social interests in this way: "The tyrant God with his mask of benevolence was incorporated into the social structure. The determinism implied in the story of the Fall—that the human race must forever suffer for the wilful disobedience of its progenitors, except for whatever alleviation God in his mercy is willing to provide—was used to achieve acquiescence of the individual in his particular lot and to ensure the preservation and stability of traditional social organization. Any probing or questioning of

the myth became a threat to the social order and to individual tranquility, and so all persons combined to turn on the questioner and silence him or drive him out." Ibid., 286–87. See also Steffan's essay in his *Lord Byron's "Cain,"* 26–65; and W. Z. Hirst, "Byron's Lapse into Orthodoxy: An Unorthodox Reading of *Cain*," 151–72.

59. All quotations from *Heaven and Earth* are taken from Byron, *Works of Lord Byron: Poetry*, vol. 5. Act, scene, and line numbers are cited parenthetically in the text.

60. It should be noted that this sentiment recalls the Romantic preoccupation with the dying world and the last, isolated individual in that world. See, for instance, the writings of Thomas Campbell, Mary Shelley, and Byron himself (in *Darkness*).

61. See Chew, *Dramas of Lord Byron*, v. Note also Robert F. Gleckner's more recent comment that *Werner* is mainly "melodramatic claptrap," in *Byron and the Ruins of Paradise*, 318n. A more positive and to my mind more credible assessment of the play has been offered by Manning in *Byron and His Fictions*, 159–70.

62. For contemporary negative assessments see the reviews in *The Edinburgh Monthly Review, The British Critic, Lady's Magazine, Literary Chronicle and Weekly, Monthly Censor, Monthly Magazine, Monthly Review, New Monthly Magazine*, and *Scott's Magazine*, compiled in Donald H. Reiman, ed., *The Romantics Reviewed: Contemporary Reviews of British Romantic Writers. Part B: Byron and Regency Society Poets*.

63. Quoted in Reiman, *Romantics Reviewed*, 4:1656.

64. With respect to psychological readings of the play, E. H. Coleridge's introductory comments are typical: "the *motif*—a son predestined to evil by the weakness and sensuality of his father, a father punished for his want of rectitude by the passionate criminality of his son, is the very key-note of tragedy" (Byron, *Works of Lord Byron: Poetry*, 5:328). As appealing as this assessment may be, it is entirely misleading. Note, for instance, that Ulric is a bandit *before* he is faced with his father; and Werner is strong rather than weak insofar as he defies convention in marrying beneath himself. Further, it is important to remember that Werner's weakened character is that of a man who has been penniless for twelve years. Such personal and social facts as these, I believe, determine the meaning of the play, yet they are ignored by most psychological interpretations.

65. Although he does not explore it in detail, Knight has recognized this connection in the play between individual crime and social reality: "*Werner* comes near to suggesting that we are all potentially, or perhaps inevitably, responsible, directly or indirectly, for crime." See Knight, *Byron and Shakespeare*, 180.

66. There have been numerous, mostly negative, studies of Byron's use of

his sources. I am relying on E. H. Coleridge's introductory comments to the play in Byron, *Works of Lord Byron: Poetry*, 5:325–33; but also see T. H. Vail Motter, "Byron's *Werner* Re-estimated: A Neglected Chapter in Nineteenth Century Stage History," 243–75.

67. It should be noted, however, that Byron is not completely consistent in ordering his materials. References to Prague do appear in these scenes (see, for instance, V.ii.49), violating in some degree the play's coherence. Note E. H. Coleridge's remark: "The Thirty Years' War dates from the capture of Pilsen by Mansfeld, November 21, 1618, and did not end till the Peace of Westphalia, October 24, 1648. The incident recorded in act v, a solemn commemoration of the Treaty of Prague, must have taken place in 1635. But in *Werner* there is little or no attempt 'to follow history' " (Byron, *Works of Lord Byron: Poetry*, 5:340).

68. See Theodore K. Rabb, *The Struggle for Stability in Early Modern Europe*, 119.

69. Georges Pages, *The Thirty Years' War 1618–1648*, 250.

70. Ibid., 17.

71. Hauser, *Social History of Art*, 3:107, 102.

72. Quotations from *Werner* are taken from Byron, *Works of Lord Byron: Poetry*, vol. 5. Act, scene, and line numbers are cited parenthetically in the text.

73. Marx's insight on this subject is helpful: he understands that crime "is not the result of pure arbitrariness," but rather is a sign of "the struggle of the isolated individual against the predominant relations." See Karl Marx, *The German Ideology*, 349.

74. See Marx, *Contribution to the Critique of Political Economy*, 21; note also Louis Wirth's comment that "The most important thing . . . that we can know about a man is what he takes for granted, and the most elemental and important facts about a society are those that are seldom debated and generally regarded as settled." Quoted in the preface to Karl Mannheim, *Ideology and Utopia: An Introduction to the Sociology of Knowledge*, xxii–xxiii.

75. From Karl Marx, *A Contribution to the Critique of Hegel's Philosophy of Right*, in *Karl Marx: Early Writings*, 244.

76. My discussion of the social dynamics of family life is indebted to Eli Zaretsky, *Capitalism, the Family, and Personal Life*.

77. It should be noted that in the context of Werner's world the unspoken horror of Ulric's conduct is not simply that he commits acts of violence, but that he plunders the nobility rather than the lower orders; this is the major distinction between his attitude and Werner's: Werner shows regard for a fixed, hierarchical social structure (note, for instance, his penance for stealing Stralenheim's gold), while Ulric pays allegiance only to individual strength. This constitutes a difference of degree rather than of kind.

78. Mannheim, *Ideology and Utopia*, 3.

79. Erdman's essays on Byron, and Leslie A. Marchand, *Byron: A Biography*, provide excellent discussions of these matters.

80. See, for example, Chew, *Dramas of Lord Byron*, 147; Charles E. Robinson, "The Devil as Doppelgänger in *The Deformed Transformed*: The Sources and Meaning of Byron's Unfinished Drama," 177–202; Manning, *Byron and His Fictions*, 170–74; Bernard Blackstone, *Byron III: Social Satires, Drama and Epic*, 32; and Marchand, *Byron's Poetry*, 94.

81. All quotations from *The Deformed Transformed* are taken from Byron, *Works of Lord Byron: Poetry*, vol. 5. Act, scene, and line numbers are cited parenthetically in the text.

82. Quotations from "Ode from the French" and "Napoléon's Farewell" are taken from Byron, *Complete Poetical Works*, vol. 3. Line numbers are cited parenthetically in the text.

83. Quotations from *Childe Harold* are taken from Byron, *Complete Poetical Works*, vol. 2. Line numbers are cited parenthetically in the text.

84. For the standard critical attitude toward the Stranger see, for example, Marchand, *Byron's Poetry*, 94; or Manning, *Byron and His Fictions*, 170.

85. This point is forcefully stated by the Chorus of Spirits who introduce Part II of the play (II.i. 1–122).

86. E. H. Coleridge mentions in his introduction to *The Deformed Transformed* that "it is evident that he [Byron] was familiar with Cellini's story" (5:471), but he does not pursue Cellini's influence; and Charles E. Robinson's definitive source study of the play fails altogether to mention Cellini.

87. I am quoting from Benvenuto Cellini, *The Life of Benvenuto Cellini, by Himself*, 117–24.

88. My generalizations about Cellini's art are taken from George Henry Chase and Chandler Rathfon Post, *A History of Sculpture*, 343–45; and from Herbert Read, *The Art of Sculpture*, 62–63, 82.

10 Conclusion

1. Daniel P. Watkins, *Keats's Poetry and the Politics of the Imagination*, 121–34.

2. See William Fordyce Mavor, *Universal History, Ancient and Modern: From the Earliest Records of Time, to the General Peace of 1801*, 17:23. For a full discussion of Keats's use of his historical sources in writing *Otho*, see Watkins, *Keats's Poetry and the Politics of the Imagination*, 123–25.

3. Otho explicitly describes to Gersa the reason behind the pardon:

> Still understand me, King of Hungary,
> Nor judge my open purposes awry.
> Though I did hold you in my esteem
> For your self's sake, I do not personate

The stage-play emperor to entrap applause,
To set the silly sort o' the world agape,
And make the politic smile; no, I have heard
How in the Council you condemn'd this war,
Urging the perfidy of broken faith,—
For that I am your friend. (I.ii.139–49)

Quotations from *Otho* are taken from John Keats, *The Poems of John Keats*, ed. Jack Stillinger.

4. Raymond Williams, *The Long Revolution: An Analysis of the Democratic, Industrial, and Cultural Changes Transforming Our Society*, 263.

BIBLIOGRAPHY

Ades, John I. "Charles Lamb, Shakespeare, and Early Nineteenth-Century Theater." *PMLA* 85 (1970): 514–26.

Aristotle. *Politics*. Book 2. Translated by Benjamin Jowett. In *Works*. Edited by W. D. Ross. London: Oxford University Press, 1921.

Ashton, Thomas L. "*Marino Faliero*: Byron's 'Poetry of Politics.' " *Studies in Romanticism* 13 (1974): 1–13.

Atiya, Aziz Suryal. *Crusades, Commerce, and Culture*. Bloomington: Indiana University Press, 1962.

Baillie, Joanna. *DeMonfort*. In *British Theatre: Eighteenth-Century English Drama*. Selected and arranged by Natascha Wurzbach. Vol. 20. Frankfurt: Minerva GMBH, 1969.

Barnett, George L. *Charles Lamb*. Boston: Twayne Publishers, 1976.

Beauvoir, Simone de. *The Second Sex*. Translated by H. M. Parshley. New York: Vintage Books, 1952.

Becker, Carl L. *Modern History: The Rise of a Democratic, Scientific, and Industrialized Civilization*. New York: Silver Burdett, 1931.

Beddoes, Thomas Lovell. *The Brides' Tragedy*. In *The Works of Thomas Lovell Beddoes*. Edited by H. W. Donner. London: Oxford University Press, 1935.

Beechey, Veronica. *Unequal Work*. London: Verso, 1987.

Beer, John. *Coleridge's Poetic Intelligence*. New York: Barnes and Noble, 1977.

Blackstone, Bernard. *Byron III: Social Satires, Drama and Epic*. London: Longman, 1971.

Bloom, Harold. *The Visionary Company: A Reading of English Romantic Poetry*. Revised edition. New York: Cornell University Press, 1971.

Bostetter, Edward E. *The Romantic Ventriloquists: Wordsworth, Coleridge, Keats, Shelley, Byron.* Revised edition. Seattle: University of Washington Press, 1975.

Bullock, Alan, and Maurice Shock, editors. *The Liberal Tradition from Fox to Keynes.* London: Oxford University Press, 1967.

Burwick, Frederick. *Illusion and the Drama: Critical Theory of the Enlightenment and Romantic Era.* University Park: Pennsylvania State University Press, 1991.

Byron, George Gordon, Lord. *Byron's Letters and Journals.* Edited by Leslie A. Marchand. 12 vols. Cambridge, Mass.: Belknap Press of Harvard University Press, 1973–82.

––––––. *Lord Byron: The Complete Poetical Works.* Edited by Jerome J. McGann. Vols. 2, 3, and 4. Oxford: Oxford University Press, 1981, 1986.

––––––. *The Works of Lord Byron: Poetry.* Edited by Ernest Hartley Coleridge. Vols. 5 and 7. London: John Murray, 1900.

Cameron, Kenneth Neill. *Shelley: The Golden Years.* Cambridge, Mass.: Harvard University Press, 1974.

Campbell, Thomas. *Cyclopoedia of English Poetry.* Philadelphia: J. B. Lippincott, 1875.

Carlson, Julie. "Command Performances: Burke, Coleridge, and Schiller's Dramatic Reflections on the Revolution in France." *The Wordsworth Circle* 23 (1992): 117–34.

Caudwell, Christopher. *Illusion and Reality: A Study of the Sources of Poetry.* 1937. Reprint. New York: International Publishers, 1973.

Cellini, Benvenuto. *The Life of Benvenuto Cellini, by Himself.* Translated by John Addington Symonds. New York: Liveright Publishing, 1931.

Chandler, James K. *Wordsworth's Second Nature: A Study of the Poetry and Politics.* Chicago: University of Chicago Press, 1984.

Chase, George Henry, and Chandler Rathfon Post. *A History of Sculpture.* New York: Harper and Brothers, 1925.

Chew, Samuel C. *The Dramas of Lord Byron.* 1915. Reprint. New York: Russell and Russell, 1964.

Coleridge, Samuel Taylor. *Biographia Literaria, or Biographical Sketches of My Literary Life and Opinions.* Edited by James Engell and W. Jackson Bate. Princeton, N.J.: Princeton University Press, 1983.

––––––. *Collected Letters of Samuel Taylor Coleridge.* Edited by Earl Leslie Griggs. Vol. 1. Oxford: Clarendon, 1956.

––––––. *The Complete Poetical Works of Samuel Taylor Coleridge.* Edited by Ernest Hartley Coleridge. Vol. 2. Oxford: Clarendon, 1912.

Colmer, John. *Coleridge: Critic of Society.* Oxford: Clarendon, 1959.

Courtney, Winifred F. *Young Charles Lamb, 1775–1802.* New York: New York University Press, 1982.

Cox, Jeffrey. "Ideology and Genre in the British Antirevolutionary Drama of the 1790s." *ELH* 15 (1991): 579–610.

———. *In the Shadows of Romance: Romantic Tragic Drama in Germany, England, and France.* Athens: Ohio University Press, 1987.

Curran, Stuart. "The I Altered." In *Romanticism and Feminism.* Edited by Anne K. Mellor. 185–207. Bloomington: Indiana University Press, 1988.

Dangerfield, George. *The Strange Death of Liberal England, 1910–14.* 1935. Reprint. New York: Putnam's, 1961.

Doherty, Francis M. *Byron.* New York: Arco, 1969.

Donohue, Joseph W., Jr. *Dramatic Character in the English Romantic Age.* Princeton, N.J.: Princeton University Press, 1970.

Ehrstine, John W. *The Metaphysics of Byron: A Reading of the Plays.* The Hague: Mouton, 1976.

Eisenstein, Zilla R. *The Radical Future of Liberal Feminism.* Boston: Northeastern University Press, 1981.

England, A. B. "Byron's *Marino Faliero* and the Force of Individual Agency." *Keats-Shelley Journal* 39 (1990): 95–122.

Erdman, David V. "Byron and Revolt in England." *Science and Society* 11 (1947): 234–48.

———. "Byron and 'the New Force of the People.'" *Keats-Shelley Journal* 11 (1962): 47–64.

———. "'Fare Thee Well'—Byron's Last Days in England." In *Romantic Rebels: Essays on Shelley and His Circle.* Edited by Kenneth Neill Cameron. 203–27. Cambridge, Mass.: Harvard University Press, 1973.

———. "Lord Byron." In *Romantic Rebels: Essays on Shelley and His Circle.* Edited by Kenneth Neill Cameron. 161–202. Cambridge, Mass.: Harvard University Press, 1973.

———. "Lord Byron and the Genteel Reformers." *PMLA* 56 (1941): 1065–94.

———. "Lord Byron as Rinaldo." *PMLA* 57 (1942): 189–231.

Evans, Bertrand. *Gothic Drama from Walpole to Shelley.* Berkeley: University of California Press, 1947.

Fekete, John. *The Critical Twilight.* London: Routledge and Kegan Paul, 1976.

Finley, M. I. "Utopianism Ancient and Modern." In *The Critical Spirit: Essays in Honor of Herbert Marcuse.* Edited by Kurt H. Wolff and Barrington Moore, Jr. Boston: Beacon, 1968.

Foucault, Michel. *Discipline and Punish: The Birth of the Prison.* Translated by Alan Sheridan. New York: Vintage Books, 1979.

Frye, Northrop. *A Study of English Romanticism.* New York: Random House, 1968.

Gaull, Marilyn. *English Romanticism: The Human Context.* New York: W. W. Norton, 1988.

Gleckner, Robert F. *Byron and the Ruins of Paradise.* Baltimore: Johns Hopkins University Press, 1967.

Godwin, William. *An Inquiry Concerning Political Justice and Its Influence on Morals and Happiness.* Edited by F. E. L. Priestley. 3 vols. Toronto: University of Toronto Press, 1946

Goldmann, Lucien. *Towards a Sociology of the Novel.* Translated by Alan Sheridan. London: Tavistock Publications, 1975.

Gottlieb, Erika. *Lost Angels of a Ruined Paradise: Themes of Cosmic Strife in Romantic Tragedy.* Victoria, B.C., Canada: Sono Nis, 1981.

Gramsci, Antonio. *Selections from the Prison Notebooks.* Translated and edited by Quintin Hoare and Geoffrey Nowell Smith. New York: International Publishers, 1971.

Gregory, Horace. "The Gothic Imagination and the Survival of Thomas Lovell Beddoes." In Horace Gregory, *The Dying Gladiators and Other Essays.* New York: Greenwood, 1968.

Harris, R. W. *Romanticism and the Social Order, 1780–1830.* New York: Barnes and Noble, 1969.

Harvey, A. D. *Britain in the Early Nineteenth Century.* New York: St. Martin's, 1978.

Hauser, Arnold. *The Social History of Art: Rococo, Classicism, Romanticism.* Vol. 3. Translated by Arnold Hauser and Stanley Godman. New York: Vintage Books, 1951.

Hazlitt, William. *Complete Works of William Hazlitt.* Edited by P. P. Howe. Vol. 9. London: J. M. Dent and Sons, 1930–34.

Hirst, W. Z. "Byron's Lapse into Orthodoxy: An Unorthodox Reading of *Cain.*" *Keats-Shelley Journal* 29 (1980): 151–72.

Hoagwood, Terence A. *Byron's Dialectic: Skepticism and the Critique of Culture.* Lewisburg, Penn.: Bucknell University Press, 1993.

———. "Prolegomenon for a Theory of Romantic Drama." *The Wordsworth Circle* 23 (1992): 49–64.

Jack, Ian. *English Literature 1815–1832.* Oxford: Clarendon, 1963.

Jameson, Fredric. *The Political Unconscious: Narrative as a Socially Symbolic Act.* Ithaca, N.Y.: Cornell University Press, 1981.

Johnson, Edward Dudley Hume. "A Political Interpretation of Byron's *Marino Faliero.*" *Modern Language Quarterly* 3 (1942): 417–25.

Joseph, M. K. *Byron the Poet.* London: Victor Gollancz, 1964.

Keats, John. *The Poems of John Keats.* Edited by Jack Stillinger. Cambridge, Mass.: Harvard University Press, 1978.

Kelley, Theresa. *Wordsworth's Revisionary Aesthetics.* Cambridge: Cambridge University Press, 1988.

Kinnaird, John D. *William Hazlitt: Critic of Power.* New York: Columbia University Press, 1978.

Knight, G. Wilson. *Byron and Shakespeare*. New York: Barnes and Noble, 1966.

Kramer, Dale. *Charles Robert Maturin*. New York: Twayne Publishers, 1973.

Kucich, Greg. " 'A Haunted Ruin': Romantic Drama, Renaissance Tradition, and the Critical Establishment." *The Wordsworth Circle* 23 (1992): 64–76.

Lamb, Charles. *The Complete Works and Letters of Charles Lamb*. New York: Modern Library, 1935.

Levinson, Marjorie. *Keats's Life of Allegory*. Oxford: Basil Blackwell, 1988.

Levinson, Marjorie, Marilyn Butler, Jerome McGann, and Paul Hamilton. *Rethinking Historicism: Critical Readings in Romantic History*. Oxford: Basil Blackwell, 1989.

Liu, Alan. *Wordsworth, The Sense of History*. Stanford, Calif.: Stanford University Press, 1989.

Lockhart, J. G. *Memoirs of the Life of Sir Walter Scott, Bart.* 2 vols. Philadelphia, 1838.

Lougy, Robert E. *Charles Robert Maturin*. Lewisburg, Penn.: Bucknell University Press, 1975.

McGann, Jerome J. *"Don Juan" in Context*. Chicago: University of Chicago Press, 1976.

———. *Fiery Dust: Byron's Poetic Development*. Chicago: University of Chicago Press, 1968.

———. "The Meaning of the Ancient Mariner." *Critical Inquiry* 8 (1981): 35–67.

———. *The Romantic Ideology: A Critical Investigation*. Chicago: University of Chicago Press, 1983.

McKenna, Wayne. *Charles Lamb and the Theater*. New York: Harper and Row, 1978.

Magnuson, Paul. *Coleridge and Wordsworth: A Lyrical Dialogue*. Princeton, N.J.: Princeton University Press, 1988.

Mannheim, Karl. *Ideology and Utopia: An Introduction to the Sociology of Knowledge*. Translated by Louis Wirth and Edward Shils. New York: Harcourt, Brace and World, 1936.

Manning, Peter. *Byron and His Fictions*. Detroit: Wayne State University Press, 1978.

Marchand, Leslie A. *Byron: A Biography*. 3 vols. New York: Knopf, 1957.

———. *Byron: A Portrait*. Chicago: University of Chicago Press, 1970.

———. *Byron's Poetry: A Critical Introduction*. Cambridge, Mass.: Harvard University Press, 1968.

Marx, Karl. *Capital: A Critique of Political Economy*. Translated by Samuel Moore and Edward Aveling. Edited by Frederick Engels. Moscow: Progress Publishers, 1954.

———. *A Contribution to the Critique of Political Economy*. Translated by S. W. Ryazanskaya. Moscow: Progress Publishers, 1970.

————. *A Contribution to the Critique of Hegel's Philosophy of Right.* In *Karl Marx: Early Writings.* Translated by Rodney Livingstone and Gregor Benton, 243–57. New York: Vintage Books, 1975.

————. *The German Ideology.* Moscow: Progress Publishers, 1976.

Mathur, Om Prakash. *The Closet Drama of the Romantic Revival.* Salzburg, Austria: Institut für Englische Sprache und Literatur, Universität Salzburg, 1978.

Maturin, Charles Robert. *Bertram.* In *British Theatre: Eighteenth-Century English Drama.* Selected and arranged by Natascha Wurzbach. Vol. 19. Frankfurt: Minerva GMBH, 1969.

Mavor, William Fordyce. *Universal History, Ancient and Modern: From the Earliest Records of Time, to the General Peace of 1801.* Vol. 17. London: R. Phillips, 1802–4.

Mennie, Duncan M. "Sir Walter Scott's Unpublished Translations of German Plays." *The Modern Language Review* 33 (1938): 234–39.

Milman, Henry Hart. *History of Latin Christianity, Including That of the Popes to the Pontificate of Nicholas V.* Vol. 1. London: John Murray, 1864.

————. *The History of the Jews from the Earliest Period Down to Modern Times.* Vol. 1. Boston: William Veazie, 1864.

————. *The Poetical Works of the Rev. H. H. Milman.* Vol. 3. London: John Murray, 1839.

Monsman, Gerald. *Confessions of a Prosaic Dreamer: Charles Lamb's Art of Autobiography.* Durham, N.C.: Duke University Press, 1984.

Motter, T. H. Vail. "Byron's *Werner* Re-estimated: A Neglected Chapter in Nineteenth-Century Stage History." In *Essays in Dramatic Literature: The Parrot Presentation Volume.* Edited by Hardin Craig. 243–75. 1935. Reprint. New York: Russell and Russell, 1967.

Nichol, John. *Byron.* 1880. Reprint. London: Macmillan, 1936.

Nicholes, Joseph. "Politics by Indirection: Charles Lamb's Seventeenth-Century Renegade, John Woodvil." *The Wordsworth Circle* 19 (1988): 49–55.

Otten, Terry. *The Deserted Stage: The Search for Dramatic Form in Nineteenth-Century England.* Athens: Ohio University Press, 1972.

Pages, Georges. *The Thirty Years' War 1618–1648.* Translated by David Maland and John Hooper. 1939. Reprint. New York: Harper and Row, 1970.

Parker, Reeve. " 'Oh Could You Hear His Voice!': Wordsworth, Coleridge, and Ventriloquism." In *Romanticism and Language.* Edited by Arden Reed. 125–43. Ithaca, N.Y.: Cornell University Press, 1984.

Plekhanov, G. V. *Art and Social Life.* Moscow: Progress Publishers, 1977.

Rabb, Theodore K. *The Struggle for Stability in Early Modern Europe.* New York: Oxford University Press, 1975.

Rambler, The. Edited by Donald D. Eddy. New York: Garland Publishing, 1978.

Read, Herbert. *The Art of Sculpture*. Second edition. Princeton, N.J.: Princeton University Press, 1961.

Reiman, Donald, editor. *The Romantics Reviewed: Contemporary Reviews of British Romantic Writers. Part B: Byron and Regency Society Poets*. 5 vols. New York: Garland Publishing, 1972.

Renwick, W. L. *English Literature 1789–1815*. Oxford: Clarendon, 1963.

Richardson, Alan. *A Mental Theater: Poetic Drama and Consciousness in the Romantic Age*. University Park: Pennsylvania State University Press, 1988.

Robinson, Charles E. "The Devil as Doppelgänger in *The Deformed Transformed*: The Sources and Meaning of Byron's Unfinished Drama." *Bulletin of the New York Public Library* 74 (1970): 177–202.

Rutherford, Andrew. *Byron: A Critical Study*. Stanford, Calif.: Stanford University Press, 1961.

Said, Edward W. *Orientalism*. New York: Vintage Books, 1979.

Schlegel, Friedrich. *Lectures on the History of Literature Ancient and Modern*. Edinburgh: William Blackwood and Sons, 1846.

Scholten, Willem. *Charles Robert Maturin: The Terror-Novelist*. Amsterdam: H. J. Paris, 1933.

Scott, Sir Walter. *The Poetical Works of Sir Walter Scott*. Boston: Ira Bradley, n.d.
———. *Scott: Poetical Works*. Edited by J. Logie Robertson. London: Oxford University Press, 1967.

Scrivener, Michael H. *Radical Shelley: The Philosophical Anarchism and Utopian Thought of Percy Bysshe Shelley*. Princeton, N.J.: Princeton University Press, 1982.

Shelley, Percy Bysshe. *The Letters of Percy Bysshe Shelley*. Edited by Frederick L. Jones. Oxford: Clarendon, 1964.

Siskin, Clifford. *The Historicity of Romantic Discourse*. Oxford: Oxford University Press, 1988.

Sperry, Stuart. "Byron and the Meaning of 'Manfred.'" *Criticism* 16 (1974): 189–202.

Steffan, Truman Guy, editor. *Lord Byron's "Cain": Twelve Essays and a Text with Variants and Annotations*. Austin: University of Texas Press, 1968.

Strachey, Lytton. "The Last Elizabethan." In Lytton Strachey, *Books and Characters: French and English*. New York: Harcourt, Brace, 1922.

Strauss, David Friedrich. *The Life of Jesus*. Translated by George Eliot. London, 1846.

Taborski, Boleslaw. *Byron and the Theatre*. Salzburg, Austria: Institut für Englische Sprache und Literatur, Universität Salzburg, 1972.

Tandon, B. G. *The Imagery of Lord Byron's Plays*. Salzburg, Austria: Institut für Englische Sprache und Literatur, Universität Salzburg, 1976.

Thompson, E. P. *The Making of the English Working Class*. 1963. Reprint. New York: Vintage Books, 1966.

Thompson, James R. *Thomas Lovell Beddoes*. Boston: Twayne Publishers, 1985.

Thorndike, A. H. *Tragedy*. London, 1908.

Watkins, Daniel P. *Keats's Poetry and the Politics of the Imagination*. Rutherford, N.J.: Fairleigh Dickinson University Press, 1989.

———. "Social Hierarchy in Matthew Lewis's *The Monk*." *Studies in the Novel* 18 (1986): 115–24.

———. *Social Relations in Byron's Eastern Tales*. Rutherford, N.J.: Fairleigh Dickinson University Press, 1987.

Watson, Robert. *The History of the Reign of Philip the Second, King of Spain*. Vol. 1. London: A. Strahan and T. Cadell, 1794.

Weimann, Robert. *Structure and Society in Literary History: Studies in the History and Theory of Historical Criticism*. Baltimore: Johns Hopkins University Press, 1984.

West, Paul. *Byron and the Spoiler's Art*. London: Chatto and Windus, 1960.

Williams, Raymond. *Culture and Society, 1780–1950*. New York: Harper and Row, 1958.

———. *The Long Revolution: An Analysis of the Democratic, Industrial, and Cultural Changes Transforming Our Society*. New York: Columbia University Press, 1961.

———. *Marxism and Literature*. Oxford: Oxford University Press, 1977.

———. *Problems in Materialism and Culture*. London: Verso, 1980.

———. *The Sociology of Culture*. New York: Schocken Books, 1982.

Wilner, Eleanor. *Gathering the Winds: Visionary Imagination and Radical Transformation of Self and Society*. Baltimore: Johns Hopkins University Press, 1975.

Wolfson, Susan. " 'A Problem Few Dare Imitate': *Sardanapalus* and 'Effeminate Character.' " *ELH* 58 (1991): 867–902.

———. "Couplets, Self, and *The Corsair*." *Studies in Romanticism* 27 (1988): 491–513.

Wollstonecraft, Mary. *The Works of Mary Wollstonecraft*. Edited by Janet Todd and Marilyn Butler. Vol. 5. London: William Pickering, 1989.

Woodring, Carl. *Politics in English Romantic Poetry*. Cambridge, Mass.: Harvard University Press, 1970.

———. *Politics in the Poetry of Coleridge*. Madison: University of Wisconsin Press, 1961.

Wordsworth, William. *The Borderers*. Edited by Robert Osborn. Ithaca, N.Y.: Cornell University Press, 1982.

———. *The Fourteen-Book* "Prelude." Edited by W. J. B. Owen. Ithaca, N.Y.: Cornell University Press, 1985.

———. *The Prose Works of William Wordsworth*. Edited by W. J. B. Owen and Jane Worthington Smyser. Vol. 1. Oxford: Clarendon, 1974.

Zaretsky, Eli. *Capitalism, the Family, and Personal Life*. New York: Harper and Row, 1976.

INDEX

✦

Hatred: social meaning of, 40, 41, 57, 58
Hazlitt, William, 128, 227*n9*
Hoagwood, Terence A., 214*n9*, 214*n21*
Hobbes, Thomas, 182
Hobhouse, John Cam, 138, 139, 227*n10*, 228*n15*
Hobhouse, Leonard, 228*n19*
Hunt, Henry "Orator," 138, 139
Hunt, Leigh, 128, 150
Huntington, Robert, Earl of (Robin Hood), 72

Ideology, 1, 2, 10, 18, 19, 22, 23, 26, 36, 38, 58, 69, 103, 109, 113, 119, 122, 126, 163, 167, 168, 169, 170, 172, 173, 180, 187, 189, 196, 197, 204, 205, 206, 208, 209
Iffland, August Wilhelm, 225*n1*
Imagination, 3, 4, 111, 143, 144
Incest: social meaning of, 33–35, 51–52, 66, 219*n7*
Individualism, 102, 116, 125, 140, 141, 202
Inheritance, 194–95
Inquisition, 24

Johnson, Edward Dudley Hume, 228*n16*
Johnson, Samuel, 145; *Lives of the Poets*, 28; *The Rambler*, 227*n7*

Keats, John, 5, 6, 132, 141, 152, 207; *Eve of St. Agnes*, 129; *Fall of Hyperion*, 7; *Hyperion*, 124; *Lamia*, 119; *Otho the Great*, 88, 207–9
Kelley, Theresa, 12, 216*n24*
Kinnaird, John, 136, 139, 141, 142, 144
Knight, G. Wilson, 231*n65*
Kucich, Greg, 214*n9*

Lamb, Charles, 214*n7*; *John Woodvil*, 4, 60–76
Lamb, Mary, 220*n4*
Language, 11, 12–19, 72–73, 159, 186
Law, 53, 55

Lee, Sophia, 181; *German Tale*, 181
Lewis, Matthew, 62; *Castle Spectre*, 66, 220*n7*; *The Monk*, 111, 222*n7*, 223*n10*, 224*n1*
Liberalism, 140
Llandaff, Richard Watson, Bishop of, 11
Locke, John, 182
Love, 73, 144–45
Luddites, 138
Lukács, Georg, 8
Lyric poetry, 1, 3, 6, 10, 40, 61

McGann, Jerome, 149, 161, 167, 216*n6*
Madness: social meaning of, 87–88, 96, 103, 104–5, 106, 115
Maier, Jacob, 225*n1*
Malthus, Thomas, 141
Mannheim, Karl, 194
Marchand, Leslie, 149
Market economy, 8
Marriage: as a social relation, 97–98, 101, 114, 116, 118–19, 120, 121, 184
Mary Tudor of England ("Bloody Mary"), 24
Marx, Karl, 191, 221*n4*, 232*n73*
Marxism, 5, 6
Mathur, Om Prakash, 218*n2*
Maturin, Charles Robert, 54, 94–110, 145; his *Bertram*, 5, 54, 94–110
Mill, James, 141
Mill, John Stuart, 141, 228*n19*
Milman, Henry Hart, 77–93, 187; his *Fazio*, 5, 10, 77–93
Milton, John, 106
Mitford, William, 138
Money, 78, 80, 81, 82, 83, 86, 87, 88, 89, 91, 92, 121
Moore, Thomas, 142
Murray, John, 136, 156, 157, 229*n39*, 230*n47*

Natural order, 186–87
Nature, 5, 73
Nostalgia: its social meaning, 30, 133, 134

Novel, the, 8, 9, 10

Otten, Terry, 3

Pages, Georges, 182
Parker, Reeve, 12, 216n24
Parties: as sign of social decay, 47–48
Past, the, 153
Patriarchy, 27, 28, 29, 30, 31, 32, 33, 49, 50, 51, 56, 75, 84, 85, 86, 88, 104, 105, 107, 115, 116, 118, 119, 120, 121
Personal life, 115, 116, 191, 192, 194
Peterloo Massacre, 196
Phillip II of Spain, 23, 24, 25, 26
Plekhanov, G. V., 5
Pope, Alexander, 144
Private property, 116
Punishment: social meaning of, 102–3

Regency, English, 127, 128, 196
Religion, 26, 33, 36, 53–55, 107, 108, 126, 127, 129, 130, 154, 173, 174, 176, 179, 180, 182, 189–91, 202, 205
Renwick, W. L., 61, 218n2
Ricardo, David, 141
Richardson, Alan, 3, 4, 213n6
Robinson, Charles E., 233n80
Romanticism, 1, 2, 3, 4, 5, 6, 73
Ruskin, John, 140
Rutherford, Andrew, 160
Rymer, Thomas, 145

Sanuto, 138
Schiller, Friedrich von, 225n1
Schlegel, Friedrich: *History of Literature*, 143
Scott, Sir Walter, 138, 227n9; *Auchindrane*, 123; *The Doom of Devorgoil*, 123; *Halidon Hill*, 4, 123–33, 209, 210; *MacDuff's Cross*, 123, 124
Shakespeare, William, 7, 39, 134, 220n4
Shelley, Mary, 66, 199, 226n4, 231n60; *Frankenstein*, 66, 111
Shelley, Percy Bysshe, 62, 128, 132, 136, 137, 183, 196, 226n4; *The Cenci*, 10; *Prometheus Unbound*, 7, 220n7

Sheridan, Richard Brinsley, 7, 21, 140, 216n4; *The Critic*, 228n17
Siculus, Diodorus, 138
Social class, 6–7, 8, 10, 11, 26, 31, 38, 41–43, 47, 49, 50, 51, 52, 56, 62–65, 74, 85, 97, 98, 99, 100, 101, 112–15, 154–55, 159–60, 183–86, 187–88, 193, 209
State, the, 90, 91, 92, 93, 100, 110, 116, 159, 167–68, 169, 170, 208
Strauss, David Friedrich, 221n2
Suicide: social meaning of, 108, 109, 166

Thelwall, John, 21
Thirty Years' War, 181, 182, 195–96
Thompson, E. P., 139
Thomson, James: "City of Dreadful Night," 224n1
Thorndike, A. H., 219n1
Thucydides, 143
Tudor, Mary, 24

Usury, 80, 81, 82

Violence: social meaning of, 35, 36, 160–62, 163–65

Washington, George, 142
Wasserman, Earl, 1
Watson, Robert, 217n9
Weimann, Robert, 22
Williams, Raymond, 7, 9, 73, 140, 210, 220n3; *The Long Revolution*, 6
Wirth, Louis, 232n74
Wolfson, Susan, 226n2
Wollstonecraft, Mary, 219n6
Wordsworth, William, 5, 39, 73, 141, 154; *The Borderers*, 4, 10–20, 75, 209, 215n22; *Lyrical Ballads*, 11, 17, 19; "Preface to the *Lyrical Ballads*," 17, 19; *The Prelude*, 215n22

Zaretsky, Eli, 109, 116, 117, 224n13; *Capitalism, the Family, and Personal Life*, 115